Virtual Morality

Graham Houston

Virtual Morality

Christian ethics in the computer age

APOLLOS

APOLLOS (an imprint of Inter-Varsity Press),
38 De Montfort Street, Leicester LE1 7GP, England

First published 1998

British Library Cataloguing in Publication Data
A catalogue record for this book is available from the British Library.

ISBN 0–85111–461–X

Set in 11/13pt Bembo

Typeset in Great Britain by The Midlands Book Typesetting Company.
Printed and bound in Great Britain by Creative Print and Design (Wales), Ebbw Vale.

Contents

Acknowledgments

I had the privilege of serving as Chaplain to Heriot-Watt University, Edinburgh, from 1990 to 1998, and I am very grateful to the university for the opportunity afforded to me as a member of staff to engage in part-time research for the degree of PhD. Having recently begun work as Executive Director of the National Bible Society of Scotland, I continue to lecture part-time in Moral and Social Philosophy at H-W U. This book is based on my doctoral thesis of 1996. I am particularly grateful to my supervisor, Professor Keith Cornwell, presently Director of Quality at the University, who encouraged me to set out on the project when he was serving as Dean of the Faculty of Engineering. I am also indebted to Dr David Cook, Fellow and Chaplain of Green College, Oxford, and Director of the Whitefield Institute, who acted as my specialist adviser in ethics and kindly wrote the Foreword to this book.

Professor Ray McAleese of the H-W U Centre for Combined Studies provided invaluable advice about accessing the Internet, and found a number of important articles for me in the process, Dr Veronica Pantelidis of East Carolina University sent me her collection of papers on Virtual Reality and education, and Professor Egbert Schuurman of the Delft University of Technology sent me his unpublished papers relevant to the topic. To them I offer my sincere thanks.

Above all, my wife Irene and our children Rachel, Rhoda and Stephen have shown great fortitude and tolerance, especially during the writing up of the dissertation, and I record my thanks with affection, having expressed it personally.

Edinburgh 1998   *Graham Houston*

Foreword

When Gutenberg invented the printing press, he could have had little idea of the impact of his invention. The extent and degree of that impact is still being seen, in the development of IT – or *information technology* to the uninitiated. The world of computers, the Web, E-mail and cyberspace is a very foreign place to most of us over fifty. To the young, it is a natural habitat; they understand how to use it and how to communicate. As with so many technological developments, moral and ethical questions are raised both by the techniques and equipment themselves and by what we are able to do with them. Our problem is twofold: we have too little grasp of the nature of technology, and even less understanding of morality and how to make good moral decisions. This is an issue not just at the personal and individual level; it is also a social, political and communal question. How shall we regulate information technology? What moral rules should guide and direct us?

Graham Houston is well qualified to guide us through the moral mazes of IT. He was, until recently, Chaplain to Heriot-Watt University. The nerve, the history and the reality of Heriot-Watt is as a centre of technological excellence set in the rolling hills near Edinburgh. But Graham's work involved not just dealing with staff and students' personal and communal issues, but also helping everyone to reflect critically on the nature, application and limits of technologies. It was no surprise, then, to find Graham successfully completing a PhD on the ethical issues around Virtual Reality.

None of us can be totally ignorant of the computer world, where you pit your wits, skills and intelligence against some kind of devious opponent. The better you do, the more difficult the game becomes as you move from level to level. The recreational application is in danger of concealing the benefits of creating virtual realities for training pilots, doctors and a whole series of professionals, who need practice which is as near to the real thing as possible. The untold benefits of saved lives must result from surgical or flight techniques practised in the laboratory world rather than on real people.

To understand technology we need to set it in the real world of the practice of science. That must be placed in the context of philosophy of science, theology, ethical and cultural reflection. Graham does not fail us. He inducts us into the worlds of philosophy, theology, ethics and cultural analysis. He is not hesitant to examine the Judeo-Christian perspectives on human nature, ethics and theology. He does not shirk from addressing the crucial issues of tolerance, censorship, manipulation, pornography and addiction. His account is balanced, recognizing the advantages and benefits of technology, but also critical and prophetic.

The kind of moral rules we need in the worlds of virtual realities must have some link with the moral decision-making we practise in real situations. Drawing on the work of Oliver O'Donovan, Jacques Ellul and Philip Wogaman, Graham offers us a theological and ethical framework for dealing with the wide variety of moral issues raised by IT and Virtual Reality.

We ignore his insights at our peril.

February 1998   *David Cook*
Whitefield Institute and Green College,
Oxford

Introduction:
Christian concern in an age of simulation

An age of simulation

As we approach the end of the twentieth century, there is a surprising lack of millennial fever in the Western world. Few people seem to be debating the imminence of the end times or of some brave new world order now in process of gestation. Instead, many are retreating into, or being fascinated by, alternative realities which have been made possible by the development of computer technology. Daily, thousands of intelligent people (or so we imagine) are entering worldwide into MUDs (multi-user dungeons) on the Internet and are engaging in fantasy relationships with other players, most often by typing text which describes actions, dialogue and emotions. There, in a MUD, words are deeds and imagination rules (Turkle 1995: 15). We can pretend to be other than we really are, in such an environment. We can swop gender and engage in the kind of role-play which absorbed us as children. Others are more content to use computer networking in a more informative way, exchanging interests through newsgroups and joining virtual communities of people who want to contact others with similar concerns throughout the world.

All of this resonates with the social atomization which is growing apace in the Western world as individualism takes its toll – the belief that the individual's personal choice and fulfilment should take precedence over communitarian values such as social cohesion or community spirit. In our middle-class suburbs, many of us no longer know our neighbours very well. We are strangers who commute to distant offices or out-of-town shopping malls. We rarely frequent downtown entertainments or hostelries and prefer to visit cinema complexes built beside motorways and by-passes. We enjoy watching the daily interaction of *Neighbours* on TV because it depicts a situation which is strange to most of us who don't actually pop in to our neighbours' homes to pour out our hearts to one another or pass on the gossip. But it's an attractive alternative world, and perhaps it happens like that in Australia. Who knows? Does it matter? Some of us are choosing mail-order fashions over the Internet, and others are seeking relationships through personal ads in the media or through computer dating, presumably because we find it hard to find a secure place where we can meet others and form friendships.

Technoptimists may believe that computer networking will reverse such trends and bring about a new kind of community which satisfies human needs and aspirations. However, the psychologist Sherry Turkle has challenged this as a false hope, in a recent book. Her question is this: 'Is it really sensible to suggest that the way to revitalize community is to sit alone in our rooms, typing at our networked computers and filling our lives with virtual friends?' (1995: 235). She suggests that, for many, the simulation has become more compelling than real life, and wonders whether direct experience is being devalued because of its messiness and lack of clarity regarding its meaning or significance. Virtual Reality technology offers vivid and compelling interaction within computer-generated, man-made environments which can reflect only some of the grain and complexity of real life, due to the limitations of computer power and computing time. It may, in due course, replace the text-based MUDs and offer visually convincing places in which to meet and interact with other avatars (representations of other users). At the moment, VR is in its infancy, and synthetic environments have a long way to go before they reach their potential as places of interactivity, perhaps replacing colour TV as the opium of the people and enabling a much less passive involvement with electronic stimuli. But, like TV viewers, cybernauts who enter virtual worlds are exploring *other people's* versions of reality. As Turkle rightly notes, 'Interactive multimedia comes already interpreted' (1995: 238). Virtual experience can enable us to engage with certain impressions of aspects of real-life experience. But we can walk away or pull out the plug if bored or upset by what we find, unlike most real-life encounters.

Turkle suggests that this age of simulation – the Computer Age – is marked by both *psychological compensation* and *political criticism* (1995: 249).[1] We live, in the Western world, in an age where many of our young people cannot find the work which they feel able and equipped to do. They may be forced to live away from the middle-class neighbourhoods in which they grew up and get out of touch with their roots and ways of interaction. For them, virtual worlds may provide compensatory experiences. There they may also find alternatives, in virtual communities, to failed Western societies which they perceive to be increasingly devoid of meaningful relationships and social responsibility. They may also seek to give expression to new kinds of human imaginative creativity as they become involved in developing online characters who inhabit a number of virtual communities. Those who live parallel lives with such multiple identities seem to be abandoning ideas of the self as real and unitary, yet they continue to face the facts of their limitations in a physical existence with its 'desires, pain and mortality' (Turkle 1995: 267).

We can see how this trend of seeing the self as decentred and diffuse is a characteristic of an age of simulation. It is also a warning sign for Christian theology and ethics in postmodernity, and an important reason for engaging in the kind of discussion found in this book. As John Calvin long ago began his *magnum opus*: 'Without knowledge of self there is no knowledge of God' (1960: 35). The poet Burns spoke of seeing ourselves as others see us, but Christian anthropology has sought to see human beings as *God* sees them. That is thought of, by Christians, as ultimate reality in terms of personal knowledge. Virtual Reality appears to be a concept which is questioning such basic notions of what is real about ourselves and the world around us, and the technology may be offering alternative realities which are thought of as valid 'places' to visit and explore. There, interests are aroused, attention is engaged, absorption is evoked, experience is transformed and expectation is transcended (Lynch 1996: 151). In other words, our exposure to multimedia involves patterns of behaviour similar to that

---

[1] In a UK context, the author suggests that political *cynicism* is a more apt term.

in which we engage in real life. Ethics, the study of principles of conduct and their foundations, has traditionally been based on our notions of reality, as we shall see in Chapter Three. In our enquiry, we seek to establish whether Christian ethics, as classically formulated, can have anything distinctive to offer in the analysis of the ethical implications of living in an age of simulation, where '*Virtual Morality*' may be a new category with which ethicists must reckon. But first we must examine how ethics and technology may be meaningfully related to each other.

Ethics and technology

This study is at the 'interface'[2] between philosophy of technology and Christian ethics. While the latter has an ancient pedigree, the former is a comparative newcomer on the academic scene, developing during the last hundred years. Carl Mitcham[3] is a leading philosopher of technology who has traced the development of the discipline and distinguishes between *engineering philosophy of technology*, or 'analyses of technology from within and oriented toward an understanding of the technological way of being-in-the-world as paradigmatic for other kinds of thought and action', and *humanities philosophy of technology*, or 'the attempt of religion, poetry, and philosophy to bring non- or transtechnological perspectives to bear on interpreting the meaning of technology' (1994: 39). He also outlines the philosophical questioning of technology, and focuses on some of the ethical issues raised.

Traditionally, ethics has been concerned with interpersonal behaviour, defining principles of conduct, and has propounded three general theories: natural law theory, teleological theory and deontological theory. The first focuses on a pre-existent framework (law or order versus disorder), the second on consequences (goods versus harms), and the third on the inherent character of actions

---

[2] 'The locus of communication between two systems, applied to either hardware or software or a combination of both . . . *Interface* is a key term in the philosophy of technology because it designates the connecting point between human and digital machine' (Heim 1993: 155). 'An interface occurs where two or more information sources come face to face. A human user connects with the system and the computer becomes interactive' (Heim 1993: 77).

[3] See Mitcham 1994: 17–134; *cf.* Mitcham & Mackey (1982) and Mitcham & Grote (1984).

(rational or right versus irrational or wrong) (1994: 100).[4]

Due to the revolutionary technological developments of the past three hundred years, traditional theories have been applied in new ways, and the scope of ethics has been expanded to include relations between humans and the nonhuman world of animals, the environment and technological artefacts. Computer ethics was initially restricted to concerns about individual privacy and corporate security, as it became technically possible for individual users to be monitored and for hackers to gain access to databases or networks. Recently, ethicists have become aware that there are *moral* questions about the computer-generated environments which have been created, as well as *general* questions about moral responsibility and computer use.[5]

The discussion in this book belongs to the humanities approach, and yet it explores some of the implications of an engineering approach to philosophy of technology. It is not a work of social science, and no attempts are made to justify conclusions on the basis of the author's empirical research. It is a philosophical examination of the way in which a Christian ethical critique may be applied to technological issues, and the author also enquires whether the concept of Virtual Reality in particular has anything to say about the foundations of Christian ethics. The argument seeks to relate ethics of technology to wider issues of values, and emphasizes the relationship between human nature and the drive for technological control.

One of the creative connections discovered in the course of research for this book is that philosophy of technology is to Christian ethics as philosophy of science is to systematic theology. Thomas F. Torrance (1969), John Polkinghorne (1986, 1991) and Nancey Murphy (1990) have made major contributions, with others, in developing the interface between theology and philosophy of science, following the seminal philosophical work of Michael Polanyi (1962, 1964) and historical work by Reijer Hooykaas (1972).

---

[4] In addition, there are, of course, approaches which focus on *virtue*, which may be thought of as related both to natural law and deontological theories. 'We may understand a *virtue* to be a disposition of the will toward a good end. It is a tendency to think or behave in accordance with goodness' (Wogaman 1989: 29). *Cf.* MacIntyre (1985) and Carr (1991).

[5] See Johnson (1993), Forester & Morrison (1993) and Gould (1989).

Connections between philosophy of science and theology

In contrast to those commentators who have supposed that technology is essentially amoral, value-neutral, and merely an instrument which humans can use for good or evil,[6] we will argue in this book, in concert with the majority of philosophers of technology, that modern technology is not merely *applied science*. As science itself has been shown to involve valuing and to be more than an outworking of a step-by-step inductive method, the claim that technology *is* just applied science would seem, at any rate, to be a red herring. Thomas Kuhn (1970) noticed that research on specific problems was always based on assumptions and convictions produced by previously existing science. He suggested that normal science operates within frameworks (*paradigms*) which involve clusters of beliefs, theories, values, standards for research and exemplary research results. Such paradigms are adopted as pre-commitments in the scientific endeavour and they influence the interpretation of empirical data. If a significant number of anomalies occur which threaten the paradigm's acceptance, a *paradigm-shift* may take place. The new paradigm will then be the basis of the next phase of normal science. In this way there is no absolute objectivity in science, based on logic, Kuhn suggested.

This confirmed, for a number of philosophers and theologians, that, despite the popularity of the conflict theory proposed by Thomas Huxley in the late Victorian debate over Darwin's *Origin of Species*, the methodologies of science and theology might be closely related.[7] John Polkinghorne, formerly Professor of Mathematical Physics at Cambridge, and now a Church of England priest and president of Queen's College, notes that both science and theology involve the acceptance of paradigms which are 'neither impervious to experience nor vulnerable to ready falsification by it' (1991: 4). By this he means that, while the religious apologist is often criticized for providing, for example, slick answers for questions about the existence of evil in a world created by a good God, the physicist is also involved in promoting beliefs which seem not to square with appearances – for example, in invoking the property of 'confinement' to explain our inability to demonstrate by experiment the existence of particles like

---

[6] See below, pp. 38–43.
[7] See Russell (1985, 1989).

quarks and gluons. Polkinghorne concludes that science and theology 'have this in common, that each can be, and should be, defended as being investigations of what is, the search for increasing verisimilitude in our understanding of reality' (1991: 4). This follows the theological dialogue with philosophy of science carried out by Thomas F. Torrance (1969), who speaks of science and theology as both engaged in an interrogative form of inquiry which is directed ultimately to the self-disclosure of the object. He compares *discovery* in science with *revelation* in theology (1969: 130–131). We will now engage in a critique of this comparison, to demonstrate the kind of way in which the interface between philosophy of science and theology may provide fruitful insights.

Polkinghorne's thesis is that theology is to religious experience as scientific theory is to ordinary experience; that revelation in theology is akin to discovery in science, and that understanding undergirds beliefs which lead to further understanding. Yet he believes that the scientific enterprise is easier to undertake than the theological, as it is limited (or should be) to concern with certain impersonal and largely repeatable phenomena. The most successful exploratory schemes in science are found in subjects with the least degree of complexity. He is critical of physicists such as Stephen Hawking who hope to discover a 'theory of everything' and to explain that the universe exists in terms of mathematics alone. Polkinghorne believes that there is more to the mind of God than the physicist can ever discover.[8]

In order to develop connections between philosophy of technology and Christian ethics, we need first to explore the implications of Polkinghorne's thesis, and offer a revision of it which, we believe, resonates with the major thrust of the thesis of this book. Let us look, first of all, at the relationship between discovery in science and revelation in theology. We must welcome Polkinghorne's defence of the rationality of the theological process and his affirmation of the debt owed to Christian thinking by modern scientific method. He clearly recognizes that, on the basis of a biblical worldview of an orderly and uniform creation, which is grounded in the being of a rational Person who has created freely so that empirical investigation is required, science must engage in an open-minded investigation of phenomena with, as far as possible, no constraint from our prejudices

[8] *Cf.* Davies (1984, 1993).

and expectations. But what does he mean by 'revelation'?

> I do not mean a divinely guaranteed set of propositions, made available to us by their being written on tablets of stone, or whispered into the mental ear of the human writers of scripture . . . Religion depends upon those revelatory moments of divine disclosure which cannot be brought about by human will alone, but which come as a gracious gift (1991: 54).

For Polkinghorne, God has revealed himself through the life of the man Jesus Christ so that the Word of God is not propositional but personal. He does not deny that God could have revealed himself through propositions, but asserts that full personal knowledge must be open and involve the risk of encounter, which may include paradox and ambiguity. How, then, is this understanding of revelation to be compared with scientific discovery?

Polkinghorne affirms that science is not an entirely objective, impersonal process which might well be conducted by a computer. He follows Michael Polanyi's account of science as involving 'personal knowledge',[9] which means that tacit skills are required which imply that the task could never be delegated to a computer, however ingenious the programming. Yet Polkinghorne rejects the notion that the scientific worldview is just a paradigm socially agreed by the scientific community, which enthusiastic interpreters of Kuhn took him to imply. In other words, science is done by persons who *know more than they can tell* (Polanyi 1962) and who bring to their observations ways of knowing which are not entirely explicable in terms of empiricism. Scientists, in addition to making experimental observations, follow hunches and trends, and operate within a community which influences the choices they make about methods and whether to accept results if they are novel or contradictory. While discovery is about '*I–it*', revelation is about '*I–thou*', suggests Polkinghorne.[10] In other words, the biblical text does not mediate information or opinion but *encounter*.

We must now enquire whether there is, in fact, such a gulf between the *propositional* and the *personal*, and whether this kind of comparison

---

[9] Polkinghorne (1991: 55) following Polanyi (1962: 315).
[10] *Ibid.*, following Buber (1970).

between discovery and revelation is a valid one.[11] The matter is complicated by the fact that the idea of *revelation*, as used by the biblical writers, must be interpreted in context and does not always have the same meaning or significance.[12] Paul refers to the phenomenon of prophecy in the Corinthian church as speaking a message to the congregation 'if a *revelation* comes' to one who prophesies (1 Corinthians 14:30–31). On the surface this seems like the instances of revelation found in the Old Testament. For example, the prophet Nathan is described as bringing a message from God to David about the future building of the temple, and as reporting all the words of the revelation he had received (2 Samuel 7:17). One of the writers of the Proverbs lamented that where there is no revelation the people cast off restraint (Proverbs 29:18). The prophet Habakkuk was commanded, we are told, to write down the revelation entrusted to him (Habakkuk 2:2). In the New Testament, the apostle Paul claimed that the gospel (good news) he preached was not man-made but that he had received it by revelation from Jesus Christ (Galatians 1:11–12). The idea is clearly that of God revealing to people, by unspecified means, insights and information which would otherwise remain concealed.

Yet in the New Testament the words associated with the idea of revelation have other nuances. Paul encourages the Philippians to have a mature perspective on the Christian life, which will involve the clarification of the teaching they have received from him and the other apostles, rather than the revealing of new truths (good news): 'And if on some point you think differently, that too God will *reveal* to you' (Philippians 3:15, author's translation). A similar usage is found in Ephesians 1:17, where Paul prays for the Ephesians that God might give them 'the Spirit of wisdom and *revelation*, so that you may know him better', which seems to mean that they might enter more deeply into their relationship with God and discover more depths of his love. There are other instances where revelation refers to God's acts of judgment in history (Romans 1:18–32) or to the developing of an intimate relationship with God (Matthew 11:25–27).

In this way, to reduce the biblical ideas of revelation to bare *encounter*, as Polkinghorne wants to do, seems inadequate. In addition,

---

[11] See G. Houston (1994); *cf.* Prickett (1986).
[12] See G. Houston 1989: 87–97.

connections between notions of revelation and discovery may not be so straightforward as he alleges, for a number of reasons. First, we must ask whether scientific discovery leads to the reporting (in journals and books) not of information or opinion but encounter. It may be that the flash of insight which constitutes the moment of discovery for the scientist cannot be explained purely in rational terms, but that insight must be tested and verified by experimentation. It must be presented to the scientific community for corroboration. Its effects must be repeatable. Critical realists, one of whom Polkinghorne confesses himself to be, believe that scientists are indeed encountering aspects of reality in the setting-up and observation involved in their work. But they bring to the experimentation prior commitments which involve information and opinions. Presuppositions are brought to bear on the study in question, and the results must be expressed in relation to them, in a way that is acceptable to the scientific community, who expect that claims to discovery will indeed be backed up by information and opinions. Without that, the idea of discovery is meaningless.

Secondly, Polkinghorne does not attempt to demonstrate the validity of his presupposition that revelation is personal rather than propositional. In fact, such a demonstration is impossible. For no reputable philosopher of religion would deny the possibility that a Supreme Being could, having created humankind with the ability to communicate with each other by means of information and opinions, then inspire humans (without needing to use mechanical means) to pass on divine information and opinions which could not be gleaned otherwise.[13] In addition, the biblical notion that humankind is made in the image of God strongly suggests that such a feat is not only possible, but probable.

Thirdly, Polkinghorne seems to confuse the doctrine of inspiration with what John Calvin (1960: 78) called 'the inner witness of the Holy Spirit'. Calvin held that the words of Scripture were the result of a mysterious working (inspiration) of the Holy Spirit who guided the writers to communicate information and opinions (revelation) from God to people, so that Paul could claim 'All scripture is God-breathed' (2 Timothy 3:16), *i.e.* the origin of Scripture is in God's Spirit. But Calvin also emphasized that the message of Scripture

---

[13] *Cf.* Evans 1982: 92–117.

had to be impressed upon the mind and conscience of the hearer or reader so that the truth revealed to the apostles and prophets had an effect in people's lives. In that sense the Bible had to *become* the Word of God: its truth had to be illumined existentially to the believer who had to make it his or her own. That phenomenon is much more like the idea of discovery which Polkinghorne has – the encounter with the given reality which initiates a response and an explanation.

While we have criticized some of the connections made between the ideas of revelation in theology and discovery in science, this does not invalidate the basic position for which Polanyi, Torrance and Polkinghorne have argued. We have suggested a revised version which, we believe, is more consistent with Christian tradition, in its comparison of scientific discovery with *illumination* rather than with revelation. As scientific discovery is the realization of knowledge of *that which* is there, so illumination is the realization in experience of the God *who* is there, as mediated by the Spirit through the given revelation in Christ and the Scripture which bears witness to him.[14]

The significance of this introductory discussion is to demonstrate the creative links which have been made between theology and philosophy of science and some of the ways in which models of scientific method may be paralleled in natural science and theological science. Such connections are well established and have been fruitful in the encouragement of scholarly dialogue, thus enabling both scientists and theologians to understand more clearly their own and each other's methods.[15] One of our concerns in this discussion is to explore the extent to which this kind of fruitful relationship may be found also in connections between philosophy of technology and Christian ethics.[16]

Connections between philosophy of technology and Christian ethics

A number of important studies which touch on the interface between philosophy of technology and Christian ethics have been produced by Jacques Ellul (1965, 1976, 1990), Ian Barbour (1992), Frederick Ferré (1988, 1993), and a multi-disciplinary group of scholars writing in a

[14] See Schaeffer (1968).
[15] See Poythress (1988).
[16] See below, pp. 179–180.

symposium edited by Stephen Monsma (1986). The present study began with an exploration of that interface, and Virtual Reality was chosen as a topical example of a technological development which provides a useful focus for discussion, partly because of publicity given to the phenomenon in its early manifestations which alleged that there were distinctive ethical implications involved, but largely because it is a young technology which is still open to formative direction.

Paul Goodman has made the radical affirmation that 'Technology is a branch of moral philosophy, not of science' (1976: 6).[17] By this he meant to carry through to a logical conclusion the implications of viewing technology as not simply applied science, but rather as the result of moral and social decision-making. For the purposes of this discussion, we will adopt the definition of technology proposed by Monsma as 'A distinct human cultural activity in which human beings exercise freedom and responsibility in response to God by forming and transforming the natural creation, with the aid of tools and pro-cedures, for practical ends or purposes' (1986: 10–23). We can see in this definition many of the concerns of moral philosophy: freedom and responsibility, autonomy and authority, ends and means. Technology clearly involves moral choices and decision-making processes. Does this lend credence to Goodman's assertion? Is technology a logical extension of ethics? In this discussion we will see that many scholars argue that technological developments may be reflections of the philosophical outlooks of particular human cultures. How can ethical theory help us to answer such questions?

Frederick Ferré has examined such questions in some detail. He notes that ethical theory can pinpoint what questions should be asked in order to make responsible decisions, but that it cannot provide us with a 'uniquely ethical policy for action' (1988: 75). Ethical theory cannot guarantee moral behaviour or even agreement on what such behaviour should be. An adequate ethical theory should propose, first, the *goals* for the good life that we should seek, and, secondly, the *principles* by which we should rightly regulate our seeking. In other words, we must ask of technology, as of every aspect of human activity, 'What is *good*? . . . What is *right*? . . . What *ought* to be done?' (1988: 76). Let us examine these questions more closely.

---

[17] *Cf.* Monsma 1986: 27.

In addressing the first question, Ferré distinguishes between *intrinsic* and *extrinsic* goods. An example of the former would be the enjoyment of health, which is desired for its own sake and not merely as a means to an end. In contrast, the accumulation of wealth is most often pursued as a means to other ends. Clearly, good health is an important condition for the enjoyment of other goods, yet its value is often most appreciated when illness invades for a time. The important point to note is that both intrinsic and extrinsic goods are 'nonmoral',[18] *i.e.* to have health or wealth does not necessitate a response of moral praise, and to lack them does not incur blame. Clearly, technology is, in many ways, an expression of the value placed on these goods.

It follows that, if people generally value the above goods, they should be as widely available as possible. The *right* action will be that which helps people to attain and develop such goods. The *wrong* action will be that which prevents people from benefiting from such goods or frustrates the enjoyment of them. Yet, in the distribution of nonmoral goods, there is a need for some principle of distribution, which Ferré finds in John Rawls's theory of social justice (fairness).[19] Rawls argues that justice begins with the examination of questions of social policy from the standpoint of the least privileged members of society. Just policies are those which can be regarded as being in the interest of such people (*e.g.* children, the disabled, ethnic minorities, *etc.*).[20]

Questions of what is good are in tension with questions of what is right: 'The quest merely to maximise the acknowledged goods of life is, by itself, heedless of the formal limitations of fairness' (Ferré 1988: 79). Questions of what ought to be done, or moral obligation, highlight this tension. We need other principles to guide us in this area, and William Frankena proposes three: first, the principle of *non-maleficence*, which should express our sense of obligation to refrain

[18] See Frankena (1971), ch. 5. Ferré (1988: 77) summarizes the nonmoral goods as: survival; health; material security, comfort, wealth; society; individuality, agency, creativity.

[19] 'The formal principle of justice, then, requires that our actions, to be morally right, be non-discriminating unless there is a justifying difference.' (Ferré 1988: 78). *Cf.* Rawls (1972).

[20] See Wogaman 1989: 93–94.

from doing anything which will diminish the good in the world or which will harm any persons who are in need of the basic goods of life; secondly, the principle of *beneficence*, by which we are obliged to do that which will add to the goods in the world and seek to help others to attain them; thirdly, the principle of *justice* helps us to get a balance in our actions, all things being equal. To summarize, Frankena is suggesting three basic answers to questions about moral obligation: we ought not to destroy good; we ought to try to create good; and we ought to be fair (1971: 45–48).[21]

In the course of our discussion, we will note that some commentators have alleged that such value-judgments are irrelevant to our understanding of technology, but that people may be held responsible for what they do with technology which is itself merely a tool, and neither good nor bad. Yet we see that technological systems are loaded with potential goods and harms which must be set against each other (Ferré 1988: 83). For example, automation in the workplace continues to be controversial, and many people in both academic and business worlds are concerned about connections between high-technology and unemployment.[22] The goods of increased production and efficiency have to be balanced with potential harms. Human dignity may suffer as people begin to feel part of the machinery. Loss of self-esteem may result, as well as de-skilling. Autonomy, craft and wholeness may be under threat. As every culture has its arts and crafts, its ways of doing things, technological choices may not only threaten individual well-being, but also societies and cultures themselves.

The operation of modern scientific culture is radically different from that of craft traditions. Research and development have replaced apprenticeship; application of explicit natural law has replaced tradition (Ferré 1993: 127–136). Philosophy of technology provides

---

[21] *Cf.* Frankena (1973), where he argues that ethical thinking should not be based on religious beliefs, pointing out that tying ethics to religion would make it more difficult to come to agreement on moral principles. As there is as much disagreement over ethical views as over religion, it may be that Frankena is mistaken in imaging that agreement in ethics is more easily achieved than in religious studies; see Wogaman 1989: 11–26. For example, Rawls's argument, outlined above, is based on criteria of self-interest which, suggests Wogaman, can be presented even more powerfully with a theological orientation based on faith in God and a deep sense of human mutual responsibility (1989: 94).

[22] *Cf.* Davis & Gosling (1985).

Christian ethics with powerful insights for the analysis of attitudes and actions in a technological society, the chief of which is the exposure of *technicism*, or *technology for technology's sake*.

Jacques Ellul (1965) was the first philosopher of technology, or Christian ethicist, to provide a penetrating analysis of this concept. He calls our self-conscious, deliberate and highly rationalized way of doing things *technique* (technical operation), which is more than just methods. Machines are examples of technique, in this sense, as they must be consciously designed and deliberately put to work; so much so that the machine has become paradigmatic of a clearly reasoned way of doing something.[23] But physical machines are not the only focus of technical operation; technique is seen in every consciously designed methodology, in the organizational structures of companies, and in the detailed formulation of forward plans and behavioural objectives in primary education. These are also 'machines', in a social, biological or psychological sense. Ellul's concern is that we have come to be so dominated by fascination with technique that it has become the popular religion. The idol of the machine, physical or otherwise, is rooted in a deterministic worldview of a universe which is reliable, predictable and intelligible: 'No unforeseen randomness, balkiness or ambiguity is permitted in the image of the perfect technique. The world of technique is in principle a soluble, a controllable world' (Ferré 1993: 128).

It is here that we immediately see the possible connections with Virtual Reality as a concept which may vividly embody the values of technicism. We are only too aware that the technicistic worldview is, as yet, far removed from the stark reality of daily life. Yet the behavioural psychologist B. F. Skinner recognizes that humans tend to play to their strengths, which for Western humankind today is science and technology, rather than philosophy or psychology. He asserts (1972: 3–25) that we need *a technology of behaviour*:

Almost all our major problems involve human behaviour, and they cannot be solved by physical and biological technology alone. What is needed is a *technology of behaviour*, but we have been slow to develop the science from which such a technology might be drawn. One difficulty is that almost all of what is called behavioural

---

[23] See Ferré 1993: 127; *cf.* Pirsig (1974).

science continues to trace behaviour to states of mind, feelings, traits of character, human nature, and so on. Physics and biology once followed similar practices and advanced only when they discarded them . . . As the interaction between organism and environment has come to be understood, however, effects once assigned to states of mind, feelings, and traits are beginning to be traced to accessible conditions, and a *technology of behaviour* may therefore become available. It will not solve our problems, however, until it replaces traditional prescientific views, and these are strongly entrenched. Freedom and dignity illustrate the difficulty. They are the possession of the autonomous man of traditional theory, and they are essential to practices in which a person is held responsible for his conduct and given credit for his achievement. A scientific analysis shifts both the responsibility and the achievement to the environment. It also raises questions concerning 'values'. Who will use a technology and to what ends? Until these issues are resolved, a *technology of behaviour* will continue to be rejected, and with it possibly the only way to solve our problems (1972: 24–25).

In this book we will propose that the *Ethics of Christian Realism,* as defined in Chapter Three,[24] can offer an effective critical analysis of a technology of behaviour, *i.e.* of *technique.* According to Skinner, evils resulting from technique are to be resolved by yet deeper faith in technique. In contrast, Christian ethics as represented by our paradigm is not committed to providing solutions and control mechanisms, which is the language of manipulation. It does not see the seat of evil in the environment – spiritual, physical or computer-generated – but in the inner being of humankind. Yet Christian ethics also recognizes that environmental influences play on that over-centred self, affecting character, attitudes and actions. It explores the good, the right and the 'ought'; it examines the consequences of action and agency; and it seeks categorical imperatives. But all of this is understood in relation to God. The context of this critique of a technology of behaviour is not the human will to power, but the dynamics of the kingdom of God, of learning to live in harmony with God's gracious reign. This delivers the exponent of Christian ethics from becoming enslaved to

[24] See pp. 79–105.

techniques for moral decision-making, which may in fact be expressions of a technicistic worldview, where the overriding concern is the 'how' question rather than the 'who' or the 'why'.[25]

The context: postmodernity

The discussion is set in the context of *postmodernity* as defined by David Lyon (1994a), rather than that of *postmodernism*. 'Postmodernity' is a provisional concept which emphasizes the social aspects of the perceived end of modernity, and which refers to a climate or condition rather than a period of history.[26] Postmodernity involves perceived social changes and may be indicative of the evolution of a new kind of society or a new stage of capitalism. In postmodernity, previous methods of social analysis and political practice are questioned. Its key issues include the increasing prominence of information and communications technology on a global scale, and the all-embracing influence of consumerism.

Modernity questions all traditional ways of doing things, replacing the authority of tradition with authorities supposedly based on science, economic growth, democracy or law. 'It unsettles the self; if identity is given in traditional society, in modernity it is constructed' (Lyon 1994a: 21). In postmodernity we are free to 'pick 'n' mix' from the available authorities within a pluralistic frame of reference.

'Postmodernism' is a movement which finds expression for the postmodern condition in philosophy, literary criticism, social and cultural theory, performance arts, fine arts and architecture. In philosophy of science this involves a rejection of foundationalism (the theory that science is built on a firm base of observable facts), and a questioning of some of the key commitments of the Enlightenment. Postmodernists believe that the concept of universal hierarchies, of knowledge, taste and opinion, has collapsed and that only a local focus

[25] See D. Cook (1983: 82–84) for an approach to moral decision-making which offers a helpful framework rather than a technique, in the context of a theological approach to ethics. *Cf.* Wogaman (1989) who proposes a method of Christian moral judgment based on manifest presumptions.

[26] 'Gianni Vattimo sees contemporary society as characterised primarily by "generalised communication". It is "the society of the mass media". The passing of modernity occurs, in his view, when history can no longer be seen as unilinear; it is just the past from a series of different viewpoints. The demise of history drags progress down with it as well' (Lyon 1994a: 49).

is attainable or desirable. This means 'incredulity towards metanarratives' (Lyotard 1984: xxiv), or a loss of belief in the large-scale interpretive frameworks afforded by the grand ideologies such as Marxism or Christianity.[27] In addition, postmodernism emphasizes the shift from word to image, from discourse to figure, and from logocentrism to iconocentrism, typified by the exchange of the printed book for TV and multimedia computer.[28] In postmodernism, *reality* is in question; modernism's world of solid scientific facts and purposeful history (products of Enlightenment thought) are perceived as mere wishful thinking or even a manipulation of ideas by the powerful.[29]

Lyon concludes his discussion by noting four characteristics of *postmodernity* (1994a: 84–86). First, it is a concept which invites discussion about the nature and direction of contemporary societies, in a global context, rather than one which describes an existent condition. The term helps us to focus on the unprecedented social and cultural shifts which are currently under way. Secondly, in postmodernity, social and cultural analysis belong together, especially with reference to information and communications technology.

Thirdly, the debate over postmodernity stimulates a reappraisal of modernity as a socio-cultural phenomenon, and especially of the impact of consumerism, of which we need to understand the cultural and religious roots and fruits. Fourthly, we need to make judgments about modernity's emphasis on progress (the secularization of providence) and ask if we can still work with it or should seek to live beyond it. Lyon concludes that we should live in a complex interaction between the premodern, modern and postmodern (1994a: 86).

---

[27] Lyon comments: 'Are we left only with postmodern pastiche, fragments and photos on a collage? Do our self-constructed photofit identities connect us with any bigger story?' (1994a: 3).

[28] 'For Baudrillard, the new electronic media presage a world of pure simulacra, of models, codes and digitality, of media images that have become the "real", or rather, that erode any distinction between the "real" world and that of the pervasive media' (Lyon 1994a: 48). 'The very items that modernity used in order to banish ambivalence and uncertainty – techniques such as managerialism, or science and technology – now help to undermine the modern sense of reality. Modern mass technologies of communication, for instance, allow for great expansion of services and leisure industries and for mushrooming simulations of reality. This is especially true of Baudrillard who announces, "TV is the world" ' (1994a: 74).

[29] 'The idea that reality is being broken down into images is common within postmodern discourse' (Lyon 1994a: 48).

In this book, we will attempt that kind of approach.

How, then, does awareness of postmodernity as a socio-cultural phenomenon bear upon the relationship between Christian ethics and technology, and in particular *information technology*? Computers and telecommunications are central to the vision of those who believe that we are moving into a post-industrial society where the class divisions resulting from earlier capitalism are being challenged and will eventually be replaced by a new social condition based on knowledge. However, as postmodern thought challenges ideas of *progress*, information technology is seen as a tool of social control; a means certainly of managing, and perhaps also of manipulation. Data-processing, electronic surveillance and virtual realities seem to dominate a technically obsessed world bereft of answers to questions of meaning and purpose, and this calls for rigorous questioning from the Christian ethicist. What can the future of humankind be if we are increasingly immersed in such artificial worlds? What is happening to us? What is real and what is simulacra? It may be that computer-generated worlds will increasingly be those in which we live and move and have our being. But what will happen to our common humanity? And what of our relationship with a Creator of moral and natural order? These are just some of the issues we must discuss in exploring a Christian ethical interface with technology in postmodernity.

Outline of discussion
The first chapter introduces Virtual Reality and questions of values which are basic to the argument. This is followed by an exploration of humanness in relation to technology. We then adopt a particular paradigm of Christian ethics, in creative tension with the climate of postmodernity, and examine eschatological connections; next we argue that Christian ethics rightly belongs to the public domain. There follows an application of the ethical insights gained to the ethical dilemmas associated with the concept and application of VR in particular. We conclude by seeking to establish the significance of VR for Christian ethics and vice versa, and thereby to develop the connections between philosophy of technology and Christian ethics in the context of postmodernity.

Chapter One:
Values and Virtual Reality

1.1 Morality in a technological age

1.1.1 Are computers changing people?

Craig Brod is a psychotherapist who is interested in the emotional and mental disorders which may be the result of computer use by ordinary people who could not be classed as psychologically abnormal. One patient, an experienced computer programmer, reported his feelings of rejection and burnout along with his marital problems. He likened his wife to a *peripheral* (like a printer is to a computer) and joked that she wasn't very good at being one. Brod came to believe that the root of his patient's problems was not in his past or his personality type, nor that he was overworking, but in the nature of human–computer interaction. He then began a three-year study in which people of all ages, from age five upwards, were interviewed. Different age groups, occupational groups and people who were at different levels of adaptation to computers were asked about the effects computers were having on their professional and personal lives. The most significant effects were in their personal relationships. Brod records a number of examples from his research, two of which we will cite as examples (1984: 101–120).

First, a young married couple called Linda and Richard reported that the husband's computer skills and job responsibilities had overtaken his life and that he was no longer a warm and emotional person, but cold and calculating. He no longer shared his feelings but merely exchanged information. Efficiency had become his obsession, even in the way he walked. Eventually the marriage broke up.

Secondly, Ron and Alice had been married for eighteen years, during which time he had worked with computer payroll systems for a large local authority. She had become increasingly aware of his totally analytic outlook on life. Although this is a common complaint of women about their partners, in this case it seems that Ron was obsessed with the need to find solutions for all the problems they faced and could not be comforted if solutions were not forthcoming.

It is difficult to determine whether computer use had made these men like that, or whether they had been attracted to computers because of inherent tendencies in them which might have been expressed even if they had not become so involved with computers. Emerson and Forbes comment that Brod's findings concerning those who have become over-identified with computers note an unusually high degree of factual thinking, an inability to feel, an interest in efficiency and speed, a lack of empathy for others, an intolerance for the ambiguities of human behaviour and communication, and a reduced ability to think intuitively and creatively, along with an obsession for order and predictability. Brod reported that it is possible to break the cycle of machine-dependence, and that obsessive-compulsive people who are attracted to computers can be re-orientated towards empathy and affection (Emerson & Forbes 1990: 86).

Brod also reported significant effects of the interaction of young people and children with computers. One thirteen-year-old said, 'Work with the computer is like being in a bubble. Once my bubble's broken all the liquid flops out, and then I can be outside again. I shake once or twice and I'm back in the real world again, trying to function like normal' (1984: 129). Brod had discovered the psychological phenomena associated with re-entry into the real world from a computer-generated environment, five years before 'Virtual Reality' as a technical term came into coinage.

Psychologist Sherry Turkle conducted a broader study, looking not just at those who were feeling harmful effects or suffering emotional disorders from involvement with computers. She tried to determine how computers affect psychological development in positive as well as negative ways, in a study based on observations of more than 200 children and a similar number of adults. Her most interesting conclusions emerged from her work with children in primary school classrooms where computers were being used, and in playing with children using computer toys, sometimes asking them questions and sometimes just listening. She also recorded conversations with university students, and monologues by others who expressed their innermost thoughts about their interactions with computers. Turkle was often asked whether she thought computers were good or bad for people, especially children. Her response is that, 'Computers are not good or bad. They are *powerful*' (1984: 338).[1] This power is seen not only in their instrumental use but also in their subjective influence; it includes 'their power to fascinate and disturb, to evoke strong feelings or precipitate thoughts' (Emerson & Forbes 1990: 88). Turkle became aware that computers are not *value-neutral*, in other words. Neutrality is certainly not an idea conveyed by concepts of power. Turkle comments:

> If the reader is surprised by the intensity or the range of responses I report, this is only to the good if it leads to a critical re-examination of what each of us takes for granted about 'the Computer' and to an attitude of healthy scepticism toward any who propose simple scenarios about the impact of the computer on society (1984: 338).

Turkle surmised that computers cause children to think profound thoughts about life, people, themselves and God – thoughts that most people obtain secondhand in university courses in philosophy, psychology or religion. Repeatedly she makes the point that we should not look for a single, universal effect of computers on the psychological and emotional lives of children. Yet she proposes that children do tend to move through three stages, or ways, of relating to computers. She calls the first stage (normally between four and seven years of age) 'metaphysical', during which children want to know whether computers think, feel and are alive. In other words they are

[1] *Cf.* Emerson & Forbes 1990: 87.

asking, '*What is this thing?*' The second (age eight to adolescence) she calls the 'mastery' stage, when children are interested in using the computer as a means to be more competent and effective in daily life. They are asking, '*What can I do with computers?*' The third (from adolescence to adulthood) involves the use of computers to explore issues of self-discovery, what Turkle labels the 'identity' stage, when young people are asking, '*Who am I?*' (see Emerson & Forbes 1990: 89–99).

Something else came across quite clearly in Turkle's conclusions. These thoughts are not superficial. They arise naturally and spontaneously in the minds of children and seem to have nothing to do with teachers, course outlines or the adult world; the issues definitely enter into children's mental and emotional development. Turkle demonstrates that computer issues are not just of academic interest, but are of intense concern to children. She reports that children ascribe other psychological attributes besides talking and consciousness to computers, such as intelligence, feeling and morality; for many children, computers are *alive*. If this may have been demonstrated by empirical study in the early 1980s, it is clear that our perceptions of reality are likely to have been further influenced by the brave new world of computer-generated environments and Virtual Reality.

1.1.2   What is VR technology?

IMMERSIVE VIRTUAL REALITY is an innovation in human–computer interaction which has received considerable publicity since it was first marketed in the early nineties. It eliminates the normal separation between user and machine, and facilitates more direct and intuitive involvement. Users wear head-mounted audio-visual displays, position and orientation sensors, and (where applicable) tactile interface devices which enable them to enter into immersive computer-generated environments. Through VR software they can create virtual worlds and step inside to see, hear, touch and move their components around, using devices such as a DataGlove.

DESKTOP VIRTUAL REALITY is a simplified version of the technology which enables some impression of the three-dimensional manipulation of environments to be experienced, in architectural and engineering design, for example, without the immersive dimension. Users interact with the virtual environment through a normal desktop PC and VDU, with the aid of a device known as a Spaceball instead of a mouse.

CAVE VIRTUAL REALITY is a projection type of virtual environment and has been developed by the Electronic Visualisation Lab of the University of Illinois at Chicago. The CAVE is a surround-screen, surround-sound system which enables groups of users to experience immersion in a virtual world by the projection of 3D computer graphics on to a 3m × 3m × 3m cube composed of display screens that completely surround the viewer(s). Head and hand tracking systems produce the correct stereo perspective and isolate the position and orientation of a 3D mouse, with a stereo sound system providing feedback. One of the viewers is in control of the exploration of the virtual world, and the users do not wear helmets as in immersive VR, but lightweight stereo eyeglasses.[2]

The word 'virtual' was applied in computing to describe the facility of 'virtual-memory', whereby use could be made of memory function outside the conventional and extended memory provision.[3] Computer-generated environments may be representations of physical reality or imaginary worlds, and so some prefer the terms *'synthetic environment'* (SE) or *'virtual environment'* (VE) rather than VR.[4]

VR technology is being applied to a number of technical problems in industry, from design to assembly planning to manufacture to robotics (Fang *et al.* 1995; R. Stone 1992, *etc.*). It is also becoming popular as a medium of entertainment, where users can experience *presence* in a virtual environment, whether by flying a virtual helicopter, exploring a virtual art gallery, or destroying virtual aliens (Horizon 1991). Clearly, patterns of virtual behaviour may be developed by those who engage in such activity, and this leads us to ask whether we can create, through technology, virtual environments in which the rules of 'this' world no longer apply. Devotees of the latest computer games say that, in a virtual world, one can attack people, rip out their hearts and watch them pulsating before one's

---

[2] Heim 1995: 71; *cf.* C. Cruz-Neira in *5CYBERCONF* 1996: 7.

[3] 'Memory that isn't really there. *Windows*, by virtue of its swap file, is able to pretend that it has more RAM available to it than is actually present in the computer' (Lowe 1995: 210). *Cf.* Pimental & Teixeira (1993); 'VR is an event or entity that is real in effect but not in fact' (Heim 1993: 109).

[4] Durlach & Mavor (1995), ch. 1. See also Krueger (1991, 1993) who uses the term *'Artificial Reality'*.

eyes.[5] One can crash one's virtual race car and walk away unscathed. Is this any different from the worlds of imagination or other media of entertainment? In reading a book, one can enter into a story and see oneself as one of the characters who may be a racing driver or a murderer. The same would be true of watching a film or a play. One might get ideas from such sources. One might become a 'copycat' murderer and re-enact the crime portrayed on film. One might attempt to drive one's car at breakneck speed and crash, or to run along the sands like Eric Liddell, the 1924 Olympic Games champion athlete portrayed in the opening credits of David Puttnam's 1981 film *Chariots of Fire*, only to collapse with a heart attack.

1.1.3 What may be the moral implications of computer-generated environments?

The moral philosopher has to consider the extent to which environment determines morality, and it is a moot point to suggest that we take our ethical cues chiefly from experience in everyday life. The influences upon human actions are among the major issues in ethical discussions. Are we free to act, or are we determined by forces beyond us, such as heredity or environment? However, moral philosophy must also ask questions about metaphysical concerns. What is the nature of reality? Is the 'virtual' world less 'real' than what we call reality? Or is it just part of 'real' reality or real life (RL) (*cf.* Hasker 1983)?

Clearly, if a person spends the majority of her waking hours watching TV, it is possible that the characters of *Neighbours* from 'Ramsay Street, Erinsborough' may seem more real to her than her next-door neighbours whom she seldom sees. The models for her actions may not be family or friends, church or society, but the

---

[5] *Cf.* Ellul: 'I am firmly convinced that the whole system of technical games and amusements and distractions is one of the most dangerous factors for tomorrow's people and society. It leads us into an unreal world, and since we have here a passion or fascination, this unreal world is not the one that is necessary for a day . . . The unreal world here is one of fantasy from which there is no longer any reason to return' (1990: 364); and 'Technical games correspond very well to Pascal's "diversions". They direct us radically from any preoccupation with meaning, truth, or values and thus plunge us into the absurd. They also take us out of reality and make us live in a totally falsified world. This is for me the greatest danger that threatens us as a result of technical development' (1990: 365).

storylines of her favourite 'soap'. In the same way computer games and Virtual Reality systems might model the actions of their users. Such perceptions of reality encourage us to enquire 'What values lie behind modern technology?' Philosophers of technology are one in declaring that all technology is 'value-laden' and not 'value-free',[6] and that this statement applies not only to the application of technical systems and products, but also to the rationale behind them. Technology is not neutral, but expresses human values. Technology is the result of human choices; morality is about choosing from alternatives; ethics analyses the principles behind such choices. Valuing is involved in every aspect of technological activity, from the choice of analytical frameworks, through the processes of design and manufacture, to the tools and products which issue from them. Those who assert that technological systems and products are value-free accept that valuing is involved in the *uses* to which people put technology but somehow imagine that the earlier stages are exempt from valuing. We need to expose the weakness of this view, but first must ask what we mean by *values* in technology.

1.2   Morality, reality and values

1.2.1   VR's underlying values

In this book, one of the concerns is to explore morality in relation to our concepts of reality. We must examine the extent to which our attitudes and actions, as expressive of ethical principles, are bound up with our appreciation of the nature of reality as a whole. Yet this might be seen purely as a formal matter, following Aristotle. The *formal cause* of an action is what I think I am hoping to achieve in expressing my values, tastes and ideas. What, then, is the formal cause of a phenomenon such as Virtual Reality? An architect has, in his mind's eye, the form of the building he is designing. His imagination is the formal cause of the final form which the structure will take, and this is constrained by the brief to which he is working: the client's wishes and cultural factors which influence the design.

What is the big idea, the 'formal cause', behind VR? This youthful phenomenon has captured the imagination of many who believe that we are on the crest of a new wave in human–computer interaction. Is

[6] See Monsma 1986: 31–36.

its formal cause – its underlying values – clear? Are these values constant or in a process of evolution? Later in this chapter we will address the question of whether *values* can be considered to be objective in any meaningful sense, rather than merely expressions of personal preference. Here we simply intend to illustrate what is meant by values in technology. VR and the response it typically engenders among enthusiasts seem to be expressive of certain key values in contemporary Western civilization.

First, its very *novelty* is appealing. The idea that one can enter into computer-generated worlds, which are not subject to the familiar limitations of the physical universe we inhabit, is attractive to some who like to explore new experiences. Originating as VR does from California, it is not surprising to find one of its pioneers, Jaron Lanier, comparing it with LSD, although there is no evidence that immersion in a virtual environment can impair brain function, whereas drugs like LSD do interfere with the chemistry and electronics of the brain to induce their novel effects (Zachary 1990).

Secondly, VR offers the possibility of *escape* from the harsh realities of normal experience. Computer-generated worlds can be appealing to those who find daily life a threat or a bore. The fascination of being let loose in a simulator illustrates this. Thirdly, it beckons us to the *adventure* of extending our consciousness, from the experience of flying to the possibilities of virtual travel to the planets or within the human circulatory system.

Fourthly, VR may enable us to enhance *health and safety* by the use of telepresence in robotics, research for which is being under-taken, for example, by the Advanced Robotics Research Centre laboratory at Salford University (R. Stone 1992). Application potential includes VR-controlled vehicles for firefighting and subsea exploration, and the manipulation of radioactive materials in the nuclear industry. The development of new methods in surgery is also being researched using VR as a training tool. One psychiatrist proposes to use VR in psychotherapy as a diagnostic tool and training aid (Tart 1990).[7]

Fifthly, VR promotes *profit*, as the manufacturers of computer games, Nintendo, demonstrated in their keenness to market a fairly crude version of the DataGlove interface before the technology had

---

[7] See also du Pont (1992).

become sophisticated enough to satisfy adult users. Golf-course architects and kitchen designers have also been swift to recognize the
potential of using VR to sell their products to clients so that they can
visualize alternative schemes at the design stage.

Sixthly, *efficiency* is a value underlying the provision of simulation
technology which can save time and expense and avoid some of the
danger in which conventional experimental methods involve scientists and technologists. VR can be used for molecular modelling,
which can enable scientists to interact with and manipulate a representation of a molecule in an attempt to understand and model the
relationship between the three-dimensional structure and the
function and properties of the molecule. This technique employs
molecular visualization, by means of which one can be immersed in
the model and 'move around'. It allows interrogation of the structure;
one can reach out, wearing a DataGlove, to manipulate parts of the
model. This saves some of the cost and time involved in setting up
physical experiments, while providing a much more salient tool for
conceptual work.

All these values may be seen behind the phenomenon of VR. But
perhaps the most significant is, seventhly, the concept of
user-friendliness, which is at the heart of the quest for appropriate
human–computer interaction. The idea is that, by use of
head-mounted displays and DataGloves, *etc.*, the cybernaut can
navigate the channels of *cyberspace*[8] without recourse to keyboarding
or mouse-clicking (which lack features of spatial control) and interact
more meaningfully with data by means of more intuitive and appropriate interfaces.

---

[8] 'An information space in which data is configured in such a way as to give the
operator the illusion of control, movement and access to information, in which s/he
can be linked together with a large number of users via puppet-like simulation which
operates in a feedback loop to the operator. VR represents the ultimate extension of
this process to provide a pure information space populated by a range of cybernetic
automatons, or data constructs, which provide the operator with a high degree of
vividness and total sensory immersion in the artificial environment' (Featherstone &
Burrows 1995: 3). *Cf.* Heim: 'Cyberspace is more than a breakthrough in electronic
media or in computer interface design. With its virtual environments and simulated
worlds, cyberspace is a metaphysical laboratory, a tool for examining our very sense
of reality' (1993: 83).

1.2.2   *Technology as value-laden*

Some commentators, however, are wary of such a focus on values. They regard technology as value-free, and believe that it is what people do with technology that causes the ethical dilemmas: 'Guns are not the problem, but people' is their typical adage. As Sherman and Judkins assert with reference to VR: 'Virtual reality itself is as neutral as the ball in a tennis match. It is what people, individually and collectively, do with it that matters' (1992: 207).[9]

Fundamental to the argument of this book is the contrary view that, like military hardware, VR is a powerful technology which is *value-laden*, both in conceptual and applicatory terms. Built-in to the technology are certain values which will influence the way VR is developed and used. Human values are clearly expressive of human nature and objectives, and are culturally defined. But what do we mean by the 'value-ladenness' of technology?

Those who argue that values are largely bound up with techno-logical *ends* but not with *means* do so as follows:

> There is no doubt that many of the components in electronic systems, for example, are software modules which do not more than operationalize basic mathematical principles. The only values they embody are those inherent in the mathematics; *i.e.*, belief in order, systematicity, *etc.* The values inherent in the larger artifact which those components comprise may be of a different order, for example a desire to conquer and dominate. All technology may be value-laden, but surely it is only the *outermost layer* of value which is relevant in the context of this discussion. A gun, for example, is an end-technology which is designed to be used for specific purposes in defence or deterrance. In contrast, VR is an enabling technology which is designed to be turned into some application and it is at this point that its outer layer of value is added. In other words, in choosing certain applications for the generic VR technology, decisions are taken to apply the technology for good (*e.g.*, emergency procedure simulations) or ill (*e.g.*, violent games). These outer values are embedded in the VR applications, not the enabling technology (Anonymous).

---

[9] *Cf.* Negropont (1995).

However, this expresses what is called the *emotive* view of values, which has a number of weaknesses. According to this view, ethical values do no more than express *preferences* for certain outcomes. The outer layer of valuing involves preferring one application over against another, perhaps on a purely utilitarian basis in terms of predicted pleasure or pain as a consequence. Yet Christian ethics has consistently sought to ascertain whether there are *normative principles* which can be derived from biblical and theological sources and which should guide the selection of means as well as of ends. The inner layers of value do not merely embody mathematical assumptions. They, like the outer layers, involve evaluation of a moral nature which touches upon personal, social and environmental concerns. Choices are made which are not based purely on scientific facts or possibilities but on the kind of world envisaged by the technologist as good. It is that moral drive which underlies all technological formation and assessment, and normative principles must be sought in order to make possible a process of evaluation. We will explore such principles in Chapter Five.

Some, however, argue that the concept of value-ladenness arises simply out of the fact that technology is undeniably a social and cultural construct. For example, the evolution of the motor car has changed transportation patterns and affected human interaction in leisure and employment. As people now have choices which were not available before the advent of the private car, they may develop a different approach to social organization and values to that which was possible in generations prior to the widespread availability of the car. In this way, many families in the USA and Europe have become 'travelling people' at weekends throughout the summer, as they pursue leisure activities with the aid of cars, caravans, boats and tents. While formerly they might have used weekends to visit family, talk to neighbours, or grow vegetables, they spend time with other social groupings of those who share common interests. They may value the pursuit of leisure more highly than close family ties or horticulture. But while it is clear that such effects can be demonstrated, there is more to the concept of the value-ladenness of technology. In fact, values are intrinsic to technology, as they are to science (Monsma 1986: 31–34).

Modern science developed within the framework of Western culture following the Renaissance and Reformation. It did not develop within civilizations influenced by Eastern philosophies or religions. Scientists engaged in study of the universe on the basis of two assumptions or beliefs: first, that the world is *orderly* and that observations made at different times in different places can be correlated; secondly, that the world is *contingent* and that causes and effects may be meaningfully related. This led to the development of certain values in science. For example, a good theory[10] should be empirically *accurate, consistent* (both internally and with other accepted theories), *broad in scope* (and extendable to new phenomena and into new domains), *simple* (in the sense of bringing together what are otherwise apparently different and unrelated phenomena) and *fruitful* (in pointing to new phenomena and uncovering new relationships among previously known phenomena).

Such values may be placed within a scale of importance, and empirical accuracy is generally held to have priority in the long run, but often not in the short-term. Theory-formation may involve intuitive leaps which cannot be tested empirically. A classic example of that is in Darwin's Theory of Evolution by Natural Selection. The theory states that the 'fittest' of a species survive and that traits are communicated through the generations. The assumption is that those who survive must be superior in some way to those who do not, and be more adapted to their environment. The successful survivor may not, however, be the best adapted to the role of hunter-killer, but may be a scavenger who relies on the skills of others. Do the *fittest* survive, or just the *most fortunate*? Darwin's theory proved attractive at a time when Britain ruled the waves and empires were being built, and when European hubris was building up to the levels which caused the disastrous wars in the first half of the twentieth century. A recent study indicates that Darwin's theory is no longer unassailable and is likely, increasingly, to come under fire until a paradigm shift takes place. A new theory of species development will seek to account for the many empirical anomalies observed which cannot be explained by Darwin's theory, but it will be received by a scientific community which, to a certain extent, has adopted more holistic values and rejects the popular view which once acclaimed them as scientist-priests in white coats.[11]

If values underlie scientific development, they are likely also to underlie technology. In fact, technology (from the Greek *technologia*,

---

[10] Ratzsch 1986: 70–71; *cf.* Kuhn (1970).

[11] See Milton (1992); *cf.* Ellul: 'The religion of science' (1976: 158).

'the systematic treatment of an art or craft') need not be applied science, and logically and temporally it precedes science.[12] Long before modern science was possible, humankind was making things and culling from the environment materials and ideas. Underlying values may well have been survival-orientated. Skills in tool-making, agricultural methods, weaponry, domestic construction, boat-building and clothing technology undoubtedly developed against a backdrop of very harsh environmental factors. The wheel became a device of strategic importance as well as of domestic convenience. Many technological wonders resulted from military requirements, as the story of Roman machine-building demonstrates.

The value-ladenness of technology is properly viewed when we consider two fundamental characteristics of technological tools and products: they are *unique*, and not universal; and they are *inter-connected* with their environments, and not isolated (Monsma 1986: 31). With regard to their uniqueness, we see that technological objects combine specific resources of practical knowledge, materials and energy into unique entities with a distinctive set of properties and capabilities. Embodied in any such object are decisions to develop one kind of knowledge and not another, to utilize energy in a certain form and quantity. 'There is no purely neutral or technical justification for all these decisions. Instead they involve conceptions of the world that are related to such issues as permissible uses, good stewardship, and justice: they involve, in other words, human valuing' (Monsma 1986: 32). The objects are also unique in the way they influence users as to how they are to be used, which often involves some degree of latitude, depending on the complexity of the object.

The inter-connections between technology and environment can be shown by two examples. First, let us consider the phenomenon of television. In order to succeed as a medium of entertainment and information, television relies on a complex network of support structures, from electrical supply, transmission stations and communications satellites, to production and maintenance facilities, government

---

[12] Monsma (1986: 10–23) deals helpfully with problems of definition. At the outset we accept the working definition of technology as 'A distinct human cultural activity in which human beings exercise freedom and responsibility in response to God by forming and transforming the natural creation, with the aid of tools and procedures, for practical ends or purposes'.

regulation and allocation of wave-bands, collection of licence fees and advertising revenue, and much more besides. Such a complex web of support structures are not value-neutral, but are bound up with decisions which affect their impact on society as a whole and the relationship of one society with others.

Secondly, Langdon Winner has noted the effect of the introduction of the snowmobile, in the 1960s, by certain reindeer-herding Lapps in Finland. These machines replaced dogsleds and skis, but the very nature of the technology and the values (such as speed and efficiency) embedded in it resulted in the breakdown of the traditional society of this group of Lapp people. They had a good reason for purchasing the equipment; to make herding faster and more efficient. But the changes which resulted were unplanned and unwanted (1977: 86–88).

In a similar way, the advent of Virtual Reality as a concept has profound implications for the way human beings interact with computers, and with other people in the real and virtual worlds, with regard to some of those values which are esteemed highly in (mostly Western) societies, and VR may produce cultural and social outcomes which are as yet unpredictable. It is not the first technological advance which may, in turn, influence cultural values. For example, David Bolter argues that, since the invention of printing, European culture has valued the sense of sight over that of touch, because seeing encourages analysis, theory and metaphysics, all of which have been developing over the last 500 years (1986: 236). In VR, the cultural value of presence is brought into focus. The possibility of immersive experiences is not essential to the concept, as the use of desktop VR in engineering design applications demonstrates (*cf.* Fang *et al.* 1995), but it is this dimension which captures the imagination of many potential users.

Immersive systems have been popularized by VR arcade games and TV demonstrations, as well as by Brett Leonard's 1992 film, *The Lawnmower Man*,[13] the storyline of which is in some ways an update of the *Frankenstein* scenario. Dr Angelo, a professor of educational psychology, believes that VR may be the ultimate learning environment, and that it may be possible to immerse a low-IQ subject in such an environment to enhance educational development.[14] The

---

[13] For critique, see Heim (1993: 143–147).

[14] 'Once the goal of magicians and alchemists, we can now use VR to actually

professor sees Jobe Smith, a simpleton mowing the lawn; a young man who is destined to perform menial tasks all his life. He is kept in his place by a crazed uncle, a Catholic priest of the old school who symbolizes the perceived resistance of traditional values to such advances in technology. The young man is enticed to explore VR and gets hooked on the latest arcade games. But the professor has a hidden agenda: of feeding him with subliminal information through VR and creating a superman. Of course, the plot has a twist and things go wrong. Jobe decides to project himself into the computer-generated environment, claiming to be 'god' of the virtual world. The resultant monster engages in a VR struggle with his creator and, in the end, suffers destruction (real not virtual).

The message of the film (if indeed there is any serious intention to offer social comment) seems to be that technology may be getting out of hand and that humans are not just machines to be programmed like computers. The virtual world may erode our contemplation of, and reflection on, the real world. Any forced acceleration of evolution will prove disastrous. The film is a foretaste of VR possibilities rather than a vehicle for specific ethical reflection.[15] Yet Dr Angelo's closing remark is, 'This technology must free the mind of man, not enslave it.' However we interpret the message of the film, it is clear that ethical concerns about the potential uses and abuses of VR are being raised by a number of commentators, and we must examine some of their claims.[16] But first, let us return to the issue of value-neutrality. There are still a few objections to our position on technology and values which need to be addressed.

1.3   Is technology value-neutral?

1.3.1   Technology's human face

As noted above, fundamental to our argument is a negative response to the question of whether or not technology is value-neutral. But

---

bring the human being up to the next stage of evolution' (Dr Angelo in *The Lawnmower Man*).

[15] 'The closing scenes spell out a bit more just what values should underpin virtual worlds research . . . the researcher knows he has a second chance . . . sheer existential thrills and ecstasy no longer govern his research' (Heim 1993: 146).

[16] See below, pp. 54–58; *cf.* Beardon (1992); Arthur (1992); Clowney (1993); Whitby (1993); social concerns are the focus of a section of *Presence* 2.2 (Spring 1993), featuring a number of leading scholars in the field.

what does that imply? We continue our discussion with a brief overview of the ways in which we have come to understand technology as a facet of human experience and expression. Modern technology is so rooted in the success of modern science that the two concepts seem almost interchangeable. Many assume that technology is, simply, applied science, *contra* Martin Heidegger (1977), who highlights sharply the clash between technology and human values. He regards technology as central to metaphysics and 'an overwhelming force that challenges the reassuring maxims of traditional morality'.[17] Heidegger died in 1976 before the microcomputer revolution got underway, but his thought is a useful analytical basis for a critique of the changes which have happened in computers since that time. He connected being with time, and believed that reality changes so that the task of thinking must also move on.

> Maybe history and tradition will fit smoothly into the information retrieval systems that will serve as resource for the inevitable planning needs of a cybernetically organised mankind. The question is whether thinking, too, will end in the business of information processing.[18]

Scientific developments have clearly increased the speed of technological change, yet technology existed long before the advent of modern science. Philosophers of the early modern and Enlightenment periods argued, initially, for the *moral primacy* of science and technology; that they are unqualifiedly good. This was replaced by a defence of *moral neutrality*, in which science and technology were considered to be outside the realm of ethics and beyond good or evil.

Of those who argued for the former position, philosophers like Francis Bacon (1561–1626) appealed to the consequences which were beginning to result from the development of science and technology in the early seventeenth century. He spoke of the 'relief of man's estate', and argued that technology should be pursued because it brought about certain benefits such as increased food production, cheaper clothing, improved transportation, better communication, *etc*.

---

[17] Comment on Heidegger by Heim (1993: 54).
[18] Quotation from Heidegger, in *ibid*. 56 (Heim's translation from original German).

This is a ***teleological*** approach.

Another version of the moral primacy argument is an appeal to the inherent rightness of science and technology. Rene Descartes (1596–1650) spoke of 'method for rightly conducting the reason' in his *Rules for the Direction of the Understanding* (1628). He held that guidelines for the proper conduct of knowing and making are inherent to the activities themselves. This is a ***deontological*** approach.

Another approach suggests that science and technology fulfil some pre-established order, that *Homo Faber* (Man the Worker) could not be authentically human without technology, as it is an expression of human nature. This we would call the ***natural law***, or moral order, theory, a famous exponent of which was Hugo Grotius (1583–1645), who claimed that 'Natural law is a dictate of right reason, which points out that an act, according as it is or is not in conformity with rational nature, has in it a quality of moral baseness or moral necessity; and that, in consequence, such an act is either forbidden or enjoined by the author of nature, God.'[19]

1.3.2   *Alternatives, possibilities, choices*

The alternative view, that science and technology *are* value-neutral, is the result of the ambiguities and difficulties associated with modern science and technology during and after the Industrial Revolution, suggests Carl Mitcham (1991). According to this view, science and technology are only means and can do nothing of themselves; it is the users who are at fault when they are misused.[20] Despite the popularity of this position, there has recently been a reassertion of the relevance of ethical discussions of technological development. Mitcham claims that all theory is *value-laden* and that there is no value-free or value-neutral methodology or theory. In choosing between competing theories or methods we appeal to values such as aesthetic beauty or simplicity.[21] The values of individuals and societies determine which research and development programmes are pursued. Mitcham also argues that theories have a bearing on human behaviour, pointing to,

---

[19] Quoted in Urmson & Ree (1991: 121–122). Note: Not all natural law theories assume the existence of God: *cf.* Wogaman (1989: 43, 49, 53). Wogaman attempts to restate the natural law on a Kantian rather than a Thomistic basis.

[20] Mitcham, in Pitt & Lugo (1991: 139); *cf.* Sherman & Judkins, see above, p. 41.

[21] As noted above, pp. 38–46. See Ratzsch 1986: 70–71.

as an example, David Hume's attempt to construct a morality compatible with Newtonian mechanics. Mitcham points out that there are practical issues at stake in all this. Technological solutions can lead to goods or harms; therefore when considering whether or not to develop a particular technology, we need to pay full attention to its social implications. Technology is not inherently right, and engineering efficiency may lead to dehumanizing effects. Because of this, limits must be set in order to minimize potential harms, by means of codes of practice and frameworks for moral decision-making (Kallman & Grillo 1996). We know only too well that environmental pollution, ecological disruption or even cultural disaster can result from scientific and technological developments, and they cannot be regarded as uniquely privileged activities. Further, they must compete for economic resources, and people must choose from alternatives. We will return to this, with specific reference to information technology, in Chapter Six.

In other words, science and technology cannot be viewed as special activities which should be treated differently from other human pursuits with respect to ethics. Technology must be subject to the same kind of scrutiny as religion, art, sport or literature. *Postmodernism* places technology among a number of equally important human enterprises, and does not single it out as the *raison d'être* of humankind's existence. Modernism tended to glorify technical achievement; now we are only too aware of some of the drawbacks.[22] But this should not mean a return to the premodern subordination of technology to nature, politics or religious belief. Postmodern pluralism, both personal and social, emphasizes the choices which are open to us, none of which can claim to be absolutely right for all. Different types of technology are the (potential) result of such choices. The watchword must be 'Consider every possible perspective. Take account of everything you can!' This, suggests Mitcham, is the new categorical imperative (1991: 143).[23] It resonates with Lyon's approach outlined above, of a complex interaction between premodern, modern and postmodern.

[22] For further discussion of postmodernism, see below, pp. 99–105.
[23] *Cf.* Jonas (1984).

1.4   The objectivity of human values

1.4.1   Introductory considerations

Our assumptions about the nature of values must be made clear at this stage. The fact–value dichotomy, popularized by the logical positivists, which is now *passé* in philosophy of science, is still influential among some exponents of Christian ethics, and in theology. Polanyi (1962, 1964) and Polkinghorne (1986, 1991) have demonstrated the weakness of a positivist approach, and the author accepts their conclusions as fundamental. From the philosophical point of view, however, it is important to demonstrate how belief in a more dynamic relationship between fact and value may be undergirded by arguments for values being in some sense objective, rather than merely subjective expressions of preference.

Current ways of thinking about morality, and values in particular, are the consequences of philosophical ideas developed in the eighteenth to twentieth centuries. Although these ideas are much older than that, originating in the earliest classical philosophy, in the past 200 years they have been accepted by many educated people as expressive of fundamental truths about the nature of reality.[24] Alasdair MacIntyre believes that the Enlightenment project has failed and that we need to return to the premodern position exemplified by Aristotle's ethics.[25] The choice for MacIntyre is between no morality (Nietzsche) and morality (Aristotle); he holds that *virtue* is the only sound basis for the governance of and interrelationships within civilized society as we have come to know it in the Western world. There therefore exists a 'right' and 'natural' way for people which can only be understood by looking beyond them. 'The education of citizens in the virtues is of central importance, because this inculcates the desirable goals' (Lyon 1994a: 82).[26]

How, then, does thinking about values connect with other aspects

---

[24] J. Haldane, 'The Nature of Values', in Carr & Haldane (1993: 9–20); *cf.* MacIntyre (1985) and Rivers (1993).

[25] 'Either one must follow through the aspirations and the collapse of the different versions of the Enlightenment project until there remains only the Nietzschean diagnosis and the Nietzschean problematic or one must hold that the Enlightenment project was not only mistaken, but should never have been commenced in the first place. There is no third alternative . . .' (MacIntyre 1985: 111).

[26] *Cf.* Carr (1991).

of thought? Some questions about values are psychological and sociological: *e.g.* 'What ideals have motivated people in the past?', or 'What
social attitudes reported in surveys are expressive of changes in
morality?' Such questions cannot settle issues about what is good or
bad, right or wrong; nor can they establish the criteria whereby we
evaluate something as good or bad. Philosophy of value (*axiology*) must
ask basic questions like, 'Is justice more important than liberty? Is
friendship good?' (Carr & Haldane 1993: 10). It explores why it is that
we deem certain activities to be wrong and others right. Although
many people are content to have values without searching too deeply
to discover their origins, values are presupposed by people's behaviour.
Action is, by definition, intentional, *i.e.* aimed at some end. So we can
ask *why* people do what they do; what is the goal in view? This does
not mean that people always have aims which have been consciously
thought out. John Haldane, Professor of Moral Philosophy at the
University of St Andrews, comments:

> Certainly we can do things with regret, even as we are doing them;
> but to the extent that we are acting intentionally there is some
> respect in which the result is viewed as desirable. It is in this sense
> that everyone who acts is concerned with values (1993: 11).

So we ask, 'What do good things have in common?' and answers
can be grouped within three general categories. First, *theological*
theories, such as voluntarism, in which something is good if God
approves of it and bad if he disapproves of it (although, as Haldane
notes, there are difficulties with this view and it is not widely held
today). Secondly, *deontological* theories: those which hold that certain
characteristics, actions and states of affairs are good (or bad) in and of
themselves; *e.g.* that lying or stealing is always morally wrong. Since
Kant, deontology has related values to the fundamental right of
respect. Kant respected rationality above all other features of
humanness. Later thinkers wanted to extend respect to all living
things, and not merely those blessed with rationality. Thirdly,
teleological theories: that actions are good in so far as they result in
good consequences. In this way, rightness and wrongness is a property
of individual actions relating to their actual or possible results. This
leads on to further questions such as, 'Is anything objectively (really)
good?' In other words, do deontological and teleological theories

merely account for the underlying patterns of our thoughts and attitudes about values, or do they describe 'an independent order of objective goods and requirements' (Carr & Haldane 1993: 12)?

1.4.2   In what ways are values objective?

Empiricism developed from the original work of Aristotle, who held that philosophy began with leisure – that people can philosophize only if they have the opportunity to distance themselves from immediate practical concerns and reflect upon the nature of reality. But the rise of modern natural science involved the development of empirical investigation through controlled experiment which was, apparently, free from any metaphysical presuppositions. Yet even this presupposed a fundamental metaphysical belief, in the *order* of the natural world and the possibility of making sense of it. Haldane argues that philosophy does not exclude the possibility that there may be a general objectivity of natural norms, over against the Humean emphasis which is subjectivist about values (Carr & Haldane 1993: 18).[27] But it goes against the flow of popular relativistic thought today to suggest that moral values may be objective, for a number of reasons.

First, it is alleged that there is widespread *disagreement about values*. Haldane replies that, while people may well disagree in their evaluation of, for example, certain actions, such disputes presuppose agreement that there *are* values. Apparent disagreements may actually be different expressions of the same beliefs, and in any case, disagreement does not mean that there can be no truth (1993: 19).

Secondly, while it is true that beliefs about values arise from *societal influences* such as education and family, the source of one's beliefs is a separate issue from their objectivity or truthfulness. Thirdly, it is reasonable to expect that value judgments will express attitudes of *approval*, because values relate to our well-being. Belief is the appropriate response to truth and approval to goodness. I may believe **x** because it is true, but this does not mean that **x** is true because of my

---

[27] Hume's view is summarized in Urmson & Ree (1991: 142): 'Just as the discovery of all matters of fact depends on relations of necessary connections which seem to be objective, but are really dispositions of the mind, so ethical judgments depend on rightness and wrongness, goodness and badness, which seem to be objective qualities of persons and acts, but are really the approvals and disapprovals of the judging mind.'

belief. Again, I may approve **y** because it is good, but **y** is not good just because I approve it.

Fourthly, it is not necessarily the case that claims about values rely on **unproven assumptions**. Persons or actions, for example, may be evaluated as 'good' as the result and proofs rest on basic assumptions, and value judgments are no worse off than other claims in this respect (Carr & Haldane 1993: 20).[28] Fifthly, it is not the case that disputes about values are **irresolvable**. Often differences of opinion about matters which people hold to be important *are* resolved. For example, the provision of education and the health service by the state is evidence of widespread agreement about their intrinsic value.

Sixthly, it has been alleged that there are no procedures for resolving disputes about values. There may be no *scientific tests* which are appropriate to some questions of value, but then we would expect aesthetic questions, for example, to be answered differently from those of physics. In most disputes about values, we may adopt the viewpoint of the impartial spectator, aiming, as far as possible, to be disinterested, impartial and free of fallacious beliefs. Seventhly, it is said that values are not found in nature. Haldane replies that they *are* natural. Values are not objects, but natural phenomena, often complex and linked with aspects of **human nature**; facts and values are not mutually exclusive.

That there is such a thing as human nature is a fundamental assumption of this discussion. It is a prerequisite of most works on Christian ethics. That does not mean that according to all Christian ethicists human nature is viewed as necessarily fixed and given. Ian Barbour (1992) proposes an approach to Christian ethical reflection, based on A. N. Whitehead's process philosophy, which views both God and humankind as undergoing a continuous process of evolutionary change. To a certain extent, Frederick Ferré (1993) is also attracted by this approach, which is characteristic of late modernity. However, in this discussion we are more concerned to relate the argument to postmodern approaches to subjectivity, theology and ethics, a task which we will address in Chapters Three and Seven.[29]

---

[28] *Cf.* Wogaman: '. . . we do not have a basis for making ethical judgments until we can ground our conception of the good and of moral obligation on an ultimate framework of valuation . . . Nothing is good just because it exists; it all depends on how it relates to ultimate reality' (1989: 15).

[29] See pp. 99–105 and 171–188.

1.5   Potential moral dilemmas posed by Virtual Reality

1.5.1   Current concerns

Much speculation is abroad about the potential ethical implications of VR. Veronica Pantelidis of the VR and Education Laboratory at East Carolina University has proposed a list of questions which, she believes, need to be asked (Pantelidis 1994). She focuses upon four principal areas of concern: first, behaviour tolerance; secondly, behaviour manipulation; thirdly, information censorship and mis-information; and fourthly, addiction to virtual worlds. Let us look at these in turn.

Behaviour tolerance in a virtual world is an ethical issue because it is unclear to what extent participants in virtual environments may tolerate types of behaviour, *in others*, which would be unacceptable in the real world. There would be degrees of toleration, no doubt, and this might be a matter of group consensus in multi-user environments. Yet the objections of those who have a low tolerance for such virtual behaviour might well have to be accepted. Those who react by suggesting that any participant has the freedom to log off at any time if the interaction becomes intolerable assume that all involved will have the strength to do so. But the attraction of the virtual world might be too strong. Casey Larijani refers to recent research at Carnegie Mellon University indicating that a participant immersed in a virtual environment is often over-tolerant of manipulative or deviant behaviour. It may be that the desire to enter the illusion is so great that users may be unaware of the ways in which they are open to manipulation (1994: 126).

Behaviour manipulation issues include whether participants may be persuaded to do something *themselves* in a virtual environment which would be ethically repugnant for them in real life; whether they might purchase something which they would not normally purchase or believe something which they do not believe in the real world, and then act upon that belief within the virtual environment; and whether thought or action in the real world might be affected, subliminally or consciously, by virtual interaction. In particular, it may be possible for thresholds of acceptable thought or behaviour to be shifted by such experience, so that actions which were repugnant become less so.

The advent of virtual communities via the Internet raises issues of *information censorship and misinformation*. If increasing numbers of people worldwide are exchanging information through cyberspace and even entering into multi-user environments, information may be doctored to further hidden agendas, misinformation may easily be spread, and global knowledge may be manipulated by pressure or power groups.

Lastly, many are concerned about potential *addiction to virtual worlds*. Already, the fascination of computer-generated environments suggests that some may prefer synthetic worlds to the real thing, especially those who find normal relationships very hard. It may be easier to relate to people over the Internet rather than to speak face to face. However, some network-users report a desire to meet regularly with their fellow participants and to have real relationships with them (Rheingold 1994: 38–64).

1.5.2   Risks and restrictions
In the discussion so far we have noted a number of potential benefits of VR, but also some risks. A case has been made for placing restrictions on certain types of activity within virtual environments (Whitby 1993: 6–10). We now relate these to the ethical questions noted above.

First, concerning *behaviour tolerance*, it is argued that activities which are held to be acceptable for other users to perform within VR may eventually become normalized. Current arcade games involve a level of simulated violence which might be interpreted as socially approved, especially by the young, even if all users do not wish to engage in such activity. Virtual pornography will doubtless become increasingly available, and come under the watchful eye of the vice squad. Why, then, should virtual violence be unrestricted?

Secondly, in response to concerns about *behaviour manipulation*, it is argued that VR-users might do in the real world things which are possible in virtuality. They might rape or murder or try to fly from rooftops. Others suggest, following the notion of *katharsis*, that to act in such ways in a virtual world would obviate the need for real acts of violence to others or self. Although it is very difficult to establish empirically causal connections between virtual and real acts, it is nevertheless a concern of many that computer games which enable users to engage in gross violence may have the effect of reducing personal sensitivity to real violence and lead to violent acts.

Thirdly, with regard to *censorship issues*, it is argued that, despite

John Stuart Mill's conviction that consenting adults should be allowed to do in private that which does not harm others, there are some activities which are not acceptable, even in private, to a civilized society. Yet Mill excluded children from his 'Harm Condition' approach, a tradition which continues in the exercise of censorship in the media such as film and TV, although computer games have avoided such oversight as yet. It is children who are likely to be among the first targets of VR-marketing, as the realism of computer games is enhanced by head-mounted displays and DataGloves.[30] Similar concerns are expressed about 'video nasties' and their potential effects on the behaviour of viewers, especially the young. This became a public issue in 1993 in the UK with the trial and conviction of two boys for the murder of toddler Jamie Bulger, following their viewing of a violent film.

Fourthly, in relation to the question of *addiction*, some believe that, as the realism of virtual environments increases, many will prefer the virtual to the real and seek to escape from hard reality. Similar forebodings were uttered about TV in its infancy, although recent research seems to indicate that, while many do spend inordinate amounts of time as 'couch potatoes', TV has not, as yet, totally undermined the fabric of society. The film director Federico Fellini, however, believes that 'TV has mutilated our capacity for solitude. It has violated our most intimate, private and secret dimension'.[31] Jacques Ellul speaks of TV as 'the great agent of transition from a society of writing to a society of pictures' (1990: 332). He cites evidence from a 1986 survey of twenty French families who were asked to do without their TV sets for a month. They reported a need to fill the time freed by the absence of television, and many felt that they had nothing to say to other people. They became marginalized in their neighbourhoods and felt an existential void within themselves for a time. But within the month they began to feel a sense of release from their bondage to TV. A few had to work through withdrawal symptoms, but most discovered that they had more time to meet and

---

[30] 'The only part of the conduct of anyone, for which he is amenable to society, is that which concerns others. In the part which merely concerns himself, his independence is, of right, absolute. Over himself, over his own body and mind, the individual is sovereign' (Mill 1859: 14).

[31] Quoted in Ellul (1990: 339).

talk to friends and to read (1990: 338). However, VR is an interactive experience which involves participation in a way which to date is impossible for the TV viewer. It invites us, potentially, to create alternative worlds and, virtually, to inhabit them; to immerse ourselves in stimuli which get the adrenaline flowing and arouse other bodily functions, and to shape the experience according to our will rather than the will of the media producer. VR is not a passive medium.

Morality is about making choices, and VR is loaded with many potential harms, which must be balanced against the good effects it may tend to promote. We must decide what are acceptable risks in the making available of a new electronic medium, and what kinds of activity can and should be discouraged, restricted or banned. This is true of the telephone and television, and it will be true of VR. However, the beneficial implications must not be ignored. In addition to the many constructive applications to which we have alluded, it may be that VR will become a medium for exploring morality and teaching ethics. We could be enabled to experience difficult moral dilemmas and to examine various behaviour patterns by entering virtual worlds. But we do have to enquire whether there are particular types of human thought and action which are inherently unsuitable for computers to represent.[32]

Another ethical concern could be added to those noted above: the level of 'hype' associated with the launching of VR – which has been heralded by some as a watershed in the history of the world, not merely in the development of computers. The late Timothy Leary, former drugs guru of the sixties, is quoted as saying:

> There are no limits on VR. It's all about access to information. The donning of computer clothing will be as significant in human history as the donning of outer clothing was in the Palaeolithic.[33]

If and when it happens, the advent of the DataSuit as portrayed in *The Lawnmower Man* will be a significant development in human–computer interaction, but other believers in the potential of VR are afraid that the technology will be tarred with the image of promises of virtual sex and holidays abroad without leaving home. Brenda

---

[32] See below, pp. 137–144, with reference to the work of Ladd (1989).
[33] In Rheingold (1991: 378).

Laurel, whose book *Computers as Theatre* reflects her interests both as an actor and computer-buff, comments:

> If we do not deliver, and deliver soon, on all the implied and stated promises, virtual reality runs the risk of falling into the same credibility, funding and profile nightmare as artificial intelligence – only much more quickly.[34]

Doubtless some people have claimed in the past that certain embryo technologies will be ultimately significant for human progress. Yet it is when a technology is in the early stages of development that ethical reflection needs to take place. When it is 'up and running' it will be too late. With the exponential increase in computer power, time is of the essence for those concerned to offer analyses of VR and values.

1.6   Christian ethical reflection

1.6.1   Which paradigm . . . What purpose?

As Chapter Three will explain, our ethical paradigm in this discussion will be an adapted version of a modern representation of classical Christian ethics which has been proposed by Oliver O'Donovan (1994), Regius Professor of Moral and Pastoral Theology at Oxford, with which Haldane's philosophical treatment of values[35] finds an immediate resonance, and which offers tools for a critique of postmodern approaches to ethics. O'Donovan's insights will be related to those of Ellul (1976) and Wogaman (1989). We shall call this paradigm the '*Ethics of Christian Realism*'.[36]

The purpose of this book is to demonstrate the distinctive contribution which Christian ethics (as represented by this paradigm) can make in the debate, and to offer a critique of the conceptual basis of Virtual Reality in the context of postmodernity, so that developments may be encouraged which enhance human dignity and responsibility as understood in terms of classical moral order theory. In particular, we will seek to answer the key questions. Does VR enhance the perception and extend the capabilities of humankind made in the

---

[34] Quoted in Arthur (1992: 22); *cf.* Laurel (1991).
[35] See above, pp. 50–53.
[36] See below, pp. 75–79.

image of God? Or does it encourage distorted conceptions of personhood and invite users to engage in activities which are hazardous to spiritual, mental or physical health?

1.6.2   *Working hypothesis*

In the discussion, we will be seeking to address other important issues, too. As the title of this book suggests, our working hypothesis is that the advent of Virtual Reality may be bound up with a new *Virtual Morality* which is expressive of postmodernity: that as our ethical principles and moral stances may reflect our perceptions of the nature of reality, so a paradigm shift may take place when we enter a virtual world. There the rules or principles which may govern action in the real world may no longer apply, and behaviour there may be carried over into real life. For Christians, this presents a dilemma, since they want to affirm the lordship of Christ over all worlds. Could it be that, through computer technology, humankind has created worlds where individuals can be free of moral responsibility to God and fellow humans? This idea raises important questions about the fundamentals of ethics as a function of our experience of reality. It brings us back to one of the all-embracing questions: Can there be any meaningful ethical framework without some ultimate reference-point, some absolute? Or do we just make up our ethics as we go along, 'inventing right and wrong', as Mackie (1974) has suggested we must?[37]

This book includes consideration of Virtual Reality both as an important concept for exploring our understanding of ethics and as itself the subject of searching ethical evaluation. The purpose of Chapters Two to Six is to analyse the issues raised by our working hypothesis. In Chapter Seven we will bring the discussion to a conclusion on the basis of that analysis, and seek to determine the significance of VR for Christian ethics, and vice versa, as well as to develop connections between philosophy of technology and Christian ethics in the context of postmodernity.

---

[37] Recently, the view that Christian ethics is purely a human construct has been asserted by Cupitt: 'The more realistic your God, the more punitive your morality' (1989: 167). *Cf.* Hart: 'Language about God is really about the self' (1993: 14). For a realist response to the humanism of Freeman (1993), see Harries (1994).

Chapter Two:
Technology and human nature

2.1 *Virtual Reality and* Homo Faber
2.1.1 *Mythology and progress*

In Chapter One we concluded that it is because technology is *not* value-neutral that it must be subject to rigorous ethical scrutiny. But, as we noted, there is a deeper reason still: technology, its artefacts, systems and concepts, can never be separated from human beings. Technology is a product of human endeavour. It is not an autonomous force which exercises rule over hapless humankind, despite the fears of Jacques Ellul.[1] Ellul (1964, 1990), the French philosopher, sociologist and theologian, analyses the phenomenon of technological development, which clearly has ambivalent outcomes for humankind. He affirms that all technical progress has a cost in human terms, that at each stage of development it raises more and greater problems than it solves, that its harmful effects cannot be separated from its beneficial effects, and that it has a great number of unpredictable outcomes. Some allege that he is unduly sceptical about technology, others that he is a prophet. However he may be judged, Ellul is clearly against any

---

[1] Ellul (1990); *cf.* Ferkiss (1969) and Bereano (1976).

crude evolutionary view of technology as humankind's highest achievement. He argues that technology is the major determining factor in contemporary society, asserting that the diverse technologies in Western society comprise a coherent system which operates according to its own laws of development and which is, in some sense, autonomous and beyond human control. As a theologian, Ellul further claims that technology has been idolized, in that modern society now depends upon continual technical advance. He believes that ancient mythology is paralleled by modern myths of progress, and that the only hope of escape from this dominance is through a form of desacralization in which people assert their uniqueness and dignity as human beings and children of God and refuse to worship technological progress. This can only be achieved, says Ellul (1990: 39), by prayer, compassion and ethical action so that humanity may be delivered from technological determinism and find true freedom.[2]

2.1.2 Prehistoric art and Plato's cave

Some commentators do indeed view technology from an evolutionary standpoint. It is suggested that the tool-making which began in the Stone Age has developed over many millenniums into the quest for ever more sophistication, and that we must see this as a continuum. But is modern high technology directly comparable with primitive craft skills? Howard Rheingold (1991) is an enthusiastic commentator on developments in computer technology who sees parallels between the advent of Virtual Reality and the cave paintings of prehistoric peoples. This analogy will help us to explore similarities and differences between modern and earlier technologies. Rheingold refers to the work of the anthropologist John Pfeiffer, who has studied and discussed the phenomena of cave art, which he believes emerged about 30,000 years ago. Cave paintings discovered in central France are located in the depths of the caves, in utter darkness far from the entrances. They are found on wide expanses of walls or hidden inside tiny chambers. Pfeiffer suggests that the paintings were probably part of rituals, ordeals or underground journeys for mystical purposes. Many of the paintings are distorted and worked on natural relief to give a 3-D impression. Others are incised in the walls and are revealed only when light is passing across them. Pfeiffer's hypothesis is that the

---

[2] *Cf.* Ellul (1976); see below, pp. 88–91.

purpose of these 'underground light shows' was to cause a specific state of *consciousness*. This might helpfully be set alongside Plato's *Myth of the Cave*, which originally illustrated his theory of forms but which has become more widely used as a tool of metaphysical analysis.[3]

In the *Republic*, Plato asks us to imagine some people living in an underground cave, who sit with their backs to the mouth of the cave. Their hands and feet are bound so that they can see only the back wall of the cave. Behind them is a high wall, and behind this human-like creatures go back and forward, holding up different figures above the top of the wall. There is a fire beyond these figures so that they cast flickering shadows on the back wall of the cave. The only impression of movement known to the cave-dwellers is this shadow-play. They have never seen the objects which cause the shadows. Plato then imagines what happens when one of the cave-dwellers manages to free himself from his bonds. He enquires what is causing the shadows, and turns round to see the figures being lifted up above the wall. He is amazed by the clarity of the figures in comparison with their shadows. He climbs over the wall and out into the open air and is dazzled by the sunlight. For the first time he sees colours and shapes, animals and plants. He could run off into the wonderful world he has discovered, but instead he decides to return to free his fellow cave-dwellers. He tries to convince them that the shadows are but reflections of the real world outside, but they do not believe him. They point to the cave wall and say that what they can see there is all that there is. In the end, they kill him. The point of the story, for Plato, was to illustrate the philosopher's discovery of the true ideas which lie behind the outward forms of natural phenomena. He was probably thinking of Socrates in particular, who suffered death because of the ignorant reaction of those who refused to accept his insights. Plato meant that the natural world is dark and dreary in comparison with the vivid world of ideas.

Ancient cave art, seen as a projection of the significance of realities

---

[3] Rheingold (1991: 378–381), citing Pfeiffer (1982); *cf.* Ucko & Rosenfeld 1967: 116–149. See also Dennett (1991), who does not consider VR to be significant in terms of expanding consciousness. For discussion of Plato's *Cave*, from *The Republic*, see Gaarder (1995: 76–78), and Heim (1993: 88–89). The idea of connecting Plato's cave with VR was suggested by Prof. G. Allport during a guest lecture in Heriot-Watt University in 1992.

outside the caves, like the shadows of Plato's myth, yet not in a dungeon, like the mythological cave, could have been an aid to the imparting of a growing body of information which was needed for the expansion of a new way of life. The development of new techniques such as seed-sowing, herbal medicine, stone tool-making, star-gazing, and animal husbandry surely meant that cultural information had to be stored and transmitted to future generations. The collective knowledge of the society was expanding, but there was no writing to aid record-keeping. In fact, writing as we know it did not appear for another 20,000 years, according to Pfeiffer and other cultural anthropologists. Cave art, suggests Pfeiffer, was used as a way of brainwashing initiates, who were taken into unfamiliar, alien and unpleasant places where their consciousness of the everyday world might be erased or undermined as completely as possible. Far from natural light, they were dramatically exposed to the transmission of the 'tribal encyclopaedia'.

What, then, is the link between this anthropological hypothesis and Virtual Reality? Rheingold suggests that the advent of VR might be a significant stage in the evolution of technology, and even of humanity. Computer-generated experiences may cause us to redefine basic concepts such as identity, community and reality. Marshall McLuhan, media guru of the sixties, followed up his famous dictum 'The medium is the message'[4] with another one-liner: 'Electronic media alter the ratios between the senses'.[5] In the case of VR, this seems to mean that, using the imagery of Bunyan's *Pilgrim's Progress*, 'eye-gate' takes precedence over 'ear-gate'. In the potential wonderland of virtual environments, language as we know it could

[4] 'To say that any technology or extension of man creates a new environment is a much better way of saying the medium is the message' (McLuhan, quoted in Molinari 1987: 309).

[5] Quoted in Rheingold (1991: 387); *cf.* 'It is one of the ironies of Western man that he has never felt any concern about invention as a threat to his way of life. The fact is that, from the alphabet to the motorcar, Western man has been steadily refashioned in a slow technological explosion that has extended over 2,500 years. From the time of the telegraph onward, however, Western man began to live an implosion. He began suddenly with Nietzschean insouciance to play the movie of his 2,500-year explosion backward. But he still enjoys the results of the extreme fragmentation that enables him to ignore cause-and-effect in all interplay of technology and culture' (McLuhan 1987: 270).

become increasingly redundant. Impressions may be more significant than information.

2.2   *Technology: ancient and modern*

Whether VR is as significant in human evolution as cave art may have been is a question which must be left to anthropologists many centuries from now. But it does lead us into a fruitful area of discussion which is important in exploring technology and humanness. Can we draw parallels between ancient and modern technologies as Rheingold does? Is there not a vast difference between primitive technology and the hi-tech world of today? Egbert Schuurman, a leading philosopher of technology who has also been an engineer and a member of the Dutch parliament, has helpfully compared modern technology with what he calls 'classical' technology (1980: 4ff.).

Schuurman defines what he means by 'technology' as 'The activity by which people give form to nature for human ends, with the aid of tools' (1980: 5).[6] This definition is not intended to be exhaustive, merely adequate for the purpose of comparing old and new technologies. Schuurman suggests that there are nine significant differences. First, the **environment** in which we live today bears the mark of technology. In ancient times, people were surrounded by a natural environment and were rarely able to distance themselves from nature. Our observations of the natural world are taken with highly developed technological instruments. Secondly, the **materials** we use today are synthetic or highly refined products rather than natural resources which we must cull and use. Thirdly, the **energy** used in early technology was produced by animals and people via tractive and muscle power, whereas modern technology derives energy from nature via fossil fuels, nuclear power, wind and water. Fourthly, modern technology is not dependent solely on the skills of human tool-handling in order to form objects, because of the advent of **machines**.

Fifthly, the **process** of technology formation has changed radically. Formerly, people merely followed rules in handling materials without the need for explanatory insight. Today the process is determined by automatic coupling and control. Sixthly, modern technology is a

---

[6] *Cf.* definition adopted above, p. 44 n. 12.

co-operative exercise between engineers, contractors and workers. Personal contact between producers and consumers may be non-existent. Seventhly, premodern technology was directed in the *here and now* and provided solutions to practical problems of everyday life. Today's engineers work first at a theoretical level and draw up their designs on the basis of mathematics, physics and technological science. The primitive approach of trial and error has been refined into sophisticated means of simulation and testing of ideas before they are transmitted into materials. Eighthly, *automation* has eliminated people from the process as much as possible, and this has been accompanied by the use of mass-production methods.

Ninthly, and finally, Schuurman notes that early technology was undifferentiated and static and changed very slowly as it was passed down from craftsman to apprentice. Modern technology, based as it is on scientific developments, is, by contrast, **highly differentiated**[7] **and dynamic** so that tremendous changes have happened in a short space of time. Yet, despite these contrasts, Schuurman wants to affirm that technological activity remains a *human* activity, even in modern times:

> One must never lose sight of the intimate connection between people and technology, especially when evaluating such a phenomenon as automation, which may sometimes appear to be rather autonomous with regard to people (1980: 8).

As a Christian philosopher, Schuurman wants to make connections not only between people and technology but also between our notions of *Homo Faber* and the biblical accounts of human origins and developments. We must now explore some of those connections, drawing upon the insights of other philosophers and theologians, notably Jurgen Moltmann, Henri Blocher, Philip Hughes, Scott Cook and Jacques Ellul.

2.3   Biblical anthropology and technology

Biblical reflection on human nature developed considerably over the

---

[7] 'The emerging industrial society was characterised by a steadily increasing division of labour, in which tasks became progressively more specialised' (Lyon 1994a: 23).

centuries during which the original ideas were transmitted verbally, written down, gathered and edited. However, there is a thread running through the unfolding accounts which is relevant to our understanding of technology and biblical anthropology, and which we now seek to trace. Recent scholarship has validated this approach in a recovery of a biblical theology of *covenant*, the unfolding account of God's relationship with his people and their ensuing responsibilities (McComiskey 1987). This is seen as the *metanarrative* which holds the biblical stories together. Of course, the use of Scripture in discussions about modern science and technology is not without its particular problems, as John Polkinghorne has pointed out (1991: 60–73).[8] For the purposes of this discussion, we will adopt a modified version of his approach which he styles *critical realism*.

Polkinghorne holds that the Bible is an indispensable way in to the story of Israel's interaction with God, to the historical figure of Jesus Christ, and to the experience of the first disciples. We are concerned, in reading Scripture, not merely with the events it purports to record, but also with the powerful symbolic images which convey the significance of what happened. As Polkinghorne says, 'As we open ourselves to the symbolic richness of scripture, we are donning those "spectacles behind the eyes" which will enable us to view the world from a Christian perspective' (1991: 69). In seeking to glean insight about a biblical understanding of the significance of technology, it seems appropriate that we adopt an approach which focuses on the meaning and significance of what the authors and editors of Scripture wrote (the approach of redaction and narrative criticism), rather than the form-critical method which focuses upon the distinction between myth and history in the stories.

2.3.1   Old Testament

To understand biblical anthropology we must begin with Genesis chapters one and two. Humankind, male and female, is created in the *image of God* (Gn. 1:27),[9] which means that God, the Father of humankind, has imparted characteristics to the race which reflect his own divine nature (Hughes 1989: 51–64). As God's vicegerents,

---

[8] *Cf.* Boulton *et al.* 1994: 15–57.

[9] Blocher 1984: 79–84; Moltmann 1985: 215–225; *cf.* McComiskey 1987: 51, 218–220; *cf.* Clarke (1982).

human beings are to have dominion over the plant and animal kingdoms and to be accountable to God as stewards of his domain (1:26). His purpose is that they may grow as fully as possible into this image in this life. Part of this purpose is that they should have knowledge, but limits are set. People have been created to live in harmony with their Maker, but this does not mean that they have immediate access to all knowledge. They must rely on God for their understanding of good and evil. The tree of the *knowledge of good and evil* bears the only forbidden fruit; this probably means that moral knowledge and ethical discernment are not to be autonomous faculties in humankind (Blocher 1984: 126–133). People are to know right from wrong as they are taught by God, and to receive from him the ability to apply their minds to moral problems. Death will ensue if they eat the forbidden fruit, and death is essentially separation from God. In other words, people will be de-humanized; they will lose their innate moral sense to some extent if they unilaterally declare themselves independent of God's will for them (Gn. 2:9, 17). Ultimately, right and wrong must either be decided by human consensus or by revelation from God. Either way, reference must be made to some absolute if sense is to be made of moral affirmations and decisions (Blocher 1984: 111–134).

According to the biblical account, humankind as originally created is a race of workers and carers (2:15) and of observers and classifiers (2:20). Even here we see the logical priority of technology over science. Man's fundamental calling is to be a good steward of the environment in which he is set, and his knowledge arises out of his daily work. However, the story relates that people chose to disobey God and to seek autonomy rather than theonomy (Gn. 3:1–9), and that this had immediate effects on their knowing (Gn. 3:10–11). The image of God in humankind was defaced, and human thinking was corrupted. Idolatry was the inescapable conclusion of this new-found philosophy. Yet, in grace, the same God who pronounced judgment gave hope of deliverance (Gn. 3:15). The fall of humankind into sin did not diminish their vocation before God. The primordial paradise may have been lost, but the human race is still accountable for its stewardship.

The philosopher of technology Scott Cook (1993) has affirmed the importance of the creation and Eden stories in exploring the relationship between nature and technology, despite the work of Lynn

White (1968) which has become paradigmatic for some critics of biblical attitudes to the environment. White claimed that the Genesis 1 – 3 myths convey a specific set of values focused on the vocation of humankind to 'subdue the earth' (Gn. 1:28) and that these values have precipitated the ecological crisis. White's conclusion was that, therefore, we must reject the myths and look for a more constructive view of creation. Cook criticizes White's analysis on two fronts. First, he argues that White is too rigid in his interpretation of the stories, which can be understood in a quite different way. Secondly, Cook wants to affirm the important place such myths can have in our understanding of technological culture and its relationship to the environment. In fact, the crucial issue is White's understanding of Genesis 1:28:

> And God blessed them, and God said to them, 'Be fruitful and multiply, and fill the earth and subdue it; and *have dominion* over the fish of the sea and over the birds of the air and over every living thing that moves upon the earth' (RSV).

According to Cook, the Hebrew for 'have dominion' (*v'yirdu*) can mean 'to rule over' but it can also mean 'to take care of'. While this point is debatable, it is not necessary to interpret the text in the way White does.[10] The meaning of 'dominion' here is not autonomous exploitation, suggests Cook, but the responsibility for something which has been entrusted into one's care. Yet Cook concedes that,

---

[10] S. Cook (1993: 36), following a modern Jewish interpretation by D. Yanow; *contra* Harris, Archer & Waltke (1980: 2: 833), who say that 'let them *rule* over the fish of the sea' (Gn. 1:28) does mean *subdue* or *subjugate*. However, this does not imply that the text is encouraging the ruthless exploitation of the environment by a race who may do as they please with it. It means that the Creator has given humankind his authority as his vicegerents over the natural world. Having taken meticulous care to create such an environment for humankind, as Genesis 1 relates, it would seem strange for the Creator then to command its predatory exploitation rather than conservation and careful stewardship. *Ruling* in the Judeo-Christian tradition often involves service rather than mere domination. *Cf.* Moltmann 1985: 20–32. Moltmann argues that the biblical charge to subdue the *earth* is nothing to do with the charge to rule over the world but is a dietary commandment; the earth is to be cultivated (Gn. 2:15) as the source of plant life which will provide food for humans and animals (1985: 29). 'The role which human beings are meant to play is the role of a "justice of the peace"' (1985: 30).

while the story may not advocate ruthless exploitation of the environment, it has been misinterpreted by some to provide encouragement for such an approval. He suggests that this is a clear example of how values underly technological formation. He argues that, while philosophical arguments may succeed in changing the thinking of individuals, it may be that stories such as those found in Genesis 1 – 3 can function at a cultural level to provide tools for the moral assessment of technological practices (1993: 42–43). Another dimension which Cook overlooks is that the call to the stewardship of the earth's resources comes before the fall of humankind into sin. Distortion of the original purpose of humanity's dominion is the theological explanation for the kind of exploitation which White rightly condemns.

The later stories in Genesis develop this metanarrative after the fall. Even after further disaster in the flood, the remnant is commanded to be fruitful (Gn. 9:1), and fruitfulness implies responsibility (9:5). This is expressed in agriculture (9:20), boat-building (10:5), weapon-making for hunting (10:9) and house-building (10:11). According to the biblical account, traditions of tool-making went back to ante-diluvian times (4:22). All these craft activities are expressions of humankind's technological vocation, an outcome of God's image stamped on human nature. Yet the dark side of that nature is never far away, and is displayed in the story of the Tower of Babel (11:1–9). The ziggurat is a well-known feature of ancient Mesopotamian architecture, and was often built with mud bricks and tar due to the scarcity of local stone. It is therefore a symbol of technology-gone-wrong, the result of the ingenuity of humankind in culling materials and using them for their own evil purposes. But it is also a symbol of their pride, their desire to make a name for themselves (11:4). Excavated inscriptions indicate that these towers were meant to serve as stairways to heaven. They had a purely religious significance and had no practical use apart from religious ritual. According to the biblical narrative, they were symbolic of the desire to usurp the authority of the landlord. They were declarations of independence from the true God, yet also expressions of underlying religious needs (S. Cook 1993: 203).[11]

---

[11] *Cf.* Ellul: '. . . man tried to get back to the absent God by every possible means – religions, vows, sacrifices, ziggurats, prayers, and magic' (1976: 80). *Cf.* Lynch: 'The Internet is in danger of being the Tower of Babel of the 3rd millennium' (1996: 74).

Technology in the Old Testament may, therefore, be an expression of the sinister aspect of humankind's nature, yet it is not necessarily a sinful activity. The skills of the craftsman are exalted in Exodus 31:2–3, when Moses speaks of those who build the Tent of Meeting for the worship of God in the desert: 'See I have chosen Bezalel . . . and I have filled him with the Spirit of God, with skill, ability and knowledge in all kinds of crafts.' Yet similar skills can be used for the casting of the golden calf (Ex. 32:1 – 33:6), another expression of rebellion. Human technical skills might glorify God or be used for idolatry. Much later, the prophet Isaiah was to bemoan this recurring failing (Is. 44:6–20 is the climax of a number of broadsides against idolatry). His comments arose from his convictions about the incomparable mystery and holiness of God:

> To whom, then, will you compare God?
>   What image will you compare him to?
> As for an idol, a craftsman casts it,
>   and a goldsmith overlays it with gold
>   and fashions silver chains for it . . .
> 'To whom will you compare me?
>   Or who is my equal?' says the Holy One.
>
> (Is. 40:18–19, 25)

Again, technology is seen at its best in the building of the temple under Solomon (1 Ki. 5 – 8), the culmination of which is the king's prayer of dedication (8:22–61). This was not an attempt to limit God to a house made with human hands (8:27) but a reminder of God's call to be fully committed to his covenant with Israel (8:61). Solomon knew that if the episodes of Babel and the golden calf were repeated, the temple would provide no safe haven for idolatry. It is significant that the temple as the focal point of the city of Jerusalem became a symbol of life lived as good stewards of the gifts of God. It was there that the people celebrated the results of their labours in the annual festivals. It was there that the rebuilding work had to begin after the exile. It was the temple which was central in Ezekiel's vision of the restored people of God (Ezk. 40 – 44). All humankind's God-given technological skills are represented there. At the temple, the image of

God in humankind as *Homo Faber* is celebrated.[12] As the theologian Jurgen Moltmann notes:

> Here we can clearly discern the development stages of modern technology. The world as God's work corresponds to human handicrafts. The subject is unremittingly active on his own account (1985: 316).

2.3.2   New Testament

In the New Testament, the Greek word *eikon* is used to develop the idea of the image of God in humankind. The word is used in various ways. For example, in Luke 20:24 Jesus draws the disciples' attention to the image of the Roman emperor on a coin. Such an image is no more than a copy or a reflection which is something other than that which it represents. But in Hebrews 10:1 we find the writer using *eikon* differently: 'The law was but a shadow of the good things to come instead of the true form [*eikon*] of these realities.' That is, the *eikon* is the reality, the law but a foreshadowing. The law has, therefore, no substantial existence of its own. *Eikon* implies the illumination of the inner core and essence of something (Brown 1976:2: 389).

In this way, Paul says, 'He [Christ] is the image of the invisible God, the firstborn over all creation' (Col. 1:15). Christ is the *eikon* of the invisible God, because he shares in God's real being and hence can be a manifestation of that being. Philip Hughes, the New Testament scholar, comments:

> We must understand that the incarnation of the Son is not the identification of us with him who *is* the Image but his identification with us who are made *in* the image . . . Thus the Son, who *is* the Image, by becoming man became *in* the image, without ever ceasing to *be* the Image (1989: 29).

Hughes goes on to suggest that the creation of humankind in the image of God is the vital bond between human beings and the Son of God, 'the archetypal Image in which man was formed' (1989: 34–35). What then are the hallmarks of this *eikon* in humankind? Hughes

---

[12] *Cf.* Moltmann 1985: 312–316.

suggests six qualities of human existence: (1) personality, (2) spirituality, (3) rationality, (4) morality, (5) authority and (6) creativity (1989:
51–64). Clearly human technological activity is an expression of
creativity, although we must not isolate this faculty from other aspects
of the *eikon*, nor should we imagine that technology is anything other
than a product of humans in their wholeness as creatures (Moltmann
1985: 225–228, 312–316).

Obviously, human creativity is not to be confused with the divine
activity which it reflects. People cannot create anything *ex nihilo* (out
of nothing), but can only bring into fresh relationship and combination the resources they have at their disposal, which are God's gifts. In
addition, all people are not equally creative in this sense. Some are
more gifted than others and some do not make good use of the gifts
they have received. And, of course, human creativity has been marred
by the fall, as have all the other faculties noted above.

Fallenness affects human creativity because it is an abuse or
deprivation of human nature as originally given by God. Hughes
suggests that evil becomes real when we use our humanness in a
manner contrary to its proper nature (1989: 77). This is demonstrated
in our chronic inability to apply scientific discoveries and technological inventions consistently for the good of all humankind. So
often, great advances in knowledge and innovatory applications have
led to disastrous consequences, as we know only too well in the wake
of Chernobyl, Bhopal, the Greenhouse Effect and ozone-layer
depletion. Perhaps we should also view the unacceptable levels of unemployment in the Western world as being due, at least in part to the
wholesale adoption of computer technology in a way which is threat-
ening to the well-being of many.

Despite that negative tendency in the race, there is no denigration
of human craft and skill in the New Testament. Paul used illustrations
in his teaching which drew on various aspects of early technology,
from armour and weaponry (Eph. 6:10–18), to household articles (2
Tim. 2:20–21), building methods (1 Cor. 3:10–15), pottery (2 Cor.
4:7) and agricultural implements (2 Cor. 6:14). The skills of the
builder are also used by Peter to illustrate the building of the Christian
church (1 Pet. 1:4–10). Believers are called 'living stones'. In the days
before the advent of modern industrial machinery, the shaping and
placing of stones was a highly-skilled operation. The technological
enterprise was a picture of the care which must be taken in the

spiritual construction work in which the first Christians were involved. The first churches were strategically planted in towns and cities as bases for outreach into their hinterlands, and believers were doubtless often reminded of this analogy as they passed building-sites.

Another associated analogy is found in the book of Revelation, written to the churches in the cities of Asia Minor. It is in the vision of the city of God that is yet to come: 'I did not see a temple in the city, because the Lord God Almighty and the Lamb are its temple' (21:22). The temple's absence is despite the many evidences of technical skill abounding in the description of the Holy City, which shone with the glory of God (21:22). That glory is not a reprise of the original creation, but a transfiguration of the world as modelled by technological humankind. 'The greatness and the wealth of the nations will be brought into the city. But nothing that is impure will enter the city' (21:26–27, GNB). Of course the genre of this writing is apocalyptic, and we do well not to read too much into such references. However, in view of John's vision of the future clearly not being in tune with the current Greek notions of history as cyclical (Cullmann 1962), it is surely significant that his vision was not of a return to Eden.

According to the biblical vision, what began in a *garden* will be consummated in a *city* (Blocher 1984: 199).[13] This indicates that the cultural mandate which leads to technological formation has eschatological implications. The question is whether the biblical story of humankind's technological quest is *world affirming* or *world denying*, as the New Testament theologian Oscar Cullmann has put it (1962: 211–213).[14] He affirms that the New Testament message is that Christ is Lord of all, and that while the death and resurrection of Jesus of Nazareth are the central moments in all human history, indeed of time itself, this should not be interpreted only in ecclesiological terms. Cullman suggests that the world has been drawn into the redemptive process. The apostle Paul criticized those in the early church who were opting out of daily work because of their belief that the Christ

---

[13] Schuurman suggested to the author that the vision of Revelation is not of an industrial city but of a *garden* city.

[14] *Cf.* Thiselton (1995: 24–26), who cites Bonhoeffer and Moltmann in support of a world-affirming approach. Moltmann says, 'Love makes life worth living' (1992: 259).

would soon return to earth (2 Thes. 3:10). That work, and therefore technical skills and technological ideas, are validated by New Testament cosmology, and eschatology is a line of thought which we will explore further in Chapter Four.

2.4   *Technology as opportunity and threat in biblical perspective*

Having outlined an understanding of the biblical material which is relevant to our discussion, we can see that technology is to be viewed as both opportunity and threat, as an expression of human nature in God's image. According to the biblical account, this is because of human disobedience to God, which has distorted the original perfection of creation (Moltmann 1985: 229–243). Moltmann notes that, according to the biblical tradition, we must refer to humans as being in God's image and as sinners at the same time. This means that humankind's essential nature, as defined by relationship to God, is now qualified negatively. Humans are neither entirely sinners nor absolutely reflective of the divine nature. The *image Dei* is neither the indestructible substance of the human being, nor can it be destroyed by human sin, suggests Moltmann (1985: 229).

Later in our discussion, the themes of 'opportunity' and 'threat' will appear again in our focus on Virtual Reality. We must now proceed to examine some of the pertinent metaphysical questions, and to enquire how Christian theologians and ethicists have sought to understand the breakdown in moral order which is implied by biblical anthropology.

Chapter Three:
Ethics and reality
(virtual or otherwise)

3.1 Morality, reality and technology

3.1.1 Origins of moral order theory

For centuries, philosophers have reflected on the nature of reality. For example, when we observe the universe, there seems to be an amazing orderliness, with many events repeating themselves day after day. The earth's revolving around the sun, and other regularities, seem to assure us that causes and effects are not mere coincidences but are the expression of some innate logic or game-plan. Thomas Aquinas (1225–74), the classical systematic theologian of the medieval Catholic Church, developed his arguments for the existence of God from such apparent orderliness. His 'Fifth Way', commonly called 'the argument from design' (better described as the argument *to* design), is considered the most convincing of the five. Beginning with the observed order within the universe, the argument concluded that there must be a Supreme Being who is responsible for that order. Such a god must be very powerful, free, non-embodied and a rational agent. Aquinas argued by analogy between the order of the world and the products of human art to a god who is responsible for the former, in some ways similar to humankind who is responsible for the latter:

The fifth way is based on the guidedness of nature. An orderedness of action to an end is observed in all bodies obeying natural laws, even when they lack awareness. For their behaviour hardly ever varies, and will practically always turn out well; which shows that they truly tend to a goal, and do not merely hit it by accident (1964: 1a, 2.3).[1]

The natural order perceived in the universe was the ground for Aquinas's theory of moral order. Oliver O'Donovan makes this observation:

> Classical Christian thought proceeded from a universal order of meaning and value, an order given in creation and fulfilled in the kingdom of God, an order, therefore, which forms a framework for all action and history, to which action is summoned to conform in its making of history. Historicism denies that such a universal order exists. What classical ethics thought of as a transhistorical order is, it maintains, itself, a historical phenomenon (1994: 67).

O'Donovan sees a link between this denial and the fundamental question of whether cosmic order really is present in the world or, rather, imposed upon reality by the human mind. Where did this idea of orderliness originate? Some, perhaps justifiably, see it as a pointer to the hand of a designer-creator, who has set in motion such patterns of thought; they hold that natural order is the basis of moral order. However, philosophers of the historicist school, including Marxists, have denied the classical view that there is a universal order of meaning and value (*cf.* Illich 1973). Such notions of a transhistorical order, so they argue, are themselves historical phenomena, and our actions must be responses to the inner workings of the historical process. In this way, such thinkers might argue that Virtual Reality was

---

[1] *Cf.* R. Swinburne, 'The argument from design', in J. Houston (1984: 51–69). *Cf.* Harries: 'We want to say that the Christian faith is a rational belief, a belief that rational beings can hold, and not just a fairy story . . . What I mean by a rational belief in religion is one that can do justice to the character of the world as a whole and make sense of it in its entirety; it helps things fall into place and discloses the meaning even of suffering . . . None of this is proof. Proof is not possible from either a philosophical or theological standpoint . . . Nevertheless there is evidence for those with eyes to see . . .' (1994: 68–69).

to be approached as a phenomenon which arises out of the evolutionary process and therefore is not to be evaluated according to the canons of some supposed universal ethical framework. But this would cause us to fall into the trap of which Jacques Ellul has warned; his trenchant analysis of *technicism* (technology for technology's sake) in post-World War Two's Western culture has been seminal (see Monsma 1986: 49–51). As Monsma comments:

> Technicism reduces all things to the technical; it sees technology as the solution to all human problems and needs. Technology is a saviour, the means to make progress and gain mastery over modern, secularised cultural desires . . . Technicism constitutes a new faith, a new religion (1986: 49–50).

Ellul (1965, 1990) argues that many have accepted the inevitability of technical development and are so fascinated by technique that technology is thought of by them as part of the historical process, having a life of its own and driving on relentlessly without the need for checks and balances, other than statutory limitations, to guide its production and application.[2] Against such historicism, O'Donovan follows Aquinas in arguing from evidence of moral order to the existence of a law-giver. Even the disastrous consequences of the fall (Gn. 3:1ff.) did not, for Aquinas, obliterate this sense of order. The brokenness of the universe is quite different from that of unordered chaos. So it is possible for all human beings to sense the need of family life, to promote virtues such as mercy and to discourage vices such as cowardice (O'Donovan 1994: 88). Following the insights of O'Donovan's revision of Aquinas's view of moral order, we can approach the evaluation of technology in a *critically realistic* way, recognizing that all human endeavour is flawed by human weakness, without becoming totally cynical about the direction taken by technological development, a tendency towards which Ellul leans in his desire to act as a watchman against the excesses of technicism. Similarly, Christian ethicists need not devalue all the moral convictions which arise from other traditions, whether they be pre-Christian, non-Christian or post-Christian. Nor need they seek to attribute anything of worth in such convictions to some supposed

---

[2] *Cf.* Schuurman (1995a).

biblical influence. But they must avoid the temptation of adopting the moral outlook of their own or any other culture. Christian ethicists

> . . . cannot set about building a theological ethic upon the moral *a priori* of a liberal culture, a conservative culture, a technological culture, a revolutionary culture or any other kind of culture; for that is to make of theology an ideological justification for the cultural constructs of human misknowledge (1994: 89–90).

In this way, Oliver O'Donovan lays the foundation for his thesis that Christian moral thought must *respond to reality*. He believes that we can only approach these phenomena critically, evaluating them and interpreting their significance, from the place where true knowledge of the moral order is given, under the authority of the gospel. From that position alone can be discerned what may be of interest or value in these various moral traditions. Like Haldane (Carr & Haldane 1993), he believes that there is a givenness, or objectivity about values, which is fundamental to reality as we know it. From the point of view of theological ethics, O'Donovan considers this givenness to be in a world order restored in Christ, which is in process of realization; it is by redemption that true reality is brought to bear upon the appearances of reality which the world presents to us (1994: 101, 104). We have termed this approach '*the Ethics of Christian Realism*'. For O'Donovan, the presence of external reality is the essential condition for the exercise of freedom, and reason is important in this only because it enables the agent to get a grip on reality. The authority we attribute to reason is better understood as belonging to reality (1994: 120).[3]

Taking this thinking into the realm of technological development and the dilemmas thereby raised, O'Donovan recognizes that technical innovation makes us ask new questions about the nature of reality. But in asserting that such developments pose new moral questions, we are really questioning the technology rather than being questioned by it:

---

[3] *Cf.* Bonhoeffer: 'The ethical cannot be detached from reality.' Christian ethics is always 'a matter of correct appreciation of real situations and of serious reflection upon them' (1955).

If we find this development morally, as opposed to technically, important, we do so by virtue of that knowledge of the moral order which we have brought with us. We did not learn from the scientists that it raised moral issues, nor did we learn from them what the moral issues it raised were. It has become the object of moral enquiry by virtue of a dynamic of thought which, simply as a technical innovation, it could not have initiated and cannot control (1994: 93).[4]

3.1.2 *Morality, freedom and knowledge*

This approach confirms the need to subject Virtual Reality, as a concept, to rigorous ethical scrutiny. Our concern here is to explore whether VR is morally significant, not just because it challenges the ethicist to scrutinize its assumptions about human nature and purposes, but also because it makes us question our understanding of the basis of our ethical reflection. If the presence of external reality is, as O'Donovan suggests, the essential condition for the exercise of *freedom*, which in turn is a prerequisite for a meaningful discussion of human responsibility as an expression of ethical principles, the concept of VR may conflict with our notions of what 'external reality' means. In turn, our notions of human freedom must come under review. This ties in with John Haldane's realist approach to values, as outlined in Chapter One, but it is in tension with the reflections of two significant philosophers of technology, Hans Jonas and John Ladd. We will tackle Ladd's thesis on moral responsibility in relation to computer ethics, at length, in Chapter Five,[5] but we turn now to the work of Jonas.

O'Donovan's view is that the classical ethical framework can readily be applied to the moral implications of recent novel technical developments. In contrast, Hans Jonas of the University of Chicago believes that modern technology has introduced such significant *factors of scale, objectives and consequences* that the traditional framework of ethics can no longer be readily applied. He alleges that the nature of human action has *de facto* changed and that humankind must now take responsibility for the whole biosphere for posterity. Ethics is no longer to be limited to questions regarding the good action for the present.

---

[4] *Cf.* J. Ladd (1989).
[5] See below, pp. 136–144.

There is a new role for *knowledge* in morality, suggests Jonas. The fact that predictive knowledge lags behind technical knowledge assumes ethical importance:

> With the latter so superior to the former, recognition of ignorance becomes the obverse of the duty to know and thus part of the ethics that must govern the evermore necessary self-policing of our outsized might. No previous ethics had to consider the global condition of human life and the far-off future, even existence, of the race. These now being an issue demands, in brief, a new conception of duties and rights, for which previous ethics and metaphysics provide not even the principles, let alone a ready doctrine (1984: 8).

O'Donovan and Jonas are offering conflicting accounts of the relationship between modern technology and ethics. The former focuses on the *metaphysical* basis of ethics, whereas the latter is more concerned with *epistemology*. The former is confident that the advent of novel techniques and applications does not bring anything significantly new to the moral debate, in that we will continue to bring to bear our sense of moral order to any dilemma. The latter is asserting that the long-term implications of technology introduce factors which were not considered by earlier ethical frameworks, especially the need for accountability to generations yet to be born. Jonas admits that the notion of *stewardship* is unique to religious ethics, and affirms that in biblical tradition it is an important aspect of the duties of humankind toward the natural world (*cf.* Ps. 24:1; Job 41:11; Acts 17:24–28; Rom. 11:35–36). According to this position, people are accountable to God for their stewardship, and this has implications for the generations yet to come. Jesus told parables in which he emphasized the need for good stewardship of God's gifts in the light of eschatological accountability (*cf.* Mt. 24:45–51; 25:14–30). Ultimately, the eschatological vision of a new earth in conformity to the will of God is a goal which informs the ethics of the kingdom, as we shall see in Chapter Four. It is Jonas's failure adequately to assess the significance of Christian ethics in the debate over modern technology with which we shall seek to argue, rather than his awareness of the new challenges faced by the moral philosopher in the advent of certain technologies. O'Donovan is surely right in affirming that new kinds of moral discourse do not arise out of the novelties as such. What changes is the emphasis on consequences (teleology) rather than principles (deontology), which inevitably leads to speculation about potential goods or harms. With Virtual Reality, it seems that our first concern must be with the conceptual rather than the consequential. We may be spurred on by Jonas's eschatological warnings and fears of what might be done with this new technology. One of the first attempts at ethical reflection on VR, by Colin Beardon (1992),[6] listed a number of possible applications of a highly speculative nature, such as virtual job interviews, virtual penal environments ('Panopticon'), and virtual psychotherapy. Such speculation does little to advance the discussion about the nature of VR and its ethical implications. Following O'Donovan's lead, we will seek to explore the relationship between virtuality and reality by looking more closely at our notions of human freedom, and our approach to ethical decision-making, with the help of Jacques Ellul and Philip Wogaman.

3.2 Virtual Reality and the ethics of Christian realism

3.2.1 Intention, imagination and desire

In some ways, Virtual Reality might be supposed to involve what O'Donovan calls 'an invasion of the absurd into our moral thought' (1994: 185). We have the freedom to choose whether or not to enter the immersive experience of VR, given the constraints upon us. To put it crudely, donning the immersive VR kit involves sticking our heads into a computer system! For a time we will be blind to the real world of sight and sound. In fact, we are opting to be 'legally blind' temporarily, as the level of vision available through VR technology would be classed as 'partial sight'. Yet we could enter a computer-generated version of a real environment like a building and negotiate it quite successfully. We could even meet other people, represented as avatars in that virtual world, and engage in conversation and other interaction. Given the software, we could choose to engage in violent virtual activity towards other persons, we could make virtual sexual advances, or we could choose to discuss the virtual weather. In so doing, have we abandoned our awareness of moral

[6] See above, p. 46 n. 16.

responsibility? Surely not, as we have, rather, chosen to abandon, for a time, our immediate awareness of *external* reality, the physical world around us, and have escaped into a world created by the human imagination where we can explore possibilities which are not open to our normal experience. Our experience of *inwardness* or subjectivity continues.

One is reminded of the saying of Jesus recorded by Mark: 'From within, out of men's hearts, come evil thoughts, sexual immorality, theft, murder . . . All these evils come from inside . . .' (Mk. 7:21–23). 'Thoughts' may indicate 'acts of thought', as O'Donovan suggests; corruptions of outward behaviour may originate in corrupt thoughts (*cf*. Mt. 5:28: 'I tell you that anyone who looks at a woman lustfully has already committed adultery with her in his heart'). This should probably not be taken to mean that every act is proceeded by thought, for people often act thoughtlessly. O'Donovan says, 'These evils arise from the *personal agency* of the one whose acts express them' (1994: 205). The individual is responsible for his own corrupt acts, including chosen thoughts and desires; as Jesus said, 'The tree is known by its fruit' (Mt. 12:33, RSV). A person's character is known through her or his acts. We see courage through courageous deeds, although it is not true that the quality of courage resides only in the acts and not in the person. Yet only the acts can show what a person is like.

This principle surely applies as much in a virtual world as in the real world. Virtual murder is not necessarily directed against any known person, living or dead, whereas the kind of hatred which Jesus spoke of as tantamount to murder is specifically focused. Yet the desire to explore the *experience of murder* through Virtual Reality may be an expression of the very kind of thought-acts which Jesus condemned. As consumption of pornography may lead to masturbation and then to obsessive sexual activity with or without others, so engaging in virtual violence may lead to sadism or masochism. Masturbation is condemned nowhere in Scripture, and yet heterosexual and homosexual lusting clearly is (Mt. 5:28; Rom. 1:24–27; 2 Pet. 2:14). From this we can deduce that pornography, which has the clear intention of arousing illicit passion, is an evil by New Testament standards. Similarly, aggressive or violent intentions are condemned in the Bible (Mt. 5:21–23; *cf*. Jas. 4:1ff.: 'What causes fights and quarrels among you? Don't they come from your desires that battle within you? . . .').

The popular contemporary notion is that freedom involves doing what one wants when one wants, especially in one's inner life, as long as other people are not actually harmed. Some existentialists have gone so far as to suggest that suicide is the ultimate affirmation of one's freedom.[7] But surely such an act obviates the possibility of any further free choices. It is a negation of the freedom for which humankind exists. Paul says, 'It is for freedom that Christ has set us free' (Gal. 5:1). Existentialist philosophers have focused upon the sense of alienation in the human condition, but, unlike the biblical writers, they have taken as a given that our lot is absurd and can only be handled by an act of will to choose for ourselves what we want. Our authenticity as humans depends on that existential choice. But is that a choice based on real *possibilities*, on human *potential*, or on mere *pretence*? Surely true freedom involves acting on the basis of reality, rather than that of unreality. The biblical notion of sin has *deception* at its heart. 'If we claim to be without sin, we deceive ourselves' says the apostle John (1 Jn. 1:8). Jesus listed deceit with sins such as greed, malice, lewdness and envy (Mk. 7:22). But the biblical writers say that deceitfulness is typical of the human condition. Jeremiah wrote, 'The heart is deceitful above all things' (Je. 17:9). The writer to the Hebrews warns his readers not to be 'hardened by sin's deceitfulness' (Heb. 3:13).

A key insight of Christian ethics is that we are responsible to God for our thoughts and thought-life, which influence our physical actions, and by which we may be deceived (Jas. 4:1ff.). This reflects Old Testament tradition as found, for example, in 1 Chronicles 28:9, where David is preparing his son Solomon to succeed him as king: 'Acknowledge the God of your father, and serve him with whole-hearted devotion and with a willing mind, for the LORD searches every heart and understands every motive behind the thoughts.'

According to the biblical writers, there is a connection between imagination, thoughts and actions. Isaiah spoke critically of the people of his own day who 'walk in ways not good, pursuing their own *imaginations*' (65:2), and who would come under judgment 'because

---

[7] Sartre, cited in Billington (1993: 171). *Cf.* Wogaman: 'Philosophers like Jean-Paul Sartre argue that we claim our authentic humanness by an act of will. It almost does not seem to matter what it is we decide, as long as we take responsibility for our own being – even if the decision is for suicide' (1989: 14).

of their actions and their *imaginations*' (66:18). Ezekiel accused false prophets of prophesying out of their own imagination (13:2, 17). Of course, these passages reflect the opposition of the true prophets to all idolatry, the ascription of worth to images which are the product of human imagination. Ethics was not to be based on such speculations but upon the revelation of God's will through his word, for, as Isaiah says as God's spokesman, 'my thoughts are not your thoughts' (55:8). Biblical ethics must have an objective basis in the givenness of what God has done in history, quite apart from our perception or appreciation of such data.

Perhaps the analogy of visual impairment, mentioned above, is a useful one if we are to think through more effectively this issue of the influence of the inner life. Although putting on the VR kit subjects one to 'legal blindness', in so doing one is not denying the existence of external reality any more than the physically blind person does. Yet we expect a blind person to remain subject to the same ethical constraints as the sighted person, despite the fact that he or she lives in a world without the benefit of visual aids to guide actions. The objectivity upon which ethical thinking and moral actions must be based is the essence of human personality which, while in process of development or recession, subsists even when certain important functions such as sight are impaired or absent. According to classical Christian ethics, it is this inner life which is the wellspring of thought and action. The blind person cannot enter virtual worlds which rely on visual representations, but must continually envisage in the imagination the unseen world around.

It is clear, therefore that *moral responsibility*, as outlined by classical Christian ethics, is not ruled out either if we are physically blind or have chosen to enter a virtual environment where we are immersed in images and sounds of a surrealistic nature. Imagined expressions of good or evil intention are held to be significant in the moral life (Carr & Haldane 1993). Therefore, to desire to commit murder in a virtual world may be no less reprehensible than to lust or covet is in response to stimuli from hard reality. Virtuality does not extend human freedom nor reduce human responsibility, according to this argument, any more than to become blind absolves one of blame for evil thoughts or intentions. We will further explore notions of moral responsibility with particular reference to computer ethics in Chapter Five.[8]

The significance of the concept of Virtual Reality is therefore (as O'Donovan suggests regarding the impact of new technology on ethical reflection)[9] not that our understanding of moral discourse is radically challenged by the development, but that it can bring into focus a factor which is often ignored in the discussion of ethics, namely the importance of the inner life and the call to that *excellence in attitude, thought and desire as well as in deed* which is at the heart of the Christian ethic. This is the ultimate meaning of freedom in Christ.[10] Jesus is portrayed in the gospels as the model of humanity, and therefore of human freedom. He promised his disciples that 'If you hold to my teaching, you are really my disciples. Then you will know the truth, and the truth will set you free' (Jn. 8:31–32).

3.2.2   A strategy of presumption
The *Ethics of Christian Realism* proposed here suggests that a holistic understanding of human nature will promote awareness of the inter-dependence which exists between the inner life and outward behaviour, even when one is indulging in fantasy. Much debate has focused on whether we can prove, by empirical means, that watching video nasties influences people to behave aggressively or to make unwelcome sexual advances, *etc.* The fact that proof is called for exposes an underlying assumption, that inner life and outward behaviour are quite discrete areas of human experience. This seems to fly in the face of common sense. The burden of proof would, rather, seem to be on the other side; we need convincing that such connec-tions are *not* likely. The concept of *burden of proof* in Christian moral judgment has been expounded at length by Philip Wogaman, and we must now engage with his argument (1989: 59–71). He bases his discussion on three key theological metaphors which resonate with our exposition of the *Ethics of Christian Realism*: first, that ultimate reality is founded in God as personal being; secondly, that this God

---

[8] See below, pp. 136–144.

[9] See above, p.79.

[10] Ellul: 'Finally, in faith we can accept the witness of Jesus to man's bondage in John 8:37. We shall have to show that freedom has its source in the Word' (1976: 50); also 'It is to the degree that he was tempted like us in all points (Heb. 4:15) that Jesus is a free man' (1976: 52).

has entered into covenant with all humanity and particularly with Israel in the Old Testament and the church in the New Testament; and thirdly, that Jesus Christ is God's visible representation (*eikon*) in human terms. Wogaman takes as his sources of authority for his approach: first the Bible, secondly Christian tradition and theology, and thirdly natural law.[11]

Wogaman proposes a Christian method of moral judgment which seeks to steer a course between perfectionism and situationalism, thereby combining the moral seriousness of the former with the flexibility of the latter. Ethical perfectionists tend to look at a moral problem with the assurance, in advance, that we can know the one correct solution, and a given moral tradition is held to be the source of the right answers. The process of judgment may involve a casuistry which clarifies the implications of the particular moral tradition for cases not clearly anticipated by the tradition itself. On the other hand, situationalists tend to weigh the available evidence without sufficient precommitment to what is *probably* the best course of action to follow. For example, Joseph Fletcher suggests that love must decide 'then and there' (in advance) what is to be done when faced with possible alternatives, and that there can be no such concept as a moral exception or a necessary evil.[12] However, this is not a very practical approach.

Wogaman suggests that it is more productive to approach moral decision-making by, firstly, recognizing our precommitments or presumptions. We should give tentative approval at the outset to the options which are apparently the strongest, with reference to our ultimate value commitments.[13] This approach is particularly useful when we have to make moral judgments which concern issues about which we may continue to be uncertain as to the right decision. We are familiar with the notion in jurisprudence of *presumption of innocence* until proven guilty. The state must prove the guilt of the accused

[11] Natural law is 'based on belief in indestructible universal moral principles that can be applied definitively to particular issues' (Wogaman 1989: 43). 'There is a moral order in the world that can be known with varying degrees of clarity apart from revelation' (J. Bennett, in Wogaman 1989: 49).

[12] 'The situationist holds that whatever is the most loving thing in the situation is the right and good thing' (Fletcher 1966: 64–65).

[13] 'We *presume* a certain kind of decision or a certain course of action to be the right one morally, unless it can be shown beyond reasonable doubt not to be' (Wogaman 1989: 60).

beyond a reasonable doubt. Again, in property cases, 'possession is nine-tenths of the law', in popular parlance and in terms of legal rights. The actual possessor of property is *presumed* to hold that property rightfully, and the burden of proof rests with any who would challenge the holder (1989: 61). This principle of presumption applies also to moral judgments, and 'The real question is not whether we have prejudices and presumptions but whether we are able to clarify and modify our initial presumptions on the basis of our ultimate value commitments' (1989: 63). We need to ask whether there can be distinctively *Christian* moral presumptions.

Wogaman proposes that there are four *positive* moral presumptions which are implied by Christian faith. First, the goodness of created existence is affirmed consistently in his sources, from the echo of Genesis 1, 'It was good', to Paul's statement in 1 Timothy 4:4, 'Everything God created is good'. This has to be counterbalanced by the doctrine of the fall, but Wogaman argues that few other religions or philosophies have the same conviction about the fundamental goodness of existence. This affects moral judgment when we are faced by issues of, for example, suicide or euthanasia. Our initial presumption must be that suicide is incompatible with Christian faith, since such an act implies that existence for the individual who contemplates suicide is no longer good. Secondly, the value of individual life is affirmed, in that our presumption must be that all people have worth, even those to whom we may be vigorously opposed. Thirdly, the unity of the human family in God is proclaimed in such texts as Ephesians 2:14, which says that Christ has 'destroyed the barrier, the dividing wall of hostility'. In this way, racism is excluded, as it is not possible for Christian realists to treat some part of humanity as a moral universe in itself, excluding all others. Fourthly, the equality of persons in God is asserted. This is not, however, an absolute equality, which Wogaman suggests is impossible and inadvisable; the distribution of the conditions of life, such as physical constitution, health and mental capacity, is clearly uneven (1989: 72–97). It may be that such presumptions are found elsewhere, for example in the Enlightenment thought of Kant about equality, but 'Christian ethics does not have a stake, finally, in the uniqueness of its insights; it does have a stake in their faithfulness' (1989: 96–97). The key issue is whether these positive presumptions reflect human aspirations and are universalizable.

To counterbalance this emphasis on the essential goodness of existence, Wogaman suggests two *negative* presumptions, which resonate with the dark side of reality as we know it. First, there is human finitude, the recognition that to be a human being is to be limited: 'In our short span of life, each of us is capable of experiencing only the tiniest fragment of reality' (1989: 99). Even the experience we do have is restricted in space and time, and our ability to act upon what we know with the wisdom we may gain is limited by time, physical location and finite power. This is true of every person under all circumstances (1989: 100). Secondly, human sinfulness – the fact that all people are to some extent disposed toward self-centredness – demonstrates the truth of Paul's dictum 'All have sinned' (Rom. 3:23; 1989: 98–115). God's grace is effective, despite our struggles with self-centredness, and affirms human freedom. In practical terms, this insight has the effect of weighting our moral presumption against self-interest and in favour of the powerless.

3.2.3   A concept of freedom

Jacques Ellul's analysis of the concept of *freedom in Christ* is essential for the development of this theme (1976: 23–132). He believes that humankind increasingly has the powerful technical means to exercise almost absolute control and that this drives the human desire to manipulate everything. People want to alter the human condition, Ellul asserts, to remove limitations of distance in space and time, to prolong human life indefinitely, and to control both birth and death. Because of this we tend to impose on every area of life a type of existence derived from the technical model, suggests Ellul, and we focus upon those aspects of interaction which involve manipulation and utilization (1976: 28). It follows that as we increasingly find the means to control the industrial and technical world, the less we see the reason for it; that *means* increase in significance, and that ends become less important (1976: 28). This may be a problem for some exponents of Christian ethics who emphasize, for example, that the end of love must be held as supreme over any means to that end. Then again, love may be thought of as a means as well as an end, a way of being as well as a goal of acting.[14] However, Ellul believes that our technological society's emphasis on means has led to the widespread

---

[14] *Cf.* Ramsey (1961).

experience of *alienation* in the modern world.

Ellul sees the experience of alienation in four main areas: first, in our awareness of *powerlessness* to modify or escape from technologically dominated society; secondly, in our awareness of *absurdity*, in which we consider events to be meaningless; thirdly, in a feeling of *abandonment* by others in society who will not or cannot support us; and fourthly, in the personal experience of *indifference* – of selves with no clear sense of destiny or purpose (1976: 29). He asserts that there are three factors in alienation: loss of control, lack of motivation, and lack of information:

> This experience of the alienated situation, lived out at the subjective level, enables us to isolate the factors in alienation. Three elements may be discerned: first, a loss of control, whether of the situation in which we are set or of our responses to it; then a lack of motivation in which man no longer knows why things are as they are but simply does what he does without knowing what it is all about; and finally a lack of information in which an individual feels isolated because the flow of information between his environment and himself (and *vice versa*) has been stopped. In sum, the adaptive function of the individual has been put out of joint in relation to the physical world, society, a group of individuals, or his partner. In consequence one cannot speak of absolute alienation or the reverse. We simply have degrees of alienation (1976: 29).

Freedom from alienation is at the heart of the Christian message, according to Ellul, and yet he is aware that people are not acutely aware of freedom as an inherent personal need. The needs of security, conformity, adaptation, happiness, economy of effort, *etc.*, are much more prominent and demanding, so much so that people are prepared to sacrifice freedom in order to satisfy those needs. In addition, scientific studies have indicated that human beings are determined by many factors, such that their possibilities of freedom are reduced. In contrast, much modern philosophy and theology, according to Ellul, magnifies freedom beyond the bounds of reasonable judgment based on the evidence (1976: 35).[15]

---

[15] Ellul is critical of Paul Tillich, among others, with regard to this issue; see Tillich (1987: 251): 'I conclude by saying, a moral action is an action in which we actualise

What is this *freedom* of which Ellul speaks, however, and what is its importance in Christian ethics? 'Freedom is not sitting back and letting God work. Freedom is knowing God's will and doing it' (1976: 62). Ellul quotes with approval this statement by Karl Barth:

> God's authority is truly recognised only within the sphere of freedom; only where conscience exists, where there exists a sympathetic understanding of its lofty righteousness and a whole-hearted assent to its demands.[16]

In this way, Ellul affirms that the Christian is truly free only in so far as he or she is bound to the Word of God and is therefore freed from all else; that to share in God's freedom is to surrender individual autonomy but to gain autonomy in relation to the world (1976: 124). Thus, for the Christian, ethical choice is not a simple matter of choosing between good and evil. It is primarily a choice between what is possible and what is not. Thus Christian ethics is essentially an ethics of means (1976: 116–117), and as such is ideally suited for a critique of technological society which is so wedded to the significance of means over ends.[17]

But is Ellul correct in this conclusion? Is our society so concerned about means rather than ends? This is hard to accept when populist utilitarianism seems to be so prevalent. Is Christian ethics an *ethics of means*? The answer may be a qualified affirmative, yet, in biblical perspective, love is *both* a means *and* an end – a way of being and a goal for action. ('Love is patient, love is kind . . .', 1 Cor. 13:4; 'Follow the way of love', 1 Cor. 14:1; 'The goal of this command is love', 1 Tim. 1:5.)

Ellul implies that Christian ethics is fundamentally, although not exclusively, deontological in character, rather than teleological, and that consequentialism such as that of situation ethics is alien to biblical

---

ourselves as persons within person-to-person encounters. Its principles are the love whose backbone is justice; the love which, though unconditional itself, listens to the concrete situation and its changes, and is guided by the wisdom of the past.' In this, Tillich assumes that we are free to love in this way, and seems not to engage seriously with the evidence for determinism, however qualified that notion may be.

[16] Ellul 1976: 123, quoting Barth (1936–69: I.2: 661).

[17] *Cf.* O'Donovan (1994: 204–225).

insights. In this he is surely correct. Bultmann stresses the relation between love and freedom and points out that love does not define the content of an action but its manner.[18] This echoes the teaching of Paul in 1 Corinthians 13:1ff. Love demands action without specifying the action to be taken. Love does not provide us with a concept of the neighbour, but enables us to identify the neighbour in each encounter, showing us what to do.

> For the free man the situation is always new. Stirred by the novelty of his discovery of the neighbour, the free man expresses his freedom in the act of specific love for the one who is thrown in his path and who seems at a first glance to be an obstacle or impediment to freedom (Ellul 1976: 206).

It is the truth which sets people free, according to John 8:31–32, and Jesus' understanding of *truth* is akin to our use of the word 'reality'. When he says 'I am the true vine' (Jn. 15:1), Jesus is using figurative language, but he is speaking about the reality of his connection with his disciples – the branches – which the analogy of the vine so helpfully illustrates. In other words, to know the truth is to know things as they really are, and to be delivered from deception or pretence. Thus, by giving human beings knowledge of the truth, Christ liberates us from unreality. Christian ethics flows from a concern that people should learn to live with as full and integrated an awareness as possible of every aspect of reality.

Virtual Reality may become a tool for exploring our consciousness of reality which ultimately enhances our human freedom, rather than being a vehicle of new bondages. If freedom is living in as close a possible harmony with reality (all that *is*), then there is some reason to believe that VR might be used as a stimulus to ethical analysis, despite the cautionary remarks made above. We suggest that the *Ethics of Christian Realism*, seen as a synthesis of the insights of O'Donovan, Wogaman and Ellul, can provide analytical tools for exploring the ethical significance of VR. But that exploration must be contextualized, a task to which we now turn.

---

[18] Ellul (1976: 205), citing Bultmann, *Glauben und Verstehen* I: 235.

3.3   Virtual Reality, surrealism and the ethics engine

3.3.1   Is VR surrealistic?

'Reality engine' is one of the terms used by the jargonauts of cyberspace to describe the computer hardware which is required to generate the artificial worlds of VR systems. As computer power increases, so the realism of the environments will develop, although, to be more accurate, one should use the word *surrealism*. The present writer's view is that the quest for 'realism' in VR is, in itself, a blind alley beyond a certain level of analogy between the real world and VR environments. We need certain cues to enable us to relate to the artificial worlds into which we may enter via VR. It would be beneficial to the architect, for example, to be able to enter into computer-generated images of his designs to gain some impression of the space he is seeking to create. But, as in the perspective drawings which such technology may replace, it is not necessary for fine detail to be included in order to achieve the desired effect. In the same way, potential applications in telepresence are unlikely to require ultra-fine tuning of the environments generated. An acceptable level will be achieved which provides an accurate representation for the purposes foreseen, whether in robotics or surgery or whatever.

Surrealism in art is a vehicle of ideas, or of that which purports to be true. The word comes from the French and means 'super realism'. In 1924, a surrealistic manifesto was published by André Breton, in which he claimed that art should come from the unconscious; that the artist should receive inspiration from his dreams and seek to express a super-realism where the boundaries between dream and reality were blurred.[19] Salvador Dali's 'Christ of St John of the Cross' is a famous surrealistic painting which hangs in one of Glasgow's public art galleries. It is an amazing 'bird's-eye view' of the crucifixion, and the perspective drawing is of the highest quality. It does not immediately strike the observer as an example of surrealism. Yet a closer look at the cross in the picture reveals that it is not placed in the ground but is hovering over the earth. Further examination reveals that there are no nails to be seen. Dali's choice of title for the work displays its inner logic. St John of the Cross was a sixteenth-century mystic who

---

[19] See Gaarder 1995: 366.

conceived of a cross hanging over the world but not touching it. Such a cross makes us question whether Christ died for this world and its people with their concerns, material as well as spiritual. It suggests that there is no real contact between the crucifixion and the real world. The absence of nails makes us question whether Christ really suffered. It is a *virtual* cross and its implications for everyday life are minimized. The only hope it seems to offer is some kind of mystical experience which lifts the contemplant out of the meaninglessness of this life.[20]

3.3.2 *VR and the difference principle*

If artists can paint pictures which express ideas and make truth-claims, then we will not be surprised if the designers of virtual environments have the same potential. In fact, we can imagine the 'reality engine' becoming an 'ethics engine'. The hardware could be used to generate scenarios which test our ethical principles and moral stances. In January 1995, the *Scotsman* newspaper featured a photograph of a VR wedding ceremony. The bride and groom were seen standing on separate rostra and between them was a giant TV monitor which displayed what they were seeing on their head-mounted displays. They were experiencing a Disney-style wedding as Prince Charming and his Princess. The virtual kiss which appeared on screen was clearly expressed by the puckered lips of the couple who were standing five metres apart! While this kind of thing can be derided as just another example of Californian excess, it demonstrates the way in which VR, as the latest expression of the computer culture, comes loaded with the value-system of technicism. The most intimate of human relationships, sealed with a kiss, can now be filtered via VR to enable us to fulfil our fantasies, and the donning of the DataSuit with tactile feedback (the next stage in interface design) will enable the 'consummation' of the marriage to take place as the ultimate expression of safe sex. The computer will have become a condom![21] VR technology will have generated a simplified, sanitized version of human life; a cartoon world which satisfies our fantasies and delivers us from outmoded notions of responsibility, and indeed (so it seems) from traditional forms of relationship.

---

[20] See Rookmaaker 1973: 159.
[21] The technical feasibility of this was demonstrated on the Channel Four programme, *Eurotrash*, January 1996.

On the other hand, the VR wedding might be just a bit of fun. It could be just a demonstration of fascination with technology, or of eccentricity. Just as earlier 'kooks' got married under water wearing aqua lungs, or on the wings of thirties bi-planes, so our VR couple are carrying on the tradition. All are examples of celebrating technology for technology's sake. They are reflections of what has come to be known as *modernity*, in which the traditions of the past can easily be discarded for that which is 'up to date'. It matters not that the couples in question are exchanging the beauty of, say, the marriage service of the 1662 *Book of Common Prayer* for a mess of technological pottage. What matters is that they are modern. The classical Christian ethics which are implied in the traditional service can easily be forgotten, as in the following parable told by Thomas Oden, an American Methodist theologian who has rejected modernism for an orthodoxy which is more resonant with postmodernity, so he believes:

> A plastic plumbing fixtures tycoon inherited from his Slavic uncle a baroque antique jewelled diadem of spectacular beauty and antiquity. He had been entrusted to take care of it but knew nothing of its actual value. He did not lift a finger to protect it. He considered it 'junk'. He hung it on an antelope horn on his mantel. Once in a while he enjoyed spinning it out of shape, getting laughs. On certain occasions when in debt, he had been known to dig a jewel out and pawn it.

> Isn't this much like the relationship modern persons have with classical Christianity? As heirs of modernity, we feel enormously superior to our Christian heritage. It is of little practical value to us, though we are still willing to keep it around. We would hardly feel good about throwing it away altogether, but it is little more to us than a mantel decoration or a souvenir of a trip taken long ago to Atlantic City (1990: 13).

A VR wedding may include elements which act as that kind of decoration or souvenir. But does the 'ethics engine' have any substantial product? Is the system encouraging us to challenge traditional values or the very reality which underlies them? The old ceremony proclaimed that they shall 'become one flesh', quoting from Genesis 2:24. The token kiss was a sign and seal on that promise which was about to be fulfilled. That they actually looked at each other and actually took the vows to each other in the presence of God and witnesses affirmed the seriousness of the promises being taken. It wasn't a play or a fantasy. This was for real, and for life, according to the traditional view.

Virtual Reality can, therefore, only be an 'ethics engine' by default. It enables us to appreciate the real world and real human relationships by providing a *differential*. It functions like the surrealistic painting, as a vehicle for truths and ideas which have their origin elsewhere. O'Donovan, to this extent, is right (1994: 93). Our sense of moral order or chaos is a presupposition which we bring with us to the technology, and our canons of ethical reasoning are thrown into relief by entering virtual worlds.

3.4   The metaphysics of Virtual Reality

3.4.1   Comparing worlds

Questions of reality, surrealism and ethics raise further metaphysical issues which require treatment. The philosopher Michael Heim suggests that Virtual Reality is an extension of the search for *artistic illusion*, which is itself the expression of a human need to create realities within realities in which we can suspend belief in one set of commitments in order to engage in an alternative set (1990).[22] Through VR we can enter symbolic space, where we can explore alternative worlds. We can do the same by reading stories, watching films or contemplating paintings. 'We enjoy being hijacked to another plane of being', suggests Heim (1990: 27).

Heim goes on to ask whether all worlds are not symbolic, including the one we call 'real'. He notes that Nelson Goodman (1978) and Richard Rorty (1980) have considered all worlds to be contingent symbolic constructs.[23] In this way, the scientific worldview can be compared and contrasted with the religious or the aesthetic. But, according to this view, they are comparable because they are all human constructs. Rorty suggests that, within its own frame of reference, each worldview is valid and meaningful, and his own approach of narrative philosophy is said to be just one story among many. Yet a recent

---

[22] Revised in Heim 1993: 128–137.

[23] It seems that Goodman and Rorty mean that all worldviews are human constructs. 'Goodman promotes the doctrine of irrealism' (Heim 1993: 130).

critique suggests that Rorty, in practice, claims that his school offers the last word, following the lead of the philosophers William James and John Dewey.[24] The possibility of a pluralistic approach to the universe in metaphysics can be traced back to Kant, who located the orderly patterns we perceive not in the given universe but in the structure of the human mind. Kant suggested that it is the human mind which drives us towards the integration of worldviews. He wanted to base epistemology on what he supposed were rational absolutes. In the post-quantum theory era of today, where it is recognized that the universe is not a closed system of cause-and-effect but open to diversity and indeterminateness, many philosophers welcome a pluralistic approach. Goodman says, 'Our passion for *one* world is satisfied, at different times and for different purposes, in *many* different ways. Not only motion, derivation, weighting, order, but even reality is relative' (1978: 20). Of course, this statement is self-contradictory. It is part of the reality defined by Goodman as being relative, yet it is an *absolute* statement, akin to the fallacy 'Everything is relative'. While we reject such nonsense, we can accept that our apprehension of reality involves *comparisons*.

Heim recognizes that virtual worlds can be *virtual* only in so far as they can be *compared* to the 'real' world. Virtual worlds need to be *not quite real*. He suggests that they should not simply be reproductions of features of reality but transformations. 'Cyberspace should evoke imagination, not repeat the world' (1990: 33).[25] Because philosophy involves looking for alternative explanations and meanings, cyberspace could be a fruitful locus for reflection. As Heim suggests:

> The ultimate VR is a philosophical experience, probably an experience of the sublime or awesome. For the sublime, as Kant defined it, is the spine-tingling chill that comes from the realisation of how small our finite perceptions are in the face of the infinity of possible, virtual worlds we may settle into and inhabit. The final point of a virtual world is to dissolve the constraints of the anchored world so we can lift anchor – not to drift aimlessly without point, but so we can explore anchorage in ever new places and, perhaps, find our way back to experience the most primitive

---

[24] See Norris 1985: 159.
[25] *Cf.* Woolley (1992).

and powerful alternative embedded in the question posed by Leibniz: '*Why* is there anything rather than nothing?' (1990: 33–34).[26]

3.4.2 Exploring metaphysics

Human knowledge, according to Leibniz, should emulate the *visio Dei*, the omniscient intuitive cognition of the deity whereby God sees all things from the perspective of eternity. He wanted to understand the way in which a divine or infinite Being knows things with 'temporal simultaneity'. God's comprehensive and immediate knowledge of everything is Leibniz's model for human knowledge in the modern world. Heim suggests that this could be a helpful metaphysical tool for analysing the concept of Virtual Reality:

> What better way, then, to emulate God's knowledge than to generate a virtual world constituted of bits of information? To such a cyberworld human beings could enjoy a God-like instant access. But if knowledge is power, who could handle the controls that govern every single particle of existence? (1993: 94).

More important for the present discussion is the associated metaphysical question, '*What* is there?', and in particular the supplementary question, 'What is *real*?' (Hasker 1983: 13). Do virtual environments really exist, or are they just electronic projections of no metaphysical significance – representations of worldviews rather than of reality? Those who enter virtual environments speak of the salience of their experience, of the surge of adrenaline and feeling of agency (Whitbeck 1993). Is this an experience of reality? Is the environment real because one can experience it, or because it is actually *there*? We might compare the experience with watching an episode of *Star Trek: The Next Generation*, in which Captain Picard and members of the crew of the USS Enterprise enter the Holodeck,[27] an (as yet) imaginary virtual environment in which they can assume other roles and play out, for example, stories from history like the mutiny on the *Bounty*. Perhaps we should regard this as a *reality in process* of fulfilment, like the robots predicted by Isaac Asimov in the 1960s, of which many

---

[26] For further discussion see Heim 1993: 92–98.
[27] See Heim 1993: 122–123, 141.

features have since been developed. The nature of reality is similarly questioned in Robert Altman's film *The Player*, in which the audience is never quite sure what is meant to be a portrayal of objective reality and what is purely in the imagination of characters, so thin is the line between reality and fantasy in the postmodern worldview of the film's director. The French postmodernist philosopher Jean Baudrillard sees in the new electronic media a world of 'pure simulacra, of models, codes and digitality, of media images that have become the "real" or, rather that erode any distinction between the "real" world and that of the pervasive media' (Lyon 1994a: 48).[28]

Metaphysics asks questions about *ultimate reality* and what the basic constituents of reality may be. If a philosopher suggests that Virtual Reality does not exist, he probably does not mean that there is no such phenomenon, but rather that the ultimate constituents of VR are electrons programmed to stimulate the brain via an interface in order to produce a state of consciousness. Yet we ask whether the constituent parts of a phenomenon are all that there is to it. For example, a physiologist might give an analysis of visual perception in VR in terms of the focusing of projected light by the lens of the eye, the reaction to this light by the rods and cones of the retina, the transmission of the visual information through the optic nerve and the processing of this information in the brain. But does this analysis include all that is involved in experiencing presence in a virtual environment? Surely not. The theory of *holism* claims that wholes, complex entities, have a reality of their own which is more than that of their constituent parts. Analysis of the whole into its parts falsifies its true nature and fails to capture that 'something more' which makes the phenomenon special (Lyon 1994a: 15). Ethical and evaluative questions are surely part of that extra ingredient. Virtual worlds have been designed and delivered. They are there for humans to explore, given the present limitations of the technology. We affirm that VR is part of total reality, objective and subjective, and that virtual environments have a temporal and psychological existence. VR should not be treated like a figment of the imagination. Conceptually, virtual worlds

[28] In this way, Baudrillard became notorious for declaring that the 1991 Gulf War had never happened and was merely a media circus. He explained his point by saying that, politically, war did not occur, but he clearly implied that the whole episode was simply unreal (Lyon 1994a: 52).

are powerful constructs of the imagination, but they should not be considered unreal. However, Heim's analysis encourages us further to explore the implications of postmodern thought in relation to VR.

3.5   Virtuality and postmodernity

3.5.1   Postmodern subjectivity

It is alleged that we now live in a 'postmodern' world, in which there is widespread reaction to the functionalism, anti-traditionalism and technicism of modernity. This is seen in the rise of the New Age movement, the popularity of alternative medicine, and the neo-classical nuances of recent architecture. In some ways, Virtual Reality might be thought of as a postmodern phenomenon, a techno-logical expression of the counter-culture. As we have noted, a number of leading figures associated with that counter-culture, including the late Timothy Leary, have made grandiose claims for the potential of VR. It is interesting that many of those who were into drugs and dropping out in the sixties look to VR for that trip into the new *consciousness* which they crave.[29]

But is VR essentially *postmodern* in its conceptual basis? The term 'postmodern' was used systematically for the first time, perhaps, in the seventies in the literary field, and then in the eighties its use was extended to the social sciences and hermeneutics. At the same time, postmodern ideas were influencing architecture. The school of modernism had banned the adoption of classical styles and motifs in architectural design since the 1920s. Postmodern architecture brought out from the file of history nuances and methods which had seemed incompatible with modern philosophy and technology. Jean-François Lyotard (1984), one of the pioneers of postmodern philosophy, spoke of the 'postmodern condition' as a challenge to the idea of modernism that the highest good is perpetual change. In architecture, this meant the possibility of recovering traditions denied by fifty years of modernism which sought the new above everything. Motifs and nuances from earlier styles were shunned.

The parallels between architecture and technology are various. Architecture has developed its forms and materials with the opening up of technological possibilities. But it has also developed its ideology.

---

[29] *E.g.* John Perry Barlow, formerly of the band 'the Grateful Dead', interviewed in Horizon (1991), *cf.* Nelson (1987), *contra* Dennett (1991).

Le Corbusier, one of the pioneers of modernism in architecture, described a house as 'a machine for living in'. His vision for design was utopian, idealist and purist. He rejected ornament, representation and metaphor. His buildings stand against all that went before. They lack humour and symbolism. The author was trained in a university school of architecture towards the end of the modernist period. Form had to be expressive of function. Functionalism was absolute. Although we were surrounded in Glasgow by the wonders of Victorian and Edwardian architecture, including the *Art Nouveau* of Charles Rennie Mackintosh, such syncretism was to be studied only in order to be avoided. It was as outmoded as Victorian moralism and out of place in the 'swinging sixties'. Today, architects in Glasgow eagerly look for motifs from bygone days to incorporate into their designs. They delight in Mackintoshesque styles and other connections with great Glasgow architects of the past like Alexander 'Greek' Thompson.

Can we see this kind of thing in developments within computer technology? Is Virtual Reality to earlier types of human–computer interaction as postmodernism is to modernism in architecture? The answer to these questions is elusive, as VR seems to embody many of the values of technicism, as a technological solution in search of a problem. It is a technology which clearly arose out of a desire to create an iconocentric interface which would enable a vivid visualization of data. Although this was initially connected with simulation technology, we have seen that research has focused on what *can* be done to make real-time representation a possibility rather than on what *should* be done. The postmodern critique of technology has been cynical about that kind of approach, and Leo Marx (1994) argues that postmodernism is, as a movement, a form of technological pessimism. For Marx, this helps to explain the controversy between postmodernism and the mainstream Enlightenment idea of progress. He notes that postmodernism holds great store by information technology and alleges that we are in the age of knowledge-based economies (1994: 24). Here we see a love–hate relationship, where postmodern pessimism about technicism seems to be blind to its reliance on advances in information technology for its existence and dissemination. Egbert Schuurman argues that postmodernism is the spirit and philosophy of the post-industrial society. The traditional view is that power is firmly entrenched and centralized, but information technologies can result in fragmentation and disorientation. 'Technological power is present everywhere but concentrated nowhere' (1995a: 12). Because of this, postmodernism recognizes no *normative* direction for technology. 'Everything is technologically possible and everything is technologically allowed (1995a: 12).[30] This leads, on the one hand, to a pessimistic and fatalistic attitude towards technology, as postmodernism acknowledges its all-embracing power and, on the other hand, to a naïve optimism which emphasizes the potential of information technology in promoting individualism.[31] Thus it appears that VR should be understood as the result of a complex interaction between modern technicism and post-modern pluralism and holism. But we need to test this provisional conclusion.

Mark Poster (1995) focuses on the new communications systems which are often presented as harbingers of human flourishing and increased equality, and notes that discussion of postmodern culture is greatly concerned about the emergence of a new individual identity which abandons the narrow scope of the modern individual with its claims to rationality and autonomy. It is in this area where we see contacts with our reflections on VR, and the reasons for connecting it with postmodernism. Immersive VR systems are surely the ultimate expression of individualism. Modern society, it may be argued, has fostered the concept of the individual as rational, autonomous, centred and stable, but postmodernity brings with it a quite different emphasis:

> If modernity or the mode of production signifies patterned practices that elicit identities as autonomous and (instrumentally) rational, postmodernity or the mode of information indicates communication practices that constitute subjects as unstable, multiple and diffuse (1995: 87).

The law, in modern society, regards this individual as reasonable, democratic institutions assume that he or she is educated, capitalism looks for a calculating, economic insight, and public education seeks to define individuals by grades and degrees. Postmodern society may

---

[30] See also below, pp. 173–174.

[31] 'Postmodernism implies a *shattering of innocent confidence in the capacity of the self to control its own destiny*' (Thiselton 1995: 11).

not place such high value on these aspects of the individual's existence. But it is not clear what part the ability to inhabit virtual environments will play in this change and whether VR is essentially a postmodern concept.

Poster argues that the key to understanding developments such as VR and the Internet is to be found in an evaluation of the type of *subject* which they encourage. He suggests that in Western postmodern culture there is a shift taking place in our sense of individuality. For Poster, this shift is powerfully illustrated by Virtual Reality as a concept which arises out of a culture which is increasingly simulational and in which the media are constantly transforming the subjects which they treat. In VR, more than one individual may experience the same virtual environment and, by virtue of the Internet, these individuals need not be in the same physical location. Transitional forms of VR which are developing on the Internet, such as MUDs or 'multi-user dungeons', have a devoted following of participants who want to engage in role-play games which are played textually (in that moves are typed as sentences) but which involve imaginary locations, characters and objects and the possibility of characters adopting fictional roles and even switching genders. Poster argues that subject constitution in the second media age (in which communications are decentralized and diffuse) occurs through the mechanism of *interactivity*, and that the Internet and VR open up new possibilities of interaction in such a way that traditional under-standings of an opposition between real and unreal community are called into question. Participants within virtual communities often express themselves with little inhibition and find it easy to develop dialogue over the Internet, so that there is a proliferation of stories, local narratives which are not set within any overarching explanatory context or metanarrative. This, for Poster, resonates with Lyotard's vision of the postmodern condition. However, he does not seem to notice the paradox highlighted by Schuurman (1995b), that the avail-ability of such an over-abundance of information is not only an opportunity for interaction but also a threat to reflection and discernment (*cf.* J. Ladd 1989). It is not surprising, therefore, if there is some ambiguity about the significance of developments in information technology.

To return to the *Star Trek* analogy, we can see how the shift from modernity to postmodernity is reflected in the underlying values of the programme. In the original series, from the 1960s and seventies, the rationalistic outlook of modernity is typified by the Vulcanian, Mr Spock, whose emotion-free analytical skills are applied to every problem. Problems, by definition, must have scientific explanations. As humankind goes boldly where no other humans have ventured before, strange and mostly hostile worlds are explored. The crew of the USS Enterprise contains token representatives of different nationalities and racial groups – the African Uhura, the Russian Chekhov, the Scot 'Scottie', *etc.* But they all reflect the values of scientism, and the work ethic of modern Western people.[32] However, in the sequel, *The Next Generation*, from the eighties and nineties, the underlying philosophy has clearly shifted. No longer is Spock the key character, but an android called Data, who longs to be human and searches for transcendent qualities such as aesthetics, erotic love or a sense of humour. The crew is no longer exclusively human. It is multi-racial, multi-galactical and even includes one of the dreaded Klingons, enemies from the earlier series. The arch enemies are now the Borg, a race of ultra-rational beings who have no appreciation of transcendence but seek to acquire and develop technology for technology's sake.

If we take seriously this example from popular media culture, modernity's conviction that *the truth is out there* (to quote from another hit TV series, the *X-Files*, itself a strange concoction of modern and postmodern mindsets), and in the potential of science to come up with explanations of all significant phenomena, has clearly been eroded since the 1960s. As we have noted, the postmodern climate is much harder to define. Truth is no longer held to be 'out there' – objective and real, waiting to be discovered. Truth is now thought of as relative, plural and subjective – one thing to you and another thing to me. According to this approach, no metanarratives from science, history, philosophy or religion can be called on to supply foundations for the understanding and communication of ideas. Postmodernists question the underlying intent of language, and words are not considered to be value-free conduits of ideas. Interpretation of texts is carried out with a presumption of there being ulterior motives behind what is stated ('a hermeneutic of suspicion'); a hidden agenda at work which influences the language chosen. Theology is also affected by

[32] N. Pratt, *Frontier Youth Trust Scottish News* (1998), 4–5.

the ambiguities of what some believe to be evidence of a major paradigm-shift (*cf.* Oden 1990).

3.5.2   Postmodern theology

Theology in postmodernity is undergoing revision due to the increasing breakdown of confidence in the Enlightenment project's legacy of absolute trust in the power of human reason to provide foundations for knowledge of reality, including God. This has ethical implications, as it is asserted that reason cannot deliver a morality which is suited to the real world in which we live.[33] Lyotard has suggested that the great biblical narratives ('les grands récits') have been interpreted in such a way as to perpetuate secular ideologies (for example, in the secularization of providence into progress) and that the Western church has merely endorsed capitalism as the current metanarrative which gives life meaning for the masses.[34] In fact, according to Lyotard, such metanarratives are no longer credible (1984: xxiv). Postmodernism, in linguistic analysis, asserts that the signifier (or signifying) has replaced the signified as the focus of orientation and value and conceives of linguistic signs as purely arbitrary. According to this view, language is purely self-referential. For such thinkers as Jacques Derrida, Michel Foucault and Jean Baudrillard, this makes fixed, absolute meanings in language impossible; language is viewed as 'whimsical and capricious'.[35] This conviction has led them to engage in the *deconstruction* of texts, a critical method which assumes that the identity and intentions of the author of a text are irrelevant to the interpretation of it, and that, in any case, no meaning can be found in the text because all interpretations are equally valid and therefore equally meaningless.[36] Following this trend, the theologian Mark Taylor argues that such concepts as truth and meaning should be rejected, as language does not refer to anything and truth does not correspond to anything.[37]

However, Thomas Oden argues that it is possible to seek and find a postmodern theological orthodoxy which recognizes, and rejoices

---

[33] See McGrath 1994: 102–105.
[34] McGrath 1994: 104.
[35] McGrath 1994: 103.
[36] McGrath 1994: 103.
[37] McGrath 1994: 105; *cf.* Taylor (1984).

in, the demise of modernism as a dead-end, but which draws on the tradition which modernity left behind or even despised (1990: 71–99). This is similar to the approach of David Lyon in social analysis, as noted in the Introduction.[38] Oden wants to adopt a holistic approach which gives credence to the metanarratives of historic Christian tradition, and to all that is good in historico-critical studies, in the context of postmodernity where it is possible to break free from modernity's proud but false claim that what is newer must be truer. But this leaves us with questions about how we should view technology and the future in postmodernity.

The crisis of our Western culture, as expressed in the postmodern condition, involves a search for the meaning of technology in the long-term as well as for sustainable applications (Schuurman 1995a; *cf.* Roszak 1988). With this future orientation in mind, we must now turn to eschatological ideas which are unique to Christian theology and ethics, in order to find a way of assessing the significance of VR in relation to the hopes and fears of the human race.

---

[38] See above, pp. 29–31.

Chapter Four:
Technology, theology and human futures

4.1 The long-range impacts of technology

4.1.1 Gutenberg and the printing revolution

We noted earlier that, according to the biblical account, what began in a garden will be consummated in a city; that there seems, even in ancient texts, to be an assumption of some kind of technological drive which moves humanity from agrarian to urban cultures. This may be connected with an eschatological vision of human futures (*cf.* Rev. 21, 22). We also noted Hans Jonas's analysis of the perceived failure of traditional ethics to consider the long-term rather than the immediate effects of action or inaction (1984: 8). It is to this future-orientated perspective that we now turn. We begin by reflecting on the kind of long-term impacts that technology can have. This will enable us to prepare the ground for discussing the possible future effects of Virtual Reality on people as individuals and societies.

Romualdas Sviedrys (1991), a historian of technology, notes that the idea that technologies might have long-range societal impacts can be traced back to Francis Bacon in the seventeenth century. Bacon argued that the invention of gun powder, the printing press and the compass did more to change society than all the ink spilled by philosophers in the preceding millenniums.[1]

It is doubtful whether Gutenberg could have foreseen the long-term effects of his printing revolution in the mid-fifteenth century. The manuscript would be replaced by the printed book as people took advantage of the availability of paper which was becoming cheaper with the development of water-powered manufacturing methods. Scribes would become unemployed or have to seek retraining. Literacy would increase. Libraries of books would be collected, and educational institutions would grow in new ways. Issues such as copyright and intellectual property rights would arise within a century.

However, new technology such as the printing press can only reinforce societal trends, suggests Sviedrys:

> The printing press did not make Spain or Russia more democratic; it only had a liberating effect in societies like Holland and Britain which were moving towards a more tolerant society anyway (1991: 37).[2]

Printing is the first example of mass production based on uniform, specialized components (typeface). When this was coupled to the steam engine, which enabled fast steam-presses to mass-produce cheap broadsheets, the modern newspaper was born. In addition, with the development of modern science and the production of scientific journals, scientists were enabled to exchange printed information and drawings in an accurate way. In the same way, technology could be taught as an academic subject and not only passed down from master craftsman to apprentice. Heriot-Watt University originated in the Edinburgh School of Arts (1821), which was a night school set up by enlightened Edinburgh businessmen who believed that mechanics should have the opportunity of understanding the scientific basis of the industrial revolution and so to develop their skills.

---

[1] *Cf.* Jiggins (1988).

[2] *Cf.* Heim: 'Just as the printing press altered culture and scholarship soon after its invention, so too the computer automates the composition, storage, and transmission of written words. And if the computer affects all written communication, will it not in turn affect the way in which we regard and use language in general' (1993: 64).

4.1.2   *Virtual Reality and communication*

Such long-term impacts can now be traced with the benefit of hindsight. But is it possible for us to forecast the likely impacts of Virtual Reality so that checks and balances may be introduced into its development? We have noted that some commentators have engaged in speculation about possible applications, some of which may be considered undesirable. But, more important, is the metaphor provided by such a development. As the printing press provided the metaphor of mass-production, we need to think hard about the potential metaphorical implications of VR; that is, the way VR may influence our perception of human existence and interaction, including leisure and work.

In computer interface design, the current trend is to replace verbal commands with icons. This tends to internationalize the software, as it can be understood without recourse to language other than compu-terese. Virtual Reality provides the metaphor for the ultimate icon: the interface which enables the cybernaut to enter into 'cyberspace' and navigate its 'super-highways'. Interestingly, such 'cybercrud' (as one critic has labelled the outflow of new terminology) is in itself a language event which is an extension of the impact of computers on the words in common use. 'Cyberspace' is a term first coined by the novelist William Gibson in *Neuromancer* (1984) as a name for an imaginary virtual environment used by IT workers in the early twenty-first century. The 'cyber' in this word comes from 'Cybernet-ics', the name for the science of control and communication coined by Norbert Wiener in the 1930s. He got the idea from the Greek word *kybernetes*, which means 'helmsman'; it describes not merely the processing of information but the use of information in a feedback system for the purposes of homeostatic control. But Gibson's 'cyber' is more about power than control. He imagines neural networks, parallel processors and artificial intelligences, which may lead not to constancy but to chaos. It should be noted in passing that Gibson, when interviewed about these ideas, warned his readers against taking him too seriously, suggesting that there were several layers of irony in his writing which he felt should be clear to the reader.[3] It is not at all clear to the author that all commentators have spotted this dimension;

---

[3] In *Horizon* (1991). For definition of *cyberspace* as understood by recent commen-tators, see above, p. 40 n. 8.

some have perhaps taken Gibson too seriously as a prophet of virtual worlds yet to come (especially Rheingold 1991).

The concept of Virtual Reality offers the possibility of further developing the metaphor of the icon at the expense of language. Jaron Lanier believes that VR is destined to replace speech and writing with a new 'post-symbolic' paradigm for communication. His idea is that VR will circumvent representation by producing experience directly. For example, if you want to understand the workings of a motor engine, you will no longer need to read a book on mechanics, but can don the EyePhones and DataSuit and become a piston (Moulthrop 1993: 78). Clearly, VR processes information or experience in ways that are very different from those of speech, writing and print. Yet it still relies on symbols. Stuart Moulthrop, who teaches and researches in the area of literature, communication and culture, makes these comments:

> If symbolism is produced by skewing the ratio of the senses toward the visual, then the omnisensory approach of virtual reality might indeed organise perception in ways that take us beyond the symbol . . . Virtual reality will not eradicate reading, writing or verbal communication of any sort. Rather, like other post-literate technologies, it will influence those practices and be influenced by them in turn (1993: 80, 84).

Even if the new technology does not threaten reading and writing, it might still contribute to a dangerous social trend: the further extension of media expertise. Like cinema, radio and television – the electronic media in whose name Marshall McLuhan announced the death of the book – VR greatly increases the demands placed on those who would be expert users or designers. In general, as communications media have grown more powerful, they have also become more complex in their workings, so that the number of expert users has become progressively smaller. This metaphor contrasts sharply with visions of VR as a democratic medium (Moulthrop 1993: 85).[4]

Clearly, it is very difficult to predict such long-term effects of new technology, but some scholars have attempted to do just that, and to build theories of what we might call *technological futurology*. One such

[4] *Cf.* McDonnell & Trampiets (1989).

is Karl Steinbuch, a German pioneer in IT. The following brief overview of his ideas will act as a catalyst for further thinking about the eschatological implications of technology.

4.2   Technology and futurology

4.2.1   Positivism and computers

Steinbuch, Professor of Communications and Information Technology at the Technical University of Karlsruhe, predicted in the 1950s that cybernetics would be the universal science of the future. Egbert Schuurman comments:

> Given the principles of cybernetics, the possibilities in this field have been brought to such an advanced stage that it is now possible to duplicate even human intellectual functions in the new machines and moreover, to improve and enhance them. This signifies to Steinbuch that in the future, man as an intellectual being will no longer be central: his place will be taken over by the computer (1980: 214).

Steinbuch distinguished between the study of the future and the control of the future. In communications technology, he expected advances in telegraphy, telephonics, radio and television, which would provide instant communication with persons and computers to access any information desired. In addition, the mass media would inform people of the opinions of others so that they would give up absolute truth-claims and relativize their own views.

Steinbuch predicted the use of computers in many areas of IT, including simulation technology, which he believed could be applied in physiology, psychology, economics and sociology. The latter two would employ models of society by which the consequences of certain decisions could be predicted. He also saw a great future in computer-based learning, although he recognized the potential problems of uniformity of thought and the universal dissemination of poor educational programmes.

Following the logical positivists, Steinbuch rejected metaphysics. In place of other-worldly thought he proposed future-oriented thought. He suggested that advancing technology was distracting people from the need for faith in an unseen world. He believed that the integrating tendency of technology would lead to the disappearance of cultural distinctives which are obstacles to technological progress. He advocated a form of futurological research which was objective, rational and free of ideology. The results of such research would be projections (various future possibilities), prognoses (the most probable possibilities) and plans (instruments for realizing particular projections). These plans would form the basis of controlling the future, and would encourage democratic institutions to develop. At the same time, outmoded ideologies such as Christianity and Marxism would easily be repudiated.[5]

4.2.2 Steinbuch's futurology

Steinbuch's is a futurology of order rather than revolution. He sees the past and present as models for the future, in that the future must be built upon what has gone before, but deficiencies must be eliminated. He believes that the people should decide from a number of alternatives proposed by the technological élite. This will involve detailed planning and fine-tuning; his thinking tends towards socialism. After the people have made their choice from the various models of the future proposed by futurologists, scientists and engineers will address the task of bringing it to fruition.

The crucial issue is whether such an approach would lead to technological-scientific control of the future and of humanity without proper respect for human dignity. In reality, Steinbuch downplays ideas of human responsibility and promotes notions of technocracy, in which we hand over the real decisions to those who know what is best for us. Strangely, Steinbuch replaces metaphysical foundations, which he rejects as outmoded, for a neo-Platonic idealism, for which he claims objectivity, but which is based on scientism and technicism, themselves belief-systems. Nowhere does he attempt to prove that the future is safe in the hands of the technological élite. For Steinbuch, this is self-evident. He seems unaware of the fact that he is employing a *belief-system*, like the logical positivists whom he follows in many ways. We must choose between belief-systems as the foundation of our futurology. Thus we now explore the eschatological claims of Christian ethics to provide normative principles which can be applied in the public arena. We suggest that

[5] See Schuurman 1980: 231–237.

the meaning and ethical implications of technology must be inter-preted eschatologically, with reference to Christian beliefs and visions of the future.

4.3   Technology, eschatology and Christian ethics

4.3.1   Christ and hope

As we have seen in Chapter Two, a study of biblical anthropology must inevitably lead us to eschatology.[6] According to Christian theology, the eternal Son of God is the image of God, but in the fullness of time he entered this world to take upon himself real humanity in God's image. Christian ethics must certainly engage with anthropology, as the New Testament presents Jesus as the model human, an example to follow in both lifestyle and character. His call is, 'Follow *me*' (Mt. 4:19, *etc.*) Yet this is no mere invitation to imitation, for this Jesus has shown himself to be the Christ, the Son of God, by his resurrection from the dead (Rom. 1:1–4). He has inaugu-rated a new age by the outpouring of the Holy Spirit (Acts 1:1–11). The 'last days' of human history have begun, the period between Christ's first and second comings (Acts 2:17; Heb. 1:2). Therefore the call to Christ-likeness, as individuals and communities (Rom. 8:29; 2 Pet. 1:1), is to share in the fulfilment of humanness as God intended it, and the Spirit as the hallmark of the new age is the source of hope that humanity in Christ can indeed aspire to such heights. The ultimate consummation of that hope is in the new heavens and new earth of Revelation (Rev. 21:1 – 22:6). Christian ethics must always have this forward-looking dimension, and some critics, including Hans Jonas (1984), have interpreted this to mean that Christian beliefs are of no earthly use, but merely serve to prepare or qualify believers for the afterlife. We must examine this claim in some detail.

4.3.2   The presence of the future

The writer to the Hebrews traces the theme of Christian hope from the time of Abraham onwards. The patriarch was a tent-dweller who was 'looking forward to the city with foundations, whose architect and builder is God' (11:10). He looked forward to the 'heavenly Jerusalem, the city of the living God' (12:22), 'the city that is to come'

---

[6] See above, pp. 65–74.

(13:14). The cities of humankind are seen as but a pale reflection of the city of God which will endure. The great cities of human history are significant in the development of technological thinking and expertise. Rome was the epitome in its creation of large spaces for human assembly, public baths and domestic heating systems, aqueducts and road networks. Yet it could also be the centre of debauchery and genocide. Its decline followed the pattern of many other centres of empire over the centuries, as absolute power led to corruption. 'Woe! Woe, O great city, O Babylon, city of power! In one hour your doom has come! . . . brought to ruin!' (Rev. 18:10–17).

The eschatological vision, however, is of God and renewed humankind inhabiting a city, within a renewed world (2 Pet. 3:13), and not of nostalgic scenes of pastoral nomadism. Humankind as *Homo Faber* is not a mere parenthesis, a meaningless phase of human development. Humankind in Christ will take into the eternal city greatness and riches which have been purged by the judgment of God (Rev. 21:26–27). Technology has a place in the kingdom of God because God himself, in Christ, is revealed as the archetypal technologist (Moltmann 1985: 312–316). Moltmann notes the references in the Psalms to *God's handiwork* (*e.g.* Pss. 8:3, 6; 19:1, 103:22); the world is thought to be the process and result of God's working activity. To see the world as God's work is to see humankind as *Homo Faber*, and vice versa (1985: 313). God is described metaphorically as the *potter* in Isaiah (29:16; 45:9; 64:8) and in Paul (Rom. 9:21). In Isaiah, the idea is of the potter's sovereign right to make of the clay what he wants. But further, the potter can see the end to which his labour is geared. He takes a natural resource and moulds it for practical use. Of course, pottery is one of the key crafts and one of the earliest forms of technology. In addition, the New Testament tells us that God freely chose to enter this world not as a farmer but as a *carpenter* (Mk. 6:3). In the ancient near east, a carpenter was not only a woodworker but also a housebuilder and maker of agricultural implements. Like the potter, the carpenter was a key member of rural and urban communities. We would be unwise to base a theology of technology purely on this evidence. And we would also be unwise to forget the important agricultural metaphors which the Bible applies to God and Jesus Christ (*cf.* the parable of the sower, Mt. 13:1–23; the good shepherd, Jn. 10:1–21, *etc.*). Nevertheless, Moltmann is surely correct to point out these important insights.

The biblical vision of *Homo Faber* as the reflection of *God the worker* indicates that Christian technological ethics must have an *eschatological* perspective, for the following reasons. Technology is an expression of humanity, which bears the divine image but is yet to be fully restored in Christ, in whom all things hold together (Col. 1:17). The alienation caused by the fall has defaced the divine image in people, but this can be removed by the One who is, supremely, the *eikon* of the invisible God (Col. 1:15). Only when his supremacy is accepted can human thinking and behaviour be brought into harmony with the mind and work of God. The kingdom of God has come into the world in Christ (Lk. 10:9; Rom. 14:17, *etc.*). It is with us now, but is yet to come in its fullness (2 Tim. 4:1; Heb. 12:28). The ethics of the kingdom are therefore the principles of conduct which will perfectly guide restored humanity in the world to come, beyond the *parousia*, the second coming of Christ. So 2 Peter says, 'we are looking forward to a new heaven and a new earth, the home of righteousness' (3:13). What, then, are the moral implications of this hope? 'What kind of people ought you to be? You ought to live holy and godly lives as you look forward to the day of God' (3:11–12).

According to Matthew, the apostle Peter was told by Jesus, 'I will give you the keys of the kingdom of heaven; whatever you bind on earth will be bound in heaven, and whatever you loose on earth will be loosed in heaven' (Mt. 16:19). In other words, the church has authority to shape human history under God. The preaching and living of the kingdom will be the key dynamic in the new age, and will have eternal ramifications. The principles of kingdom ethics must influence all of life, for all human activities are but a preparation for the renewed world to come, under the righteous rule of the King of Kings.

However, some assert that the 2 Peter passage shows no concern about humankind's cultural and social vocation, and that the author emphasizes our spiritual calling to prayer and evangelism as a preparation for death and the world to come. Why invest in the things of this world if it is transitory? Why bother about technological issues, when one day all will be engulfed in the flames of God's judgment? 'The day of the Lord will come as a thief. The heavens will disappear with a roar; the elements will be destroyed by fire, and the earth and everything in it will be laid bare. Since everything will be destroyed in this way, what kind of people ought you to be?' (3:10–11).

A superficial reading of this passage does seem to suggest a fundamental discontinuity between the fabric of this world and that which is to come. Destruction, fire and disappearance all imply finality. But the literary *genre* of such eschatological passages sheds further light upon them. Michael Green, a conservative biblical scholar, has this to say:

> The language of this passage is figurative. It is an attempt to convey in the language of this world something of the wonder of the next. But it is not so much concerned to describe the indescribable, as to act like a *Sursum Corda*, to prevent us getting earthbound, to assure us that God has a purpose and a future not only for our souls but for our bodies, not only for redeemed individuals but for a redeemed society. There is such a thing as human solidarity, alike in creation, in fallenness, and in restoration (1987: 141–142).

These words warn us against an over-literal interpretation. Fire and cosmic confusion are associated with the coming Day of the Lord in the Old Testament, as predicted, for example, by the prophet Joel:

> I will show wonders in the heavens
>   and on the earth,
>   blood and fire and billows of smoke.
> The sun will be turned to darkness
>   and the moon to blood
>   before the coming of the great and dreadful day of the LORD.
>   (Joel 2:30–31)

Yet this is quoted by Luke in Acts 2:19–20 as part of Peter's sermon on the Day of Pentecost. The outpouring of the Spirit was understood to be an eschatological sign of the inbreaking of God's judgment in advance of the final day. The nations would now be summoned to decision, and a great historical upheaval was under way. It was surely difficult for Peter's hearers to accept this message in the circumstances of his day; that is, to believe that the church of Jesus Christ would have such an impact on world history.

Therefore it is possible to see technology within the *already–not yet* tension of the kingdom (G. Ladd 1964). We can hope for a dramatic climax to human history and the inauguration of a renewed world without either denigrating technology as a merely transient phenomenon or demonizing it. According to the biblical writers, *the climax* of history must not be separated from its *process*. The invasion of God's kingly rule came with the incarnation of the Son of God, so that he could say to his disciples 'the kingdom of God is among you' (Lk. 17:21). Yet he looked forward to a time when God's rule, now behind the scenes and a secret revealed only to Christ's followers, would be self-evident. So he taught his disciples to pray 'Your kingdom come . . . on earth as it is in heaven' (Mt. 6:10). This is what New Testament scholars have labelled 'eschatology in process of realization'.[7]

The dynamic behind Christian ethics is, therefore, *the presence of the future*,[8] which is the reign of God realized by the coming of Christ and the gift of the Spirit. That presence is to be taken into every area of human life by Christ's disciples, whom he calls 'the salt of the earth' and 'the light of the world' (Mt. 5:13–16). It is difficult to believe that Christ limited this role to 'spiritual' matters. The love which he came to encourage and enable is a practical love, which influences all of life, personal and social, not least in the world of work. And if the process of history is leading to a great climax in the consummation of God's kingdom, it surely makes sense to prepare for the ultimate destiny of the human race, in Christ, by working for societies which are just, participatory and sustainable in their distribution of wealth, processes of government and technological development.[9]

4.3.3   Hans Jonas and Christian ethics

A contrasting view is that of Hans Jonas, who considers Christian ethics to be an 'ethics of fulfilment in the life hereafter' and suggests

[7] G. Ladd (1964: 19) citing Jeremias (1954: 159). *Cf.* Harries: 'On Karl Marx's grave in Highgate cemetery are carved his famous words "Philosophers have only interpreted the world; the point is, however, to change it." Christians have much sympathy with that statement. For they do not offer a philosophical answer to the problem of suffering, as though it were something to be resigned to. They offer a vision of an ultimate state of affairs which has to be worked for. It is true that the new heaven and earth of which the Bible speaks go beyond our space and time but they have to be reached for and built up on this earth' (1994: 63).

[8] Moltmann (1985: 62); also G. Ladd (1976).

[9] World Council of Churches (1980); *cf.* Kung (1991); also Francis & Abrecht (1976: 196–199).

that it attempts to give the future greater weight than the present as a motivation for morality (1984: 12–14). He agrees that ethics for a technological age must 'consider the global condition of human life and the far-off future, even existence of the race' (1984: 8). In this way, Kant's categorical imperative must be reworked thus: 'Act so that the effects of your action are compatible with the permanence of genuine human life.' If we reject individualism for holism, we have no right to choose non-existence for future generations in order to seek a better life for the present one. Christian ethics might be the key to dealing with the complex dilemmas which arise in modern technological society. Jonas recognizes that, unlike the classical theories of Kant or Mill, Christian ethics does not seem merely to offer help in making decisions for the here and now, by appealing to duty or the possible consequences of our actions. But, after further thought, he rejects Christian ethics as the hoped-for key. He asserts that ethics in an age of technology should not be eschatological in basis.

Jonas believes that, in religious ethics *per se*:

> The acting down here is not credited with bringing in the future bliss by its own causality (as revolutionary action is supposed to do), but is merely supposed to qualify the agent for it, namely, in the eyes of God, to whom faith must entrust its realisation. That qualification, however, consists of a life pleasing to God (1984: 13).

If the principal objective is the saving of the individual soul, Jonas believes that this must inevitably involve renunciation of this world in favour of the world to come, in order to gain merit which will qualify the soul for that future existence. He concludes:

> In this case, we are dealing again with an ethic of the here and now: a form – albeit a supremely egotistic and individualistic form – of the ethic of self-perfection, whose inward exertions may indeed attain to those peak moments of spiritual illumination, which are a present foretaste of the future reward: a mystical experience of the Absolute (1984: 14).

Jonas acknowledges that it is only religious approaches to ethics which have provided us with an ethic of *stewardship*. Stewardship has an essential forward-looking dimension; it is about holding resources in trust for the future when a reckoning will take place. This kind of thinking is well described in the parable of the talents (Mt. 25:14–30), where Jesus encourages his hearers to make good use of the gifts of God, to whom they are accountable. The analogy is investment, which inevitably involves time, abilities and money. If modern people recognize that technological goods are gifts of God, they can, similarly, seek to be good stewards, not only because of their responsibility to God, but out of love for the human race, their neighbours, both those who are alive now and those yet to be born. As Jonas points out, it is impossible to find such a motivation apart from the insights of a living religion.

Therefore it is disappointing that Jonas dismisses the relevance of Christian ethics for technology due to a misconception. He believes that Christianity is radically individualistic, almost selfish, in its emphasis. He imagines that the principal motivation for Christian ethics is qualification for the afterlife. We have suggested that he is wrong. Preparation for the world yet to come is a worthy motivation if it means seeking to bring human activities into line with principles which will last and which can permeate every area of human life, but this is much more than bare qualification. Qualification asks 'How can *I* get in?' Preparation asks 'How can *we* be ready?' Christian ethics is unique in providing a cosmic and eschatological emphasis which can inform personal and social life. As we noted, Jesus called his disciples to live as salt and light in society in order to enrich life, prevent corruption, and offer the truth and purity of their Lord to a world in need of enlightenment and direction. He commissioned his people to teach the nations *everything* he had commanded (Mt. 28:20).[10] This remains the *raison d'être* of Christian social, political and technological involvement, because Jesus' teaching includes an emphasis on being involved and influential in society ('salt' and 'light', Mt. 5:13–16, *etc.*). In addition, Jesus claimed to be the fulfilment of the prophetic vision of justice and peace in the messianic age (Lk. 4:14–21; *cf.* Is. 61:1–2). The cosmic Christ[11] calls his people to live out his concern and reflect his integrity. According to Paul, it is only in union with his people that Christ holds *all* things together (Col. 1:17), and this insight has informed Christian

[10] See Moberg 1973: 155.
[11] See Moltmann 1985: 94–95.

involvement in every area of human activity, including technology.

The validity of Christian ethics in the public domain must now be discussed, since many assume that, while such ethical frameworks may be instructive for individual or faith-group preferences, they can have no real significance in the public debate about the impact of technology.

Chapter Five:
Christian ethics as public truth

5.1 Basis: theology or sociology?

5.1.1 Christian ethical concern in a technological society

In our discussion so far, we have sought to establish connections between the conceptual basis of Virtual Reality and of contemporary discourse in technological ethics, and Christian theological approaches to human nature and purposes. However, some may feel that this begs a very big question which must now be addressed. It is all very well for us to seek to make such connections; but are they valid? Dorothy L. Sayers saw clearly the failure of the church in her own day (1930s) to relate the gospel to the world of work:

> In nothing has the church so lost her hold on reality as in her failure to understand and respect the secular vocation. She has allowed work and religion to become separate departments, and is astonished to find that, as a result, the secular work of the world is turned to purely selfish and destructive ends, become irreligious, or at least, uninterested in religion. But is this astonishing? How can anyone remain interested in a religion which seems to

have no concern with nine-tenths of his life?[1]

But is Sayers right in assuming that Christian theological and ethical reflection is readily applicable to the secular world of work, where modern technology is centre-stage, in such a way as to be relevant to those outside the community of faith? How can we relate the privately held beliefs (of a significant number of people, it must be agreed) to a major public issue such as the development of computer technology? A number of answers have been given to this difficult question.

Robin Gill, Professor of Modern Theology in the University of Kent at Canterbury, argues against the privatization which has characterized many approaches to ethics in recent decades. He suggests that Christian ethics arises not from individualistic reflection but is a community exercise. He is critical of modern analytic philosophy which assumes that the good can be discerned through individual enquiry alone. Christian communities, most often called 'churches', have been criticized for failing to practise what they preach, and rightly so. Gill notes that the media in a pluralistic society is often keen to point this out (which is its responsibility, he agrees). While the churches may often fail to be good examples of the values which they purport to hold dear, Gill suggests that Christian communities may yet be 'harbingers of values'.

> Christian communities may need to be reminded that they are harbingers of values which they frequently flaunt, misunderstand or fail to notice. Yet their Scriptures, lections, liturgies, hymns and accumulated sources of long-refined wisdom continue to carry these values despite their own manifest frailties. Worshipping communities act as moral harbingers, whether they realise this or not, and then spill these values more widely into society at large, again whether they realise this or not (1991: 25–40).[2]

The justification of Christian ethical reflection on technology, for Gill, must lie in this knock-on effect. Society at large may be unaware of the influence of Christian values, and the churches may similarly

[1] D. L. Sayers, quoted in Hunter (1992: 96).
[2] *Cf.* Lyon (1984, 1986, 1994a).

fail to appreciate their impact on society, but the Christian ethicist must demonstrate connections where they exist. This argument is a *sociological* justification.

5.1.2   A theological approach

Another approach is *theological* in its basis. This is seen in the work of Oliver O'Donovan (1994: 13ff.), which we have already cited.[3] His confidence in the relevance of Christian ethics to modern discourse on technology (or whatever) rests upon what God has done in human history, and, in particular, in the resurrection of Jesus Christ from the dead. O'Donovan holds that this event is as much within the public domain as any other historical event, and is open to the same canons of falsification as other events which have been reported by purported eye-witnesses. It matters not that the alleged event is quite unique in substance. It must be subjected to the same kind of scrutiny which historians apply to other alleged events in the ancient world, such as Julius Caesar's reported visit to our shores in 55 BC.[4]

O'Donovan suggests that it is the historical objectivity of the resurrection which provides a real basis for Christian ethics. Indeed, the datum of the resurrection establishes the credentials of Jesus of Nazareth as the supreme moral teacher as well as his claim to be Saviour and Lord. The universal importance of the resurrection renders Christian ethics of universal significance even to those who, as yet, do not accept the authority of Christ or that of his church.

This is a similar argument to that put forward by Lesslie Newbigin (1989, 1991), missionary elder-statesman and theologian, in his concern to affirm Christian doctrine as 'public truth' and not relevant only to private individuals who happen to believe. In this he wants to stand against those who suggest that the gospel is valid only within certain parameters; for example, that the church should not speak out in political debates but rather concentrate on personal morality or spirituality. More profoundly, he is resisting the tendency to reduce

---

[3] See above, pp. 76–79.

[4] This event is known to us only through Caesar's own account of the Gallic wars, the earliest extant MS of which dates from about AD 900. This is very slender documentary evidence in comparison with the gospel accounts of the resurrection, for which we have numerous MSS, some copied only 100 years or so after the alleged events.

beliefs to preferences which people choose to hold and which have no necessary basis in objective reality (1989: 14–51).[5]

Gill believes that those outside the Christian fold are more likely to be persuaded by his appeal to consequences as a justification for affirming the place of Christian ethics in secular worlds than by any appeal to theological criteria. If effects of the over-spill of Christian values into secular society can be demonstrated, such justification is possible. In contrast, the view of O'Donovan is that Christian ethics is inherently worthwhile because of the datum of the resurrection, quite apart from any effects which Christian ethical reflection may have.

It is this latter view which is most relevant to our discussion, for despite the fine work being done by, for example, the Society, Religion and Technology Project of the Church of Scotland, it is very difficult to measure the effects of dialogue and debate even over many years.[6] The justification for Christian ethical critiques such as we are seeking to undertake here must be in the nature of the Christian gospel and its ethical implications. As O'Donovan reminds us, Christian ethics are and must remain *evangelical* ethics; that is, they must be rooted in the gospel itself and not in legalism or codes of practice. The gospel is good news for public proclamation and dissemination rather than mysteries purely for the initiated.

The good news of the kingdom of God comes as the inauguration of human liberty (Hebrew, *shalom*) in every area of life, with the coming of Christ. The Old Testament demonstrates that technology can be formed and used for good and ill as an expression either of devotion to God or of rebellion against God, as we have noted in Chapter Two.[7] The real problem is that of human nature itself, which finds redemption only through the work of Christ. The plan of redemption is in the process of realization, and part of the scheme of God is a restoration of human crafts and skills which befit good stewards of a gracious lord. We expect to see conflict in all of this between good and evil, not in a dualistic sense, but in view of the struggle which has been begun in the sufferings and death of Christ to overcome the powers of darkness. While the battle has been won, as at D-Day, the war is not yet over (Cullmann 1962). We expect to

---

[5] *Cf.* Holmes (1984).
[6] See Ferguson (1994).
[7] See above, pp. 66–71.

see a cosmic struggle for the minds and activities of people in all aspects of life. Because we live in evil days, we are called to join in what Paul calls the *redemption of time* (Eph. 5:16). The alternative is to waste time, and not to make the most of the opportunities afforded to us, not least in the world of work (which, in the ancient world as in the developing countries today, took up even more time than it does in today's Western societies with their leisure cultures). Christian tradition affirms that the Risen Christ is Lord of time, a fact which has been established by the resurrection, and that the universality of Christian ethics depends on this evangelical foundation.

5.2   The nature of public truth

5.2.1   Plausibility structures and the gospel

Clearly, however, to affirm that Christian ethics must not be privatized is not to say that all, or even a majority of people, accept its validity. Public truth is that which belongs in the public domain and not to some esoteric group. Christianity is not a mystery religion and has been severely critical of such religions in its history. The claims of Christianity extend to a belief in the integrating influence of Christ over all things, for 'in him all things hold together' (Col. 1:17). Lesslie Newbigin notes that the gospel is *good news of what has happened*, but that there are problems in communicating this in a pluralist society where the gospel becomes but one opinion among many and cannot be 'the truth' for pluralists. They believe it may be 'true for me' but cannot be true for all people (1989: 242).

In this kind of climate, Christians and churches have been keen not to appear arrogant, and have dissociated themselves from past works of missionary endeavour which have often, unfortunately, transported Western culture, thinking it to be a reflection of the essence of the gospel itself. Reaction to this kind of error has been twofold, suggests Newbigin.

First, theologians have become timid and governed by the assumptions of modernity, which, as we have noted in passing, is itself *passé* in many intellectual circles. Christian theology has been circumscribed by the limitations of current *plausibility structures*, the paradigmatic frameworks which may be acceptable at any given time. Thus we have been told that modern man cannot believe certain things, especially in the area of the supernatural. Christianity claims that, behind the scenes of life, Christ is Lord, despite the indifference of many to the claim. The essence of the gospel is that God has revealed this truth to his people through the apostles and prophets (Eph. 3:2–11). The sharing of this truth leads people to encounter the Risen Lord for themselves. Clearly these are supernatural claims. But the experience should not therefore be privatized, as the believer is called to share the truth publicly and corporately by life and witness. In a technological society, part of that witness must be to relate the principles of evangelical ethics to the social developments of the day, including technology.

5.2.2   Pluralism and the gospel

Secondly, Newbigin focuses on the widespread anxiety in the West that the churches are in terminal decline; that Christianity may be abandoned due to lack of interest, despite the frantic activism of some Christians. In a pluralistic society, any confident affirmation of the truth is likely to invite questions as to why certain truth-claims should be believed, and it is tempting to test the significance of any truth-claim by counting the number of people who believe it. Thus, in the minds of many people, truth is consensus (1989: 244). However, following Haldane (Carr & Haldane 1993) and O'Donovan (1994), we have presented an argument for the objectivity of values and the existence of moral order which resonates with Newbigin's concern for the gospel as public truth. We need now to develop the significance of the *Ethics of Christian Realism* for the church's witness to the gospel in modern technological culture.

5.3   Prophetic witness and technicism

5.3.1   Technology, the cultural mandate and technicism

The idea that this Christian witness is essentially *prophetic* has been helpfully explored by scholars writing in a symposium which has become seminal in Christian theological and philosophical reflection on technology (Monsma 1986: 200–221).[8]

> The cadence of our culture is set by the beat of the technological drum. In and of itself, this basic fact should be cause for neither great rejoicing nor great alarm. The crucial question is, if this is so,

---

[8] *Cf.* Van Til (1972).

who or what is determining the beat? The central message of this book [*Responsible Technology*] is that in modern society this beat is largely determined by a drive for power, for human mastery apart from the will of God. Humankind has revolted against its Maker, has declared its independence from him and his will, and all too often drives ruthlessly for a salvation of material prosperity brought about by technological prowess (1986: 200).

Monsma and his colleagues argue that technology is part of the *cultural mandate* given to people by their Creator, and that it must issue from a spirit of service to others and responsible stewardship of the environment. The norm of responsible technology is the love of God, despite the fact that humankind's fall into sin has flawed human love with a tendency to be self-seeking. The temptation is to think of technology as the sole and ultimate solution to the problems of the world. This view is called 'technicism'. The prophetic witness of Christians must challenge the assumptions of technicism and offer a more realistic and fruitful alternative.

That technicism is alive and well in the hearts of those deeply involved in Western technology is demonstrated by a recent article by one enthusiastic commentator in which he says:

New developments in science and technology suggest that the pre-eminence of the human being is being challenged by the very capacity for innovation which has secured our dominance of the planet until now. There are a number of technologies undergoing intensive research which indicate that the existing relationship between humans and machines is altering. Whilst there are no machines which can yet be said to be capable of taking over the world, the distinction between humans and machines is becoming less clear. Sometimes known as CyberSpace, Virtual Reality involves the use of high-powered computers to build three-dimensional environments in which a user can be immersed in real-time interaction with a mathematically-generated world using stereoscopic headsets and spatially-sensitive input devices. Many users report that after a few minutes immersion in cyber-space, the 'reality' is just as convincing as any other interactive space *e.g.* the 'real' world. As graphics processors become more powerful in the next few years, we can expect to see a dramatic increase in the levels of hyper-realism to be found in such systems. As a result the separation between reality and virtual reality will diminish (Pepperell 1994: 35–43).

This kind of *hype* (which clearly stems from a lack of hands-on experience of VR as we know it today) is coupled with a conviction that technological advances since the Renaissance have marginalized God and promoted humanism as the underlying worldview of Western culture. In contrast, Monsma writes:

> This drive for mastery apart from God and his will manifests itself in technology in what we will call *technicism*. Technicism reduces all things to the technological; it sees technology as the solution to all human problems and needs. Technology is a saviour, the means to make progress and gain mastery over modern, secularised cultural desires. Technology thus becomes its own reason for existing (1986: 49).

5.3.2 *Prophecy, technicism and Jacques Ellul*

Technology for its own sake, therefore, must be the focus of the prophetic witness to public truth which is at the heart of the concern of this book. By 'prophetic' we do not mean 'predicting the future'. The Old Testament prophets most often were involved in relating the truth of God to their contemporary situation, *forth*-telling rather than *fore*-telling.[9] And they did not set themselves up as people detached from the weaknesses of the society they challenged. So today, we must be aware of the ways in which we are all involved in the tendency to be over-optimistic about the potential of technology to solve world problems, and admit that we can all get caught up in the desire for more sophisticated technology not necessarily because we need it, but because of its inherent fascination.

However, Monsma and his co-writers are critical of one prophetic voice, that of Jacques Ellul, whose analysis of modern technology has been rejected by some commentators as cynical and fatalistic. Ellul, in his apocalyptic interpretation of the influence of modern technology in society, argues that technology is a threat to human faith and freedom. He sees no hope of deliverance short of divine intervention

---

[9] See G. Houston 1989: 27–41.

to consummate history. The only option is a revolt against the present system. In his latest work, Ellul says:

> Is this a closed situation? Is there no way out? Is collective spiritual and material suicide the only result that is incontestably held out to us by the actual bluff of technology? . . . If we have any chance of emerging from this ideologico-material vice, of finding an exit from this terrible swamp that is ours, above all things we must avoid the mistake of thinking that we are free (1990: 411).

In this way, Ellul denies that the prophetic task is to redirect technological history, and seems to condemn it out of hand. For him, only God's intervention in judgment can effect any lasting change.

Ellul seems to rule out any hope that a prophetic call can lead others to repentance, that is, to a change of direction. In this he displays his dependence upon the theology of Karl Barth, who denied that human history has meaning or value in itself. Barth distinguished between actual historical events (*historie*) and the interpretation of those events (*geschichte*). According to this view, God is free to invade history at his own time, but full meaning and salvation lie outside of history and are experienced only through faith. Monsma sums up this view:

> Society's only hope for an authentic freedom, therefore, rests upon a terrible cataclysm at the end of historic time, one that reaches back to shatter our everyday illusions and totally disrupts the flow of history with a solution rooted outside it (1986: 207).

In contrast, the promotion of Christian technological ethics as public truth must be in tune with the ethics of the kingdom of God, which is both *already* and *yet to come*.[10]

5.4   *Criteria for evaluation*
5.4.1   *Normative principles for responsible technology*
In this chapter, so far, we have sought to establish the validity of Christian ethical critiques in the discussion of public issues such as

---

[10] See above, pp. 112–116.

technology, and how they may be justified and act as a bone fide expression of the prophetic calling. It is now our task to outline those normative principles which can be used in order to engage in such critiques, so that we can apply them in our final two chapters.

Ethical decision-making is the practice of *making principled choices* between alternative courses of action, and, because human action tends to be complex, we must recognize a number of influencing factors, each tending to bring about competing consequences. This problem is related to the issue of the public nature of the gospel and its implications, in this case ethical. Secularized Western culture is resistant to the kind of criticism of technicism which has been expounded above, and claims that technology based on hard science has alone the right to control our lifestyle. In contrast, Christian ethics proposes other normative principles.

Love alone is normative, according to Christian tradition, because love is the fulfilling of God's purposes for humankind.[11] Even the most superficial reading of the gospels will confirm this (Mk. 12:28–34; Mt. 22:34–40; Lk. 6:27–36; Jn. 15:9–17). Are there Christian principles and standards which, inspired by love, enable us to evaluate technological developments, at least to a certain extent? Clearly, it would be strange if such criteria could not be applied in the world of work, which is the arena of technology, when it is widely accepted that Christian ethics can rightly offer guidance in marriage, the family, business and politics, as well as in church matters. Ethical choices must be made on the basis of some standard or criteria, for example, the principle of harm minimization, whereby we seek to minimize the amount of harm that may be caused to any persons or organizations who may have a stake in the decisions. An unethical decision would be one which results in unnecessary harm. Monsma suggests that we should employ evaluative criteria to establish principles for the guidance of technological activities, with the

[11] Dt. 6:4, 'Hear, O Israel: The LORD our God, the LORD is one. Love the LORD your God with all your heart and with all your soul and with all your strength'; Lv. 19:18, 'Love your neighbour as yourself'; Jn. 15:12, 'My command is this: Love each other as I have loved you'; Gal. 5:14, 'The entire law is summed up in a single command: "Love your neighbour as yourself" '; *etc. Cf.* Thiselton: 'The claims to truth put forward in Christian theology, therefore, call for love where there is conflict, for service where there are power-interests, and for trust where there is suspicion' (1995: 43).

following characteristics:

First, these principles should be **adequate in scope** and not treat technology in isolation. We have established that technology is not value-free in conception or effects but is part of the complex web of human cultural expression. We must therefore explore the various contact points between technology and the rest of life and not adopt a blinkered approach. Technicism has been rejected in this discussion because it is narrow and reductionist in its vision of technology for its own sake. We see the result of this in the disastrous effects of pollution, in the dehumanization of the workplace, and in a disregard for the future inhabitants of the earth. However, another blinkered approach is that which singles out efficiency and economic growth as the only supreme values worth pursuing. It may be held that economic growth is the only true measure of social progress (hence the focus on the notion of 'living standards' as all-important in social policy) and that all economic growth is good in itself. A classic reaction to this kind of approach is found in E. F. Schumacher's study *Small is Beautiful* (1974), in which he proposes other means of increasing the quality of life. For example, he challenges the assumption that developing countries will benefit from technology transfer, which fails to appreciate the cultural and social differences between the rich north and the poor south. His call for *intermediate technology* appropriate to the developing world has received some attention in the last twenty years.

In addition to this insight, Christian theology would add that broadness of scope must be such as to include the full breadth of God's involvement, *i.e.* all things. The ultimate good news is that, in Jesus Christ, integration is possible, and every aspect of human thought and activity can be held together creatively in him.

Secondly, Christian normative principles inspired by love must **make necessary distinctions** and recognize the diversity within the created order as well as its unity. According to Christian belief, everybody is created in God's image, yet each person is unique, and there is great diversity within the human race which the anthropologist observes and records. Technology as a cultural expression is somewhat different; it cannot be treated merely as a product of natural diversity, as all technology is the product of human choices, for good and ill.

Thirdly, Christian normative principles for technology should **integrate the diverse aspects of society** so that each receives its due place. In this way, ethics must not be set against economics, nor justice against technology. 'The realisation that ethical choices rest to some extent on technological mechanisms is appropriate, but so is the recognition that one's technological choices rest upon implicit or explicit ethical criteria' (Monsma 1986: 67).

What, then, are those *specific normative principles* which, if applied together, can lead to responsible technology? Monsma suggests eight such principles: 1. cultural appropriateness; 2. openness or information; 3. communication; 4. stewardship; 5. harmony; 6. justice; 7. caring; and 8. trust.

These eight must be pursued simultaneously, as they are all aspects of love and reflections of the kingdom of God in which *shalom* reigns (the Hebrew word includes the ideas of harmony, joy, justice, love and peace). Let us now look at these principles.

5.4.2   Cultural appropriateness

Decisions about appropriate technological developments involve five areas which provide a focus for evaluation: (1) continuity and discontinuity; (2) differentiation and integration; (3) centralization and decentralization; (4) uniformity and pluriformity; and (5) large scale and small scale (Monsma 1986: 71).

How might Virtual Reality be viewed in terms of its cultural appropriateness according to these criteria? This will of course depend upon the particular culture in question. But let us imagine the adoption of a VR system for computer-based learning in a culture which has experienced the amazing developments of the last fifteen years in personal computers. Such a system might seem to foster continuity, and to be the logical next step in the development of computers in society. However, some might see it as such a radical development as to undermine the learning culture. It could lead to the establishing of the virtual university, where students and staff meet only through computer networks. Some might suggest that it could radically change the nature of learning and dehumanize education. Technicists would favour discontinuity, tending to assume that what is newer is truer and better for us.

Some years ago, the toy industry in France decided that modern children needed to play with modern materials and moved away from wood to plastic. On a visit to the toy capital of Moirans, in Jura, the author was told that a reversal is in process. Wooden toys are coming back into vogue. Similar reversions to traditional methods which were once scorned are being made in other areas of life. There needs to be greater reflection on cultural appropriateness before such major developments are planned. In the European Union at the moment, uniformity seems to have developed as a result of making economic efficiency the supreme value. When we visit France, we see fewer really French cars and many 'euro-models', which are the result of integration, centralization, and large scale. For many, this seems to be progress. In evaluating VR we need to ask ourselves whether computer-generated environments will become even more standardized and tend to deny the differentiation which real life entails. The very simplification involved in creating such worlds suggests that it will be impossible for VR to do otherwise, despite the extravagant claims noted above concerning the potential realism of virtual environments. Against this, others might say that VR will encourage users to create their own worlds and that 'off-the-shelf' worlds are unlikely to take the market by storm. Yet the amazing complexity of computing skills required for this process suggests that a more uniform approach is much more likely.

5.4.3 Information and communication

Virtual Reality has hit the headlines in recent years and much has been said about its potential. But much of this has been 'hype', as we have noted. In the early days of the development of nuclear power, some suggested that it was the ultimate solution to the energy needs of the world, and yet we are much more cautious now that we are aware of the dangers of waste and potential disasters. In the same way, claims for VR need to be scrutinized realistically. 'Without open communication there can be no knowledge; without knowledge there can be no fulfilling of responsibility' (Monsma 1986: 73).

5.4.4 Stewardship

The development of VR involves the use of resources both material and human. Questions must be asked about the amount of computer power required for VR environments to become adequately realistic. Is this an appropriate use of expensive equipment? The phenomenal amount of time required to produce computer-generated worlds which are at all convincing is another issue. Do we value this development so highly that we are prepared to encourage fellow human beings to invest hundreds of hours of work in the production of seconds of computer graphics? One exponent of computer graphics spent four days of computation time to produce fifteen seconds of footage.[12] Clearly this time will reduce with increased computer power, but intensive human input will still be involved.

5.4.5   Harmony

At the moment it is impossible to say that VR systems are characterized by harmony. Research at Edinburgh University Psychology Department, and elsewhere, indicates that nausea can result from extended periods of wearing a VR headset (Wann 1992).[13] Doubtless improved equipment will reduce such problems, but it will be a long time before VR equipment is a delight to use. The basic problem is that to don the headgear is to cut oneself off physically from the real world and to become 'legally blind' for a time. The experience is the ultimate in artificiality and leads many users to long for the grain and complexity of the real world.[14]

5.4.6   Justice

'Technology should do justice to the material things it uses by bringing out and developing the potential God has placed in them' (Monsma 1986: 74). A fundamental question about the development of VR systems is whether there is likely to be a dehumanization of the workplace as a result of the adoption of this technology, or other threats to, for example, family life. There is clearly potential for the latter if VR games become widely available, and concern has been expressed about the dangers of involvement in violent games and pornography. Yet the same technology can be used to enhance human life by promoting health and safety in hazardous work situations.

---

[12] Gareth Davies of the Moving Picture Co., quoted in Horizon (1991).

[13] *Cf.* Regan (1995) and Wilson (1995).

[14] The novelist Michael Frayn, interviewed in Horizon (1991), commented after spending some time in a (somewhat basic) virtual environment: 'It would be appalling to be sentenced to spend the rest of one's life in this [VR] world. The world is too simple, it doesn't have enough roughness and opposition in it to engage one's imagination for very long. It's wonderful as an escape from the world of mud and rain and reality, but if you don't have the mud and the rain and the reality you lose not only the sense of the outside worlds, but eventually I would think you lose any sense of yourself.'

Potential harms need to be balanced by the prospect of useful applications.[15]

5.4.7   *Caring and trust*

Caring goes further than justice or fairness, and technology which embodies care for persons is sensitive to their needs and aware of potential dangers. Trust focuses on the dependability of technological objects and whether they are, and do, what is claimed for them. Another factor is the health and safety of use. At the moment, VR equipment is in the embryo stages and suffers from a tendency to malfunction when in the hands of the non-expert. As we have noted, questions of health have been raised, and it remains to be seen whether these problems can be overcome.

5.4.8   *Harm minimization*

We continue our examination of normative principles by asking how technological projects might be structured to *minimize harm* to all stakeholders. Of course, this will depend on our notions of *harm*, and whether we accept that potential harm to others, to property or to the environment, is, in itself, a good reason for introducing sanctions or ethical guidelines, or whether risks are worth taking if some long-term benefit is in view. For the purposes of this discussion, let us explore the classical position of John Stuart Mill, the nineteenth-century English utilitarian philosopher. His view has come to be widely accepted in the Western world.[16] It is seen in the extent to which civil or criminal law may be used to enforce moral standards, with regard to, for example, sexual behaviour, pornography, racist or other literature. Mill asserted that the only good ground for the law to intervene is the causing of harm to others, a principle sometimes described as the 'harm condition'. Self-inflicted harm, potential or real, was not considered to be a justification for legal sanction. Although we are not concerned about matters of civil or criminal law as such in the ethical debate about VR, we can see how this issue of harm impinges on any analysis which might result in the establishing of professional guidelines for VR research and development.

[15] See below, pp. 149–170. *Cf.* Wolterstorff (1983).
[16] See above, p. 56 n. 30.

The question is whether the principal or only reason for discouraging or banning certain VR applications would be that they cause or are likely to cause harm to others. Here we must distinguish between *necessary* and *sufficient* conditions for such action; *i.e.* that such an application *must* cause harm before it can be discouraged or banned, and/or that if such an application causes harm that is *enough* to justify prohibition or disapproval.

Gordon Graham, Regius Professor of Moral Philosophy at the University of Aberdeen, helpfully explores this issue, and here we follow his argument, with specific application to VR issues (1988: 121–137). One argument against the sexual molestation of small children has been that it causes harm to them. However, others allege that not all such molestation invariably causes harm. It is possible that a small child may not be harmed by, for example, the fondling of genitals, but there seems to be clear and good reason for the law to forbid this. The same would be true of the activities of a 'peeping Tom'. He may cause no known harm, but he is invading privacy, and it is commonly held that the law should protect this up to a point. Theft can be harmless, in the sense that a millionaire is unlikely to be harmed by the loss of a £150 portable TV. We believe that such activities ought to be against the law, not because harm is necessarily caused but because of other factors, such as rights or duties.

Neither, Graham argues, is harm a sufficient condition for certain activities to be proscribed. There are a great many activities which societies permit and which do cause harm to others. For example, success in business may well be at the cost of a competitor going 'bust'. One scientist can ruin another's reputation by publishing a refutation of his pet theory. Recently a young boxer was killed in a professional bout in Glasgow, and his parents responded, not by suggesting that boxing should be banned or the other boxer indicted, but that their son knew the risks he was taking, that he was gambling with his own life for financial gain and personal satisfaction. This demonstrates that what matters most is not harm but *consent*. The small child in our example may not have been harmed, but she or he was not in a position to consent to such advances and was wronged because the molester had no right to act as he or she did. Similarly, theft is proscribed because it involves the taking of property without the consent of the owner, even if no harm is caused.

With regard to the debate about VR, we see how the harm

condition, if used without other analytical tools, is an inadequate tool of ethical analysis. The nature of immersive VR as a concept is that one must consent to don the EyePhones and expose oneself to a virtual environment. There are extreme possibilities where VR could be used as a torture device or a means of enforced psychoanalysis or punishment, as we noted in passing with reference to the work of Colin Beardon (1992).[17] However, these are surely speculative exceptions which prove the rule. The essential question is whether *consent* on entry to a virtual world has been freely given, a consent which is an invitation to users of the virtual environment to relate to others in the way they so choose, recognizing that all users can withdraw at any time by removal of the headset and switching off the machine. We need insights from deontology (rights, duties and the categorical imperative) as well as from the specific normative principles outlined here.

5.4.9   Moral responsibility

As harm and consent, rights and duties and other normative principles are important concepts in the analysis of VR applications, so also is that of *responsibility*. In what way(s) are designers responsible for their products and their use? Deborah Johnson has demonstrated in her study of computer ethics (1993) that there are different levels of responsibility.[18] *Accountability* for an event or mishap means that the accountable person is the appropriate one to respond when something unwanted happens, and may mean that he or she has only to offer an explanation or, perhaps, to provide compensation. *Role responsibility* refers to the duties one has in fulfilling a certain role, but not in other roles. For example, a researcher may have role responsibility for the effects of a particular project, but not for the application of its findings in other situations. *Causal responsibility* is recognized when someone acts or fails to act with the result that effects are caused, for example if a VR researcher fails to report negative effects from the use of head-mounted displays. *Blameworthy responsibility* exists where one does something wrong which leads to a negative effect, and this must be distinguished from *legal liability responsibility* which always involves the risk of claims being made for compensation even

---

[17] See above, p. 46 n. 16.
[18] *Cf.* Forester & Morrison (1993).

if blame cannot be established. For example, if a VR product malfunctions, there may be strict liability under the law for negative effects, even if the researchers did everything reasonably possible to test and modify the equipment. But in this book we are chiefly concerned about issues of *moral responsibility*; to explore why the concept of moral responsibility is essential to our analysis and who is responsible for the effects brought about by computer use.

John Ladd explores this last theme in a seminal article (1989). In contrast to the view of O'Donovan,[19] Ladd believes that information technology does raise ethical questions of a new order, so that a considerable restructuring of ethical categories is required. He alleges that philosophers of technology can no longer apply ready-made categories to new situations. The challenge in evaluating new technologies is to find new categories or new ways of interpreting old categories.

An example is the traditional category of *rights*, and in particular the right of *privacy*, which involves control over information about oneself. Formerly this was secured by, for example, drawing curtains and locking drawers. However, the advent of computer networks has made it possible for detrimental information about individuals to be gathered without violation of physical barriers. Because of this, our definition of the right of privacy needs revision. Those who willingly engage with such systems are surely abandoning their claim to the right of privacy as it has been traditionally understood. For example, possessing a credit card means willingly being subject to the test of 'credit-worthiness' and the police's being able to trace our movements. If we use electronic banking machines, 'big brother' knows where and when we have done so.

In view of this, it is likely that similar revision of categories such as *piracy* or *intrusion* is required. Formerly, hi-jacking of equipment or machinery required physical violence or forced entry. If information was to be acquired by spies, bugs would have to be located. However, Ladd's main concern is more fundamental, with our concept of *moral responsibility*. In particular, he focuses upon moral responsibility for negative outcomes, such as disastrous computer errors. He explores the ethics of what people may *unintentionally* do to harm others through the use of computers. Ladd begins his analysis by

---

[19] See above, p. 79.

restating his basic question in metaphorical terms:

> . . . there is such a long distance between the inputs of particular individuals and their significant outcomes, and there are so many different sources (designers, operators, managers, and consumers), that as far as establishing human responsibility is concerned, we find ourselves adrift in a vast sea of anonymity where responsibility has become so diffused as to evaporate into nothingness (1989: 209).

This difficulty is due not only to the technological and social complexity of computer use, but also to the fact that computers can be used for both positive and negative purposes. When we speak of the 'misuse' or 'abuse' of computers, we seem to be assuming that computers are essentially good for us and that evil outcomes are exceptional and easily recognizable or predictable. Yet computers can 'crash', sometimes with disastrous results. So our focus must shift from the purposes for which computers may be used, to what computers actually do; that is, to the *consequences* of operating them.

An underlying recurring problem in this analysis is the *myth of technological neutrality*, which we have discussed earlier.[20] According to this, whether or not a particular technology is morally acceptable depends on what it is used for and who uses it. Questions of ethics and value are considered to be external to computer technology. This surely flies in the face of the wisdom of the vast majority of philosophers of technology who hold, as we have noted, that technology is value-laden.[21] Clearly, new technology has moral implications, making certain kinds of conduct easier, and others harder. For example, computers have facilitated and encouraged new surveillance techniques, and matching and profiling. In this way, new ways of behaving and new social institutions, such as the Internet, have been developed which may be heralded as a means of support for the depressed, or condemned as an avenue for pornography (Rheingold 1994).

It is simplistic to separate ends and means in the way ethical neutralism has sought to do with reference to technology. Ladd

---

[20] See above, pp. 46–50.

[21] Including Jacques Ellul, Frederick Ferré, Carl Mitcham and Egbert Schuurman.

demonstrates that such a separation leads to a serious misunderstanding of the nature of moral responsibility in relation to computers:

> Human agents are responsible not only for the outcomes of their actions and for their uses of technology but also for how the technology itself shapes our conduct, our attitudes, and our institutions (1989: 211).

This is the key issue in any exploration of the value-ladenness of technology. It introduces a comprehensive concept of moral responsibility which departs in essential respects from traditional philosophical discussions of free will and determinism. These tend to be chiefly concerned with defining excusing conditions which imply the absence of responsibility. Similarly, lawyers are preoccupied with the conditions which may exempt a person from criminal or civil liability. Here, we join with those who treat moral responsibility in a more positive way by referring to such issues as one's duties to others with whom one has a relationship, *e.g.* children, employees or associates, and to duties of due regard for the consequences of one's actions for the health and safety of others. This breaks the traditional tie, noted earlier, between responsibility (as a virtue) and liability in any legal or blameworthy sense. This positive conception of moral responsibility differs from more negative conceptions in two basic respects. First, it is non-exclusive; a lot of people may be co-responsible for something, even if in varying degrees. Secondly, moral responsibility is often indirect and remote rather than direct and proximate. Thus this concept of moral responsibility has merit because it is both 'consequentialist' and 'agent-relative' (J. Ladd 1989: 211). It reflects the basic insights of traditional views of responsibility which link outcomes, agents and victims.

We may apply this concept to computer ethics by noting that technology adds another element to the analysis of responsibility, namely an *intermediary*. For example, in the case of a reckless driver, the technological intermediary is the motor car; in the case of the careless programmer it is the technological process of running the program and connecting it with other parts of the system. Clearly, where complex technology is involved, the interposition of intermediaries of various kinds tends to make it very difficult to assign responsibility for various outcomes. In addition, we are usually unaware of the part that a motor car or a computer system, for example, may play in determining what we do when we use them or how they may impose patterns on our actions and their outcomes. As noted earlier, we often assume the ethical neutrality of intermediaries, and because of the complexity of computers we tend to ignore our responsibility for the outcomes of computer operations. In fact, precise causal connections may be neither known or knowable.

The concept of moral responsibility surely implies that human agents are responsible for the systems themselves, *i.e.* for the way systems function, and that human responsibility for disasters is not limited to the direct input of particular individuals. This kind of indirect and diffused responsibility can be called 'collective responsibility', a term which Ladd does not find helpful as its use tends to fudge the issue of exactly which persons are responsible in any given circumstances. He notes:

> To answer this question requires tracing the causal connections and responsibility relations for outcomes to particular individuals and to their individual failures stemming from such things as self-centred projects, narrow and single-minded interests, unconcern, and moral mindlessness (1989: 216–217).

What, then, of structured human processes such as those found in formal organizations or bureaucracies? An example is the automated bank teller; this uses computer technology to carry out financial transactions which are defined through a complex set of social structures, processes and procedures. These structured processes act as intermediaries in a way comparable to the working of technological systems, and, as with machines, it is often claimed that they are ethically neutral. 'It's not the system which is at fault but the operator', is the allegation when things go wrong. But structured processes of bureaucracy, like technological systems, are themselves made by humans and loaded with human values, so that the actions of apparently autonomous individuals may be shaped by the systems in which they take place.

Applying this to concepts of corporate responsibility, is it both a conceptual mistake and a moral error to attribute moral responsibility to formal organizations? Justin Welby (1992) argues that it is reasonable to speak of the moral agencies of companies or other corporate bodies for three main reasons: the legal existence of corporate entities, their organization, and their ethos. This last factor is crucial, for a company's ethos influences many of its activities over a period of time. Even members of senior management are subject to the company's ethos while playing their part in its development and acting as servants of the shareholders, who may be its ultimate custodians. According to Welby, justice requires that accountability for the actions of a corporate body is not only a matter for those directly implicated in any particular event or course of events. A company can reasonably be expected to encourage a culture which would discourage bad practice leading to negative outcomes, and shareholders might also be held responsible for the company's sins of omission and commission (1992: 24). But Ladd is concerned that such collective responsibility should not let individuals off the hook:

> It is a bit of anthropomorphic nonsense to ascribe moral responsibility to systems, whether they be technological or social, in addition to or instead of the individuals that make and use them. Questions about who was responsible for the Nazi holocaust are not simply answered by reference to the technological machinery involved or to the bureaucratic system that carried it out; rather, responsibility must be attributed to indefinitely large numbers of individuals who in one way or another contributed quite indirectly and remotely to the outcome (1989: 218).[22]

In this way it is suggested that as individuals cannot escape their moral responsibility, either retrospectively or prospectively, by appeal to the fact that they were only obeying the orders of a superior, so computer professionals, users, operators, programmers and managers cannot dodge responsibility for negative outcomes on the grounds that they were only doing what the computer system led them to do. It does sometimes appear that we have delegated or even abdicated our decision-making powers to computers and have made computers responsible for outcomes for which human beings used to be held responsible. We now blame the computer for mistakes which were previously blamed on people, as when we hear of a 'computer error' on an electricity bill. But to do this is to avoid the issue. While

[22] *Cf.* Ladd (1970).

computer systems fail, they do not make mistakes in any moral sense, nor do they apologize for failures unless programmed to do so.

Human control over computers (like that of other intermediaries) must be seen as an example of indirect and less easily assigned responsibility. New questions arise about responsibility for the formerly human tasks now performed by computers and whether computers perform these functions well or badly in specific situations. In addition, we must ask what kind of controls should be exercised over computers in order to obtain morally responsible outputs.

So we see that the nub of the issue is the shift from human control to computer control and its effects on the assignment of responsibility. The innovation of automated aircraft landing systems, for example, has brought many benefits but also new hazards, which have led to disasters when computer failure or electronic interference has caused aircraft to crash. What, then, are the ethically significant aspects of this shift in control from humans to computers?

Clearly, there are similarities between the jobs normally done by humans in controlling intermediaries and those performed by computers (J. Ladd 1989: 221–224). As in human decision-making, computers make decisions on the basis of information-processing by the ordering of ends and means through the use of algorithms, where the means consist of operations of intermediary systems, mechanical or organizational. We might compare a computer-directed operation with a human-directed operation such as the landing of an aircraft. Computers operate at a secondary level, in that they operate on other systems (intermediaries), but the significant point to note is that neither human controllers nor computers produce their effects (negative or positive) directly, but only indirectly through the systems which they control. Because of this, we cannot evaluate computers as dangerous or safe *in themselves*. A computer-controlled nuclear power station may be dangerous because it involves nuclear fission, but not because it involves computers. Both the positive and negative value of computers depends upon the nature of the systems they are used to control. We need to ask which sort of control, computer or human, is best suited for a particular purpose or a particular kind of intermediary. As we are chiefly concerned about responsibility for avoiding negative outcomes our enquiry should be: 'What do computers do best and what do human beings do best?' Ladd proposes that we should adopt the following as a general principle:

In situations where satisfactory controls require dealing only with closed systems of factors, data, or tasks, computers are probably superior; when the systems required are open-ended and fluid, human controllers are generally preferable. In an old-fashioned terminology, human beings are better than computers where 'judgment' is required (1989: 223).[23]

The problem is that, even if this principle were to be accepted as theoretically sound, it is likely that computers will continue to be used for tasks which they are intrinsically incapable of handling effectively. Because of this, there needs to be some way to get out of a computer-controlled system and revert to human controls when computer decision-making becomes defective. This will require a loose coupling between computers and the systems they are controlling and between such systems and their output. This kind of safety mechanism is required especially where there is a chance that a computer error could lead to disastrous outcomes.

In summary, we conclude that there are at least two fundamental issues here. First, that we should not give the computer control over tasks for which it is unsuited, and, second, that there should be a means of de-coupling if things go wrong. Two examples may be cited to support this thesis. The first concerns the growing number of cases of *police misidentification* arising out of computer searches. From available databanks, adopting matching and profiling methods, it is inferred that the wanted person has certain identifying characteristics. An individual is then discovered who has, by coincidence, a number of these characteristics, even though there may be no evidence to connect him or her with the scene of the crime. In one notorious incident, French police shot and killed suspects on the basis of computer mismatching. The second example concerns the *too close coupling* between a computer system and an intermediary (in this case the Bank of New York and Wall Street). This led, in 1985, to severe financial losses when the system was down for twenty-eight

---

[23] *Cf.* Dreyfus (1979), cited by Heim (1993: 58–59): 'We are deluding ourselves if we believe that we can create machines to replicate human thought . . . Dreyfus explained his philosophical point – that he was concerned not with generic predictions but with the underlying comparison that hastily identifies intelligence with formal patterns or algorithms.'

hours.[24] The framework of moral responsibility proposed by Ladd is undergirded by these illustrations. Above all, they demonstrate that human agents must take *prospective* moral responsibility for preventing the disastrous consequences which computer operations can have for health, safety, welfare and *moral integrity*. We cannot simply adopt a crude utilitarian approach and hope that there will be a surfeit of positive over against negative outcomes; hence the need for our present discussion. Our concern is to propose certain normative principles as essential for such a prospective analysis, and to show how those principles may be applied specifically to the development of virtual environments.

5.5   Evaluation of criteria

5.5.1   *Technological faith*

The principles outlined above were originally intended to inform and guide the development of technology rather than as criteria for ethical evaluation as such. But, of course, the one implies the other. That which is good to consider in the research and design process is surely good to consider when a technological system and its products are undergoing development, production and use. The concern is to counteract the 'technology for technology's sake' approach, and to avoid being ruled by the dictum that what *can* be done *should* be done. As Frederick Ferré, philosopher of both religion and technology, observes:

So much has been staked on technological faith that the levels of anxiety produced by discovering that it has, indeed, been faith all along are inevitably high. It would be tedious and unnecessary to enumerate the ways. One obvious example, however, is the faith our society has shown in the ability of the technical experts to cope successfully with nuclear wastes that are now building up . . . Despite warnings, we went ahead with nuclear technology, creating these wastes at an ever-accelerating rate, with the blissful confidence that 'they' would come up with a solution . . . Not only was it a *sacrificium intellectus*, it also showed a readiness to sacrifice the future safety of all life on the planet on the blessed

---

[24] See Vallee (1982).

assurance that a technological fix would somehow, over more millennia than any civilisation has ever been sustained, take care of us and our progeny to the end of time (1993: 48).

The criteria outlined above are useful in determining the *limits* of any particular technology rather than whether it is absolutely right or wrong to develop certain systems. These *specific normative principles* are meant to act as guidelines in a way similar to the markings on a football pitch. They are not the invention of a spoil-sport but the necessary limitations which must be set in order for the game to be played safely, enjoyably and fairly. The rules of the game govern what may occur within those boundaries and are interpreted by the referee. By definition, the rules are more complex than the markings on the pitch and require interpretation by the officials. In technology, such oversight tends to manifest itself in codes of practice (rules) espoused by professional bodies (referees) which ensure proper standards.

5.5.2   Checks and balances

Perhaps many of us in the West have lost an awareness that such concerns are rooted in our biblical heritage. The Old Testament is not only the basis for the claim that the love of God should be normative for all human existence and endeavour: it also contains practical rules which carry through those normative principles which we have noted above. An example of building regulations can be found in Deuteronomy 22:8. To prevent accidents, new houses were to have parapets around their flat roofs, which were used for drying clothes and storage. Health and safety issues were also addressed, for example in the laws requiring the eradication of dampness, symptomatic of which was mildew on the walls of houses and in fabrics (Lv. 13:47–59; 14:33–57).

The purpose of the criteria outlined earlier in this chapter is to provide a system of checks and balances for the technologist, a framework within which responsible technology may be developed. Its validity does not rest on societal acceptance of the norms of the Judeo-Christian ethical tradition, nor is its validity lost should a society once influenced by such norms take another course. We are not arguing for the acceptance of such criteria on the basis of its consequences, but on the objective reality of a world-order restored, and in process of restoration, in Christ, as declared in the gospel as public truth.

5.5.3 *Distinctively* Christian *criteria?*

That the *Ethics of Christian Realism* can provide such specific normative criteria, there is no doubt. But are these criteria distinctively *Christian*? What does theology bring to ethics other than what R. M. Hare calls 'emotional flavour'? Hare writes:

> Since morality pertains to our concrete actions and attitudes – always within the sphere of human culture and society – our real reasons for doing something will also arise within human culture and society. Any reasons other than these are not real reasons. They are only harmless baggage. At best, they only supply motivation for doing the things we know, on other grounds, we ought to do.[25]

For example, there are good reasons for opposing war or racial discrimination on ethical grounds, and for approving peace and racial integration. Wars kill people, cause suffering and destroy property; racial discrimination undermines community and has negative psychological effects. But Hare does not tell us why these issues are regarded as moral problems. Nor does he identify the ultimate origin of our values. Philip Wogaman argues that there is explanatory power in a Christian approach to moral judgment consistent with the *Ethics of Christian Realism*.

Wogaman begins by looking at alternative approaches such as utilitarianism, which focuses on the pleasurable or painful consequences of proposed actions. G. E. Moore (1903) showed that pleasure cannot be proved to be *good* and suggested that we grasp the moral quality of goodness intuitively. He believed that moral intuition is part of human nature, but that nothing should be treated as good just because it exists (the 'naturalistic fallacy'). Again, Kant had affirmed that the ultimate good is the good will itself; but what is the good? Is it self-evident? Wogaman comments: 'It does not appear possible, in the final analysis, to speak of selfhood as a good apart from some ultimate frame of reference in which the self exists' (1989: 14). He argues that we really do not have a solid basis for making ethical judgments until we can

---

[25] Quoted in Wogaman (1989: 12).

ground our conceptions of the good and of moral responsibility on an ultimate framework of valuation (1989: 15). The question is, how do we establish what is *ultimate*?

Wogaman shows that all major approaches to moral judgment rely on some appeal to an *ultimate reference-point*, such as intuition, the good will, existential decision or a Supreme Being. He believes that it is useful to think of all ethical systems as finally based on 'revelation', by which he means that which makes everything come into focus or fall into place. A religious revelation, for Wogaman, is something which suddenly enables one to make sense out of everything else (1989: 17–18).[26] What is distinctive about Christian ideas of revelation is that notions of ultimate reality are founded on belief in God as a personal being, who has entered into covenant relationship with all humanity and particularly with Israel (before the Christian era) and with the church of Jesus who is the image of God (in the messianic age; Col. 1:15–20). Christ is seen as the decisive revelation of what goodness ultimately means: this is shown in his teaching and healing ministry, the quality of his life, and the depth of his love demonstrated in the cross (1989: 21).

5.5.4 *Transcendence and realism*

Richard Harries, Bishop of Oxford, has recently affirmed that Christian realism provides an ultimate reference-point which enables truth-claims to be discussed in the public domain. He rejects the basic outlook of the 'Sea of Faith' group that 'God' is purely a human construct, a word which refers only to human values and ideals.[27] In a dialogue with the thought of Alasdair MacIntyre, Harries challenges the widely held modern view that there can be no absolute stand-point from which to judge rival claims to truth (1994: 71–78).[28] MacIntyre believes that concepts of right and wrong are culturally defined. Notions of 'duty', for example, should not be detached from the culture in which they developed and the generally accepted norms of conduct which are valued in that culture, especially those relating to public offices or roles. Moral concepts cannot be divorced from a holistic understanding of human nature, which varies

---

[26] *Cf.* discussion in Introduction, above, pp. 19–23.

[27] Harries (1994: 1–4), responding to Freeman (1993).

[28] *Cf.* MacIntyre (1985).

according to tradition and is bound up with particular philosophical and religious understandings about the essence of humanness. Does this mean that relativism rules? Must we assume that every tradition within society and every society will have its own criteria for assessing truth-claims? Is the approach we have taken, of defining normative criteria, in fact misguided? Surely not, as Harries reminds us in his summary of MacIntyre's argument:

> Because each tradition is committed to the truth of its claims, it is thereby also committed to examining the claims of rival traditions. In order to do this it has to formulate those claims, and in order to formulate them, it has to translate them into the terms of its own tradition. This means that rival traditions will inevitably be brought together with comparable strands of rational justification. Even if one tradition comes to the conclusion that there is no real meeting, that the claims are incommensurable, this judgment of itself assumes that there has been some genuine contact, some common ground . . . Any tradition committed to the truth of its own point of view must at the same time be committed to a dialectical relationship with rival traditions, in which conversation takes place, conversation which will inevitably involve some shared understanding of what might count for and against the truth of the claims in question (1994: 71–72).

The *Ethics of Christian Realism*, in this way, and specifically in the context of postmodernity, must be seen as an affirmation of Christian ethics as public truth, in dialectical relationship with rival truth-claims, and open to revision. The specific normative principles advocated in this chapter must be seen in this light and considered as offering critical tools for a meaningful and productive conversation at the interface between philosophy of technology and Christian ethics. It is now our task to apply these principles in an analysis of the particular ethical issues which are being raised concerning Virtual Reality applications.

Chapter Six:
Virtual Reality: opportunities and threats

6.1 Review of current VR applications

Today's computer communication cuts the physical face out of the communication process. Computers stick the windows of the soul behind monitors, headsets, and datasuits . . . Without directly meeting others physically, our ethics languishes. Face-to-face communication, the fleshly bond between people, supports a long-term warmth and loyalty, a sense of obligation for which the computer-mediated communities have not yet been tested . . . The face is the primal interface, more basic than any machine mediation . . . Cyberspace without carefully laid channels of choice may become a waste of time (Heim 1993: 102, 105).

With this warning from Michael Heim in mind, we must now address the issues of opportunity and threat which have been raised in our synthesis of the *Ethics of Christian Realism*, with particular reference to Virtual Reality applications. Since VR technology became accessible to the public about 1991, the medium has been most widely marketed by leisure industries, which have produced simulation games. The goal of *virtual sports* games is to enable participants ultimately to be able to play realistic, challenging, physically exercising sports against virtual opponents or remote human opponents.[1] Impediments to progress include scarce technical, financial and entrepreneurial resources, but a number of VR sports games have been marketed, including *Full Swing*, a golf game featured on a BBC TV show, which involves striking with a real club a ball attached to an electronic interface, which computes the physical forces at play and is connected to a screen, upon which the flight of the ball is then projected by means of a computer-generated image. *Alpine Racer* is a skiing simulation which has become quite popular, and other games include virtual pool, basketball, tennis, table-tennis, volleyball, cycling and boxing.

However, the most widespread impact of VR has been in *entertainments* applications, mostly for arcades and theme parks. Early in 1995, twelve companies worldwide were offering immersive VR systems of this kind, and by the end of the year the number had grown to twenty-seven.[2] The British company *Virtuality* sold 80% of all the VR entertainments units bought in that year, at an average retail unit cost of $30,000, and had eighteen different VR games on offer in its catalogue. The vast majority of games available are of combat scenarios, racing or flight simulators, or labyrinthine fantasies, as a glance at any recent issue of a CD-rom games magazine will confirm.

Apart from leisure applications, which account for the lion's share of VR use so far, the main VR developments have been in *education and training*, and in *virtual engineering and architecture*. The former has included industrial training for safety procedures,[3] the training of surgeons in the methods of keyhole surgery, and the accurate delivery of instruments in biopsy.[4] In addition, educational material in process of development includes virtual heritage projects which enable cybernauts to visit computer-generated representations of historic buildings and archaeological sites.[5] In engineering and architectural

---

[1] *VR News* 5.4, May 1996, 28–30.
[2] *VR News* 5.2, March 1996, 18. Installed units grew from 1,005 to 1,615 in 1995 (6% increase). The average retail unit cost fell from $31,500 to $30,150 during the year.
[3] *VR News* 5.4, May 1996, 31–33.
[4] *VR News* 5.3, April 1996, 29–33.
[5] *VR News* 5.1, Jan-Feb 1996, 24–33.

applications, developments include virtual assembly-planning, design analysis, control-room design, oil-platform virtual prototyping, real-time urban design, virtual manufacturing-plant design, and prototype-vehicle usability testing.[6]

As we have noted in passing, due to the predominance of VR leisure applications, we may be tempted to play down the ethical significance of immersive VR, or, in contrast, to imagine that non-leisure applications are likely to be free of ethical implications. However, we must remember that ethics is concerned about finding principles by which we may decide, in advance of action, what ought or ought not to be done. It is about being able to give a principled defence of our moral commitments. For example, points in favour of developing VR as a surgical training aid include the principle of *harm minimization*, as surgeons can learn techniques without risk to real patients. The use of VR is consistent with the *categorical imperative*, as people are not being treated as means of experimentation, but as the ends of tests which are being carried out for their ultimate benefit, with no risk to them through being subjected to trials. It is a model of medical research which we would surely want to see extended to other areas where practicable. In this chapter we will reflect on the opportunities afforded by such applications, and also examine some of the potential threats to human well-being which may result. We will present an ethical analysis of one particular application, and seek to show how the tools of applied ethics can be honed and used in that case.

6.2   Virtual environments in an age of anxiety

6.2.1   *Imagination and its effects*

First, we will explore some of the potential and actual disadvantages of VR developments. Thomas Sheridan (1993) has expressed his anxieties about potential harms resulting from immersion in virtual environments which are supposed to be vehicles of entertainment. As an engineer at the Massachussets Institute of Technology, Sheridan affirms that VR is not essentially an altogether new concept, nor is it inherently bad for people. He wants to compare computer-generated environments with the worlds created by story-tellers and writers

---

[6] *VR News* 5.3, April 1996, 29–33. See Appendix Two.

throughout the generations, but also to note points of dissimilarity.[7]

Sheridan reminds us first of the role of *imagination* within societal groups, and how story-telling (often augmented by acting, dancing, or singing) has been used to motivate the imagination. The visual arts, from painting and relief-work, to sculpture, photography and film, have been used in the same way. These have often been accompanied by music in a desire to create an environment with visual, auditory and *haptic* components. (Haptic perception involves not only the tactile sense but also our awareness of the position of our limbs in relation to one another and to the space around us.) While children throughout the ages have delighted in this kind of imaginary environment, and on the whole it is considered culturally enriching, the intention in creating such environments may not always have been benign. Imagery can be used to arouse anger, or hatred for enemies, for negative advertising, or political smear.

Let me cite two examples. In the village of Carrbridge in the Highlands of Scotland, the Landmark theme park includes an audio-visual account of the clans of Scotland. The impression is of a rather bland, tourist-orientated account which has been created in order to engender romantic notions of Scottish origins. But one can see how such a presentation could easily be used for political purposes or to encourage hatred of the English. It might also focus on the violent chapters of the story out of all proportion to the other aspects of Scottish history.

The same could be said of the Jorvik Centre in York, which portrays the life of a Viking village in the ninth and tenth centuries, by recreating the homes and work of the time in sight, sound and smell. Again, the effect is somewhat sanitized, despite attempts to recreate the vapours from the common latrine! One is taken through a model of the village and its people by hi-tech monorail, and the presentation is clearly an attempt to tell us that the Vikings were ordinary folk like us and that their reputation for rape and pillage has been overplayed. (After all, the British later did the same kind of thing, travelling by ship to other lands and settling there despite the protestations of the locals!)

One can see how the exhibition might have been set up to communicate quite a different message. Had the Nazis succeeded in

---

[7] *Cf.* Stanney (1995).

occupying part of England for over a hundred years, one wonders if later accounts of the 'Germanlaw' would have been so favourable as the Centre's depiction of the Danelaw! Such story-telling by the creation of virtual environments of one kind or another is not value-free, but presents worlds which are interpretations of the historical evidence, often stylized and packaged for the consumer, who is unlikely to want to be overwhelmed, on a tourist trip, by a sense of the terror experienced in the past when human life was cheap. Recently, it was alleged that Mel Gibson's 1995 film *Braveheart*, a portrayal of the life of the Scottish patriot William Wallace, may have sparked off nationalistic attacks against English students at St Andrews University, although the president of the students association pointed out that such attacks were part of a wider problem, and that Scottish and overseas students had also suffered.[8]

So we may not be surprised if the very nature of electronic virtual environments tends to promote certain phenomena over others. It is easier to portray violent scenarios than to express co-operation, friendship and love. Shooting weapons, explosions, smoke, fire and resultant bodily reactions are the stock-in-trade of the most popular computer games, such as *Street Fighter*. So far we have not seen a game entitled *Mother Theresa's Street Carers*! Yet not all computer games are without constructive purpose. The popular *Sim City 2000* is about the construction of cities to meet the projected needs and wants of imaginary inhabitants ('Sims') and is open to disasters natural and man-made. It could be developed using virtual environments as a tool for learning about town-planning, civil engineering or crisis management. Sheridan, however, is concerned that there may be a very thin line between simulation and reality, so that what seems like harmless violence in a simulation may become a rehearsal for real violence in the streets (1993: 142).

6.2.2 Escape from reality
Secondly, Sheridan alerts us to the tendency of VR to become an *escape from reality*, by its very nature. He asks:

> Is the new VE technology the year 2000's step beyond Orwell's *1984* or Huxley's *Brave New World*, where real people turn off from

---

[8] *AUT Bulletin*, No 202, January 1996, 8.

society to become contented zombies, enslaved in a virtual world that panders to their whims but nurtures and encourages their growth in a human community not at all? (1995: 142).

Even if this doomsday scenario cannot be confidently predicted at the moment, there is evidence that, far from producing contented zombies, exposure to virtual environments can induce chronic fatigue, lethargy, drowsiness and nausea (Durlach & Mavor 1995: 44ff.). This is the so-called 'Sopite Syndrome'. Durlach and Mavor comment, 'Unfortunately, there are as yet no adequate theoretical models for enabling synthetic environment system designers to predict how subjects adapt to such alterations . . . (*e.g.* a distortion plus a time delay plus some jitter in time or space)' (1995: 44).[9] In addition to Sheridan's two concerns we must also note, thirdly, that threats to health and safety have recently been discussed by Professor J. R. Wilson of the VR Applications Research Team at the University of Nottingham (1995: 20–24). He makes five points which summarize the present state of knowledge about VR health and safety issues.

First, Wilson agrees that, for some people, in some circumstances, use of immersive VR has been shown to produce adverse side effects, such as dizziness, nausea, disorientation and visual fatigue. We should remember that motion sickness resulting from the use of aircraft simulators has been documented for a long time, but this has not led to the banning of such equipment. The same would be true of adverse effects associated with real sailing or flying. Secondly, he believes there to be no published evidence that these effects are serious or long-lasting, and that they usually wear off quickly and often lead to adaptation in further experiences of immersion. Thirdly, reported effects may be due to the particular hardware, software, virtual environment or the participant himself, or a combination of these. The psychological work published by Wann *et al.* (1992), for example, was based on tests using a relatively primitive head-mounted display. Fourthly, most popular media reports of adverse side effects have no basis whatsoever in published VR research. Finally, there is a need, suggests Wilson, for appropriate clarification and assessment methods, but these will take time to develop. He notes that, in the UK, the outcome of the Health and Safety Executive's two-year study on the

---

[9] *Cf.* Regan (1995).

health and safety implications of immersive VR (due to end in July 1996) was subject to a watching brief by the Department of Trade and Industry. The aims of the study were fivefold: first, to identify and clarify possible side-effects of VR use; secondly, to produce appropriate methods to assess potential VR side-effects; thirdly, to assess potential consequences of any side-effect in terms of the health and safety of participants; fourthly, to identify and evaluate possible health and safety benefits of VR use; and fifthly, to recommend guidelines for VR use where possible.

If such concerns are being expressed about health and safety issues, it is surely appropriate to attempt an ethical analysis of VR applications and to propose guidelines for the ethical use of VR systems. One problem is that current experience of VR systems is too limited to allow one to draw any firm conclusions in this area. But such uncertainties surely underlie the need for ethical evaluation. The weakness of a crude utilitarian approach is displayed. If we cannot accurately predict likely effects, how can we make any advance assessment of the happiness or harm, pleasure or pain which may result? Ernest Kallman is a computer professional who emphasizes the need for ethical evaluation in the development of VR: 'Developers need to perform an ethical evaluation of the effects of a particular VE application, then decide what actions, if any, are required' (1993: 144). But such an evaluation involves a complex interaction of ethical theories rather than the application of one in particular.

The purpose of this book is to propose one such approach to ethical evaluation which arises out of a Christian ethical concern for responsible technology, as outlined in Chapter Five. This kind of evaluation will involve philosophical notions such as *harm minimization, the public interest* and *accountability*, as we have noted. But a major problem is persuading technologists even to begin asking such questions. Ten organizations involved in VR development were asked by Kallman to respond to a questionnaire which focused on ethical issues.[10] Only two replies were received. Perhaps Kallman makes too

---

[10] Kallman's questions were: 1. Has your organization recognized any ethical issues related to virtual reality systems? 2. If so, what has been its response? If not, do you think there is merit to examining ethical aspects of VR? Are there VR applications which have questionable ethical implications? 3. What guidelines would you suggest to help developers in the appropriate design and use of VR systems? 4. Might there

much of this silence, as the organizations may have had valid reasons, such as pressure of work, for failing to respond. Kallman concluded that there was, at that time, little evidence of interest in ethical prethinking among VR practitioners. His anxieties were not shared, he felt, by many technologists. If that is the case, our search for an appropriate analytical approach is even more urgent (1993: 145–146).

6.3   Approaching an ethical analysis of a current VR application

6.3.1   Kallman and Grillo's approach

In Chapter Five we outlined criteria for the ethical evaluation of technology and related them to our theme.[11] Here we focus specifically upon the ethical issues surrounding VR. We seek to adapt (by the addition of the normative principles already outlined),[12] and apply, the approach of Kallman and Grillo (1996), whose 'four-step analysis process' provides a model for an approach to ethical decision-making in information technology.[13] This process is designed to enable defensible ethical decisions to be made when one is faced by specific dilemmas concerning the use of IT. It is similar to other approaches to ethical decision-making which have been adopted in business ethics.[14]

It involves, as **Step One** ('Understanding the situation'), a 'brain-storming' of all the *facts* involved in a particular dilemma, or a description of the research under consideration, where a choice must be made about, for example, a potential VR application. We have to ascertain, then, which of these facts raises an ethical issue, and why, and the degree to which there may be potential or resulting harm. We need next to list all the *stakeholders* who are involved: those who will be influenced, to varying degrees, by the decision. In **Step Two**, ('Isolating the major ethical dilemma'), we must first ask what is the ethical dilemma which needs to be resolved *immediately*. Should someone do or not do something? We must then isolate the *major*

---

be some legal liability issues should someone claim they were 'encouraged' to perform an illegal act through having 'performed' a similar act in a VR setting?

[11] See above, pp. 128–144.

[12] See above pp. 128–134.

[13] See Appendix One for full details.

[14] *Cf.* Ferrell & Fraedrich (1994: 94–108).

ethical dilemma, and ask the same question.

Step Three ('Analysing the ethicality of both alternatives in Step Two') involves the application of normative principles, such as consequentialism, deontology (rights and duties), and the categorical imperative. In our adaptation of the process, we will also include the normative principles already proposed in Chapter Five.

In **Step Four** ('Making a decision and planning the implementation'), we have to make a defensible ethical decision based on the analysis in Step Three, indicating the principles we have chosen as appropriate and adding reasons for the choice(s) made. Where there are conflicting rights and duties, these must be weighed up and those which take precedence must be chosen and justified. Following that, the specific steps required to implement the defensible ethical decision must be listed, and we must demonstrate which stakeholders will be affected by proposed actions. If possible, we would then consider other longer-term changes which might help us in future decisions of a similar nature (political, legal, technical, societal, organizational or concerning codes of ethics). Finally, we should ask what prethinking might have prevented this dilemma.

Our reasons for adapting the approach of Kallman and Grillo are clear. They have produced the only current model for ethical decision-making in IT which has been widely accepted by both engineers and ethicists.[15] They show that the ethical issues surrounding VR are not unique, but rather involve novel and perhaps more grandiose forms of the same generic problems with which earlier technological developments were beset. They argue that such an approach is required because the ethical implications of information technology require the attention of all stakeholders: the potential consequences of making poor choices (or not making them at all) increases the risk for all involved. Above all, it is their concern that researchers and developers should address the issues, as these are the key people who can define the trends in technological development. This approach enables the participants in ethical decision-making to avoid the extremes of excessive caution (focusing as it does on moral responsibility rather than legal liability issues, such that

[15] As demonstrated by the inclusion of Kallman's basic thesis in a special issue of the MIT specialist journal for VR researchers, *Presence*, 2.2, Spring 1993. Kallman & Grillo (1996) is in its second edition, having first been published in 1993.

experimentation and creativity are not stifled needlessly), and the 'technology for technology's sake' approach which has been criticized in this book.[16]

For the purposes of this part of our discussion, we will choose a real, and, so it seems on first consideration, a relatively non-controversial VR application which is currently being developed: a VR version of the cave of Lascaux in France, the site of prehistoric cave art of great anthropological importance which has become such a tourist attraction that the cave and its treasures are endangered.[17] This has led to its closure, so only academic anthropologists will have direct access to the cave for the foreseeable future. The idea of using VR to create virtual caves through which virtual visitors may walk and view the paintings seems, at the outset, to be an excellent example of the way in which technology can be used educationally in an environmentally friendly way.[18] It seems to be no different from the creation of virtual art-galleries on the Internet, a way of enabling many more people to 'visit' these shrines of significant art and artists. But let us look a little closer. Is there any hint of an ethical dilemma in this application? Is there any question that such a thing ought not to be done, or that there should be checks and balances built in to how it is done? Space forbids a detailed examination of how the process could be applied in this case, but we will seek to give an impression of its relevance.

6.3.2   *The facts of the dilemma posed by this VR application*
We begin by listing the relevant facts. (1) The cave is endangered by erosion and air and light pollution, so that it has been closed by the French authorities and visitors can no longer gain access. (2) The paintings are located away from the cave mouth and probably have cultural-consciousness significance rather than being art for art's sake. (3) They are a French national treasure and the most famous and significant of many similar sites in the Dordogne. (4) A VR representation embellished with text and photographs can be constructed to provide a multimedia educational 'tour' of the site. (5) This could be sold on a CD-rom or be released on the Internet. (6) Many people

---

[16] See Kallman 1993: 146.
[17] See Appendix Two.
[18] *VR News*, 5.1, Jan–Feb 1996, 24–33.

who would otherwise never have been able to see the cave will now be enabled, virtually, to do so.

Of these facts, a number raise ethical issues. Clearly, if no action is taken to protect the cave, the result may be not only closure but also the loss of artefacts. It seems to be imperative that something is done to preserve the paintings from damage and yet make them available for viewing in some way. However, even VR representation is to a certain extent selective and subjective, and there will undoubtedly be a loss of objectivity for the 'visitor', especially in the loss of ambience (smells, moisture, lighting effects, *etc.*). In addition, will the choice of Lascaux, the most famous site, for this VR project, lead to the neglect of other sites in the region and give an unbalanced impression of palaeolithic cave art? Will there be, in addition, a loss to France of cultural property, perhaps a modern equivalent of the transfer of the 'Elgin Marbles' from Greece to the British Museum in the last century? And there are specific issues raised by the application of VR technology in such a case.

Caroline Whitbeck suggests that there are two special features of VR experience which pinpoint the particular ethical issues raised by this development (1993: 147, 150–151).[19] First, there is the *vividness* of the user's experience, and secondly, the sense of *agency*. The former will become more pertinent as the technology becomes more sophisticated and present problems regarding the use of head-mounted displays are overcome. Nonetheless, VR enables one to enter fascinating worlds where some of the normal limitations of real life are suspended for a time. Unlike more passive media, a virtual environment gives the users a sense of action, and they are enabled to manipulate virtual objects. This is an experience of a different order to cinema, TV or even arcade video games. It is a distinguishing feature of VR that visual, auditory and haptic stimulation may be co-ordinated in order to produce a vivid, compelling experience of doing something. In this case, the wonder of entering an ancient site and looking around will be very compelling. But VR introduces another factor: the possibility of including in the software the ability to manipulate objects within the virtual environment and to create or re-arrange paintings, without sufficient knowledge of their purpose or significance in developing cultural consciousness, and forgetting that

[19] *Cf.* V. Stone (1993).

they are expressions of human values at a particular time in prehistory. In fact, the Lascaux reconstruction includes a human figure which comes to life and invites the viewer to receive a secret message about the hidden history of humanity. We will explore some of the ethical implications of this below.

6.3.3   List of all stakeholders

From the facts of the dilemma, we move to consider those who are likely to be stakeholders in VR applications. We have to ask, 'Who will be affected by this particular VR application?' Clearly the researchers themselves have a major stake in the outcomes, along with those who will be involved in the manufacture and marketing of the eventual product, all users and also developers of competing technology. Educationalists and students are involved, but so are the local people, who will not profit so much from visitors. If the alternative of an on-site visitor centre is replaced by the VR option, the French people and state may lose a national treasure, and the anthropologists and archaeologists may find their work being over-simplified in order to fit the virtual environment. If such technology may affect our perception of humanness, given the anthropological significance of this application, then society in France and wherever the VR product is available must also be included, and perhaps all humankind. Again, for those whose ethical analysis moves beyond humanistic reflection to the grounding of ethics in metaphysics or religious belief, there may be scope for exploring the involvement of an *Ultimate Stakeholder*. In Chapter Five, we suggested that there is good reason to include this factor among the proposed normative criteria for ethical evaluation, not least because it involves the concept of *stewardship*, which is hard to justify without some ultimate reference-point.

6.3.4   Application of normative principles

The use of ethical principles to evaluate an action 'provides a rational foundation for the ethical choice and allows competing positions to be judged on a basis other than intuition or emotion' (Kallman 1993: 145). The normative principles of cultural appropriateness, stewardship and justice would seem to be most relevant to our chosen example. The principle of *harm minimization* is not so prominent in this case, but others are important, such as *the public interest*, basic *human rights*, and commonly accepted *duties*, such as truth-telling or promise-keeping. Other normative principles have already been outlined.[20] On the basis of those principles, we affirm that Virtual Reality can and should be developed in a *culturally appropriate* way. This will mean being careful not to export, for example, Californian culture via the medium of VR, but developing systems which are flexible and adaptable to different cultures throughout the world. We see only too clearly the results of cultural imperialism through the development of computers and other electronic media. *Openness and communication* will mean that VR is promoted in a realistic way, acknowledging the limitations of the technology and the areas where its application would not be suitable. In the same way, information about potential side-effects suffered by users will be made known. *Stewardship* of material and human resources will mean that limits are set on the level of realism expected in virtual environments so that computer power and human time are not wasted on unnecessary refinement of images. *Harmony* will mean that every effort is made to develop interfaces which are user-friendly and which overcome the present problems of nausea, *etc.*, and which enable social interaction as well as individualistic exploration. *Justice* will mean that the technology brings out the potential for good in VR systems and that they are accessible not only to an élite. This is a particular concern when one considers the uneven distribution of computer access and network waveband availability, which means that the two-thirds world is disadvantaged once again.[21] *Care and trust* will ensure that VR is developed in such a way as to be sensitive to potential users, and faithful to the present state of knowledge.

6.3.5 A defensible ethical decision

In applying such principles to our example, we note the widespread belief that palaeolithic cave art reflects primitive beliefs in sympathetic magic, by which people could control or influence whatever subjects were represented. Because all the animals depicted were food sources, the theory is that the paintings were used for initiation into hunting culture. It may have been believed that by this means not only could animals more easily be killed for food, but that some of the qualities

---

[20] See above, pp. 128–134.

[21] For discussion of cyberspace justice issues, see O. Oguibe in *5CYBERCONF* (1996), 28–29.

of the quarry might be magically transferred to the hunter. For some scholars, this is the 'hidden meaning' behind cave art. It may seem appropriate to include in the VR version of the cave of Lascaux a secret message or 'revelation' from a prehistoric human about the anthropological and metaphysical meaning of cave art, in that prehistoric artists appear not to have practised their art simply for art's sake. However, clearly such a view must remain provisional, as it is rash to assume that humans living in this century can know *a priori* about the ethos of palaeolithic culture. In fact, there is a great deal of variety in cave art, in terms of distance from the cave mouth, techniques used and combinations of subjects portrayed. Ucko and Rosenfeld suggest that it is nonsensical to have expected that any one interpretation of the evidence could provide an adequate account (1967: 124, 135, 238–239). It is possible that some representations were the work of children (*e.g.* floor engraving), that some were used in acts of sympathetic magic (paintings which have been pierced with holes, *etc.*), and that some were illustrations of myths and traditions. In addition, it is clear that some paintings were created for reasons not currently understood. The danger, therefore, of implanting a secret message or revelation in the software is that it may give the impression that a particular anthropological interpretation is the key to unlock the mystery of cave art. This falls foul of our *culturally appropriate* and *stewardship* criteria. It is probably also *unjust*, in that alternative interpretations may not be allowed to get a fair hearing. The danger is that the virtual visitor may receive the impression that palaeolithic man left some hidden key by which his cave art could be interpreted. This does not square with the evidence and does not leave room for remaining mystery, thus contravening the ethical principle of *truth-telling*.

In this case, a defensible ethical decision will involve such considerations. The result may be a decision to proceed with the application while recognizing the need to modify the software in order to be sensitive to the issues noted. On the other hand, an argument could be made for a moratorium on VR archaeological heritage projects until such time as there is more widespread awareness of potential problems. Clearly, such dilemmas can be avoided if there is careful ethical pre-thinking. The problem is that when such technology becomes available it is too easy to seek suitable avenues for applications. In this case, careful balancing of the advantages and disadvantages of virtual heritage sites is required. However, we are aware that much more widespread concern is being raised about the impact of computer use in other, more controversial, areas of morality. To some, cyberspace is itself fraught with inherent dangers.

6.4 The potential dangers of cyberspace

6.4.1 Pornography, virtual sex and the Internet

Cyberspace is a concept which includes VR but is much broader, as we have noted before, and is particularly informed by developments in computer networks. At the moment, most networking is done by text, but it will not be long before multi-user virtual environments are more widely available.[22] Already, some concern has been expressed about the interaction which the Internet has made possible. In fact, the most popular Website in the UK at the time of writing is 'LoveNet', where pornography is freely on offer. The editor of *net* magazine commented in a recent TV interview that it was no surprise to him that pornography was so prevalent and popular with those who surf the Net as the greatest number of enthusiasts come from the male 18–30 age group, where hormones are most active! He estimated that 75% of the content of the Internet was pornographic.[23] Be that as it may, pornography is not the only area where concerns have been raised. For example, a New York journalist recently reported a bizarre case in which a husband was suing his wife for divorce on the grounds that she had committed adultery in cyberspace.[24] John X caught his wife Diane involved in an explicit cybersex affair on their home computer with an Internet partner who styled himself 'the Weasel'. They engaged in 'dirty talking' by modem and had never actually met each other. They were planning a physical liaison, however, in the honeymoon suite of a hotel in New England. Mr X also claimed extreme cruelty and sought the custody of their two children. His lawyer said that the case was breaking new legal ground. The dictionary may define adultery, but has new technology challenged this definition? Another lawyer asserted that it may be cruel and inhuman to act in this way, but that it cannot be seen as adultery *per se*. Clearly if Mrs X and her partner had been able to engage in such activities with the added saliency of Virtual Reality in which they

---

[22] *Cf. 5CYBERCONF* (1996).

[23] Cited by J. Allan in *NB*, Feb–Mar, 1998, p. 8.

[24] C. Laurence, in *The Daily Telegraph*, 3 February 1996.

could see, touch and hear one another, then such a question might not be out of place.

Mark Slouka, a lecturer in twentieth-century culture at the University of California, goes so far as to allege that cyberspace is proving to be a cesspool of all that is worst in human nature (1995). He had imagined that the strength of cyberspace would be its disembodied nature; it might encourage values such as mental agility, humour and character, over against physical beauty, power or colour. However, he believes that the dream has been replaced by the reality, in which virtual worlds become the home of dark 'virtues', freedom to abuse and torment, anonymity to engage in obscene net-surfing, and liberty from the physical in order to engage in virtual torture.

> All the worst in human nature quickly set up shop. What the planners failed to reckon with was that freedom only exists within certain constraints, that mortality matters only within the bounds of the physical world. There could be no morality in heaven. Or hell.[25]

In contrast to this assertion we must ask whether it is not more likely that contemporary American culture, rather than cyberspace, is the locus of the excess which Slouka bemoans. The kind of hype associated with the launch of VR, as noted in Chapter One, is mirrored in this over-reaction. We are being deliberately provocative, but it is clear that the ideology of cyberspace is the problem rather than some metaphysical category. We have also to challenge Slouka's selective indignation about the abuse of cyberspace. Is it true that synthetic environments have inevitably become places where users engage in such sordid pursuits? Is cyberspace to be viewed as essentially different from other forms of telecommunication such as the telephone? A glance at tabloid newspapers will demonstrate that all kinds of services are offered by telephone chat-lines. It seems that there is a market for sexual fantasy in our society at present, and technology clearly opens up possibilities unknown to previous generations. We have suggested that technological systems are not value-free conduits of human attitudes and behaviour, but neither should they be demonized. It may well be that the concept of

[25] Slouka, quoted in the *Guardian*, 30 January 1996.

synthetic environments is loaded with values which encourage fantasy of all kinds. But one can engage in fantasy exploration of molecular structures for the purpose of pharmaceutical research within cyberspace, using the same kind of synthetic environment in which sexual fantasy may be explored. In this respect virtual worlds mirror the real world. We cannot demonize 'real' reality because there are those who act in anti-social, obsessive or destructive ways. The real issue is whether VR clarifies the relationship of morality to reality, and brings into focus our notions of moral responsibility.

6.4.2   *Taking responsibility for cyberspace*

In what ways should the developers of VR systems take prospective responsibility for the ways in which such systems may be used? If multi-user text-based environments can lead to the problems outlined above, is it not likely that immersive virtual environments will be even more attractive to those who seek such solace?

Here it seems that arguments about human freedom are important. If we hold that the freedom of the individual is paramount, then we have to accept risk. In other words, freedom includes the possibility of self-harm and harming others inadvertently. We may freely choose to participate in systems which have the potential for negative outcomes, but we may also choose to limit the possibility of adverse effects in advance. In the UK, for example, we have a National Health Service which enhances human freedom because it provides a socially agreed safety-net which allows for the fact that many people might not for various reasons make adequate provision for private health insurance. It also exists to help those who fall ill because of their personal habits or lifestyle. One of the risks of this is that people will ignore health warnings in the belief that such a service will always be available to 'pick up the pieces' (Graham 1988: 99–120). However, with regard to potential harms caused by Internet use, there is a need to focus on the danger posed to children, who may be exposed to pornography more readily available than from the top shelf of newsagents. Mill's harm condition, as we noted, leaves children in particular out of the debate. It is what consenting *adults* do in private that concerns the classical utilitarian.

Disciplinary cases known to the author include one of a student who was accessing a pornographic site in a university computer room and taunting passing females by directing them to the images he had downloaded. Thankfully, he was dealt with severely by the authorities. Internet use may not be in private, and offence may be caused to those who inadvertently get involved. In addition, sexual harassment of the kind depicted in the 1995 film *Disclosure* (which begins with an explicitly seductive internal e-mail from a female senior executive to one of her male subordinates) may have made the monitoring of employees' e-mail a necessity to preserve human dignity instead of a threat to human liberty. It may be part of the *panopticon* society forecast by Foucault where we are all under surveillance of one kind or another.[26] Of course, while such ideas have their roots in the ideas of Jeremy Bentham, father of utilitarian thought, there is also a Kantian overtone. Why should we be afraid of being overseen in a public place if we are doing no wrong or no harm? As one book on business ethics suggests, Kant's categorical imperative could be re-written as follows:

> If you feel comfortable allowing everyone in the world to see you commit an act and if your rationale for acting in a particular manner is suitable to become a universal principle guiding behaviour, then committing that act is ethical.[27]

The problem with this view is that the pornographer probably feels no guilt about his activity and would commend others to do likewise.

The argument of this book is that there has to be some transcendent reference against which to gauge our moral stances and ethical principles, as defined by moral order theory and in particular a realist approach to Christian ethics. The subjective damage done to those who immerse themselves in pornography and encourage others to do the same is the issue at stake. Pornography, after all, is a world of intention, imagination and desire, which are characteristics of all virtual worlds.

6.5   The 'virtues' of Virtual Reality

6.5.1   Positive applications of VR

There is no doubt that synthetic environments can be used for good or evil purposes, as may the physical environment around us. To

[26] See Lyon 1994: 47.
[27] See Ferrell & Fraedrich 1994: 58.

counterbalance such potential abuses as those noted above, we could cite some of the more positive applications[28] which are unlikely to be as newsworthy as cybersex.[29] Our Western civilization's obsession with sexual activity is clearly a filter through which some commentators view trends in modern life. Other societies which do not so value sexual experimentation might encourage a different emphasis in those who reflect upon trends. For example, we might be part of a society which was obsessed by health and safety issues. It might be that issues of the long-term existence of the human race were more important by far than the seeking of momentary pleasures. We can see that Virtual Reality provides a conceptual tool for those who are concerned to engage in reflection on such issues. We could set up visual representations of the world in future generations if present environmental trends were to continue. We could create a synthetic world with no rain forests or with oceans depleted of fish stocks for human consumption. We could ask fundamental questions about our ethical duties to our children's children and the long-term outcomes of technological processes which may deplete the ozone layer and lead to carcinogenic effects.[30]

Again, we might focus on the educational applications of VR. Since 1992, research in the VIRART project at the University of Nottingham has focused upon the development and evaluation of desktop virtual environments designed specifically for students with severe learning disabilities (those with an IQ less than 50). Such students pose many challenges for teachers, not least the much broader spread of ability than would be found in a class in a mainstream school, and the wide range of sensory and physical impairments for which the teacher has to make allowance.[31] Part of the research involved the creation of a virtual supermarket to train such students in the skills of choosing and purchasing.

6.5.2   The choice is ours

The point is that certain social choices must be made in the development of VR technology, and the way that VR is envisaged will

---

[28] See Appendix Two.
[29] See above, pp. 163–165.
[30] See Haldane (1990); *cf.* Kung (1991).
[31] See Cromby (1995). Also Schroeder (1995).

depend largely upon societal values. The companies which provide Internet servers can set up access limitations and censorship of contributions if they so wish. The eruption of 'flame wars', in which aggressive or obscene text is traded-off by Internet users, means that such action is inevitable and essential. The checks and balances which we have come to see as essential in normal social interaction in real life are there in order to promote true freedom rather than to deny it.[32]

Technology is not neutral, but value-laden; yet the values of a given society are complex and in constant flux. The advent of mass telecommunications has eroded traditional cultural distinctives, and increased participation in the Internet is bound to accelerate the process of change. It may be that VR is an expression of the radical individualism which has characterized Western society in the 1980s and 90s, while the development of computer networking has sought to redress the balance from a more communitarian perspective. Howard Rheingold describes the attraction of computer conferencing through membership of a network called the WELL:

> In the traditional community, we search through our pool of neighbours and professional colleagues, of acquaintances and acquaintances of acquaintances, in order to find people who share our values and interests . . . In a virtual community we can go directly to the place where our favourite subjects are being discussed, then get acquainted with people who share our passions or who use words in a way we find attractive . . . You can be fooled about people in cyberspace, behind the cloak of words. But that can be said about telephones or face-to-face communication as well; computer-mediated communications provide new ways to fool people, and the most obvious identity swindles will die out only when enough people learn to use the medium critically. In some ways, the medium will, by its nature, be forever biased toward certain kinds of obfuscation (1994: 27).[33]

At the moment, such networking is largely text-based, but there is no doubt that networked multi-user virtual environments will become

---

[32] See Graham 1988: 28–52.
[33] See also Heim (1993: 102), quoted above on p. 149.

attractive meeting-places for those who find it harder and harder to meet people socially in real life. Yet Rheingold speaks of the need to have face-to-face meetings with some of the friends he has met over the Net (1994: 32). This need is unlikely to be obviated by the experience of seeing or even touching representations of people within virtual worlds, and there are some who suggest that it is inappropriate to represent the human form in this way (Don 1992). To do so is to convey a devalued view of humanness, of people as objects to be manipulated along with other virtual objects in the environment.

6.6   Opportunities and threats

We began this chapter with an analysis of some of the ethical dilemmas which may be brought into focus by VR technology. This was set against the backdrop of some of the concerns of computer professionals aware of the social and moral implications of their work. We have outlined some of the strengths and weaknesses, in moral terms, of the conceptual aspects of VR. We may relate this to the discussion in Chapter Two in which we described technology as both opportunity and threat, within the biblical perspective of *Homo Faber* who both reflects the divine image and is fatally flawed by sin.[34] Jacques Ellul believes that all technical progress has its price, and that at each stage of development technology raises more and greater problems than it solves. He alleges that the harmful effects are inseparable from the beneficial effects and that there are always a great number of unforeseen consequences (1990: 39–76).[35]

In our final chapter, we will seek to draw together the insights of the preceding argument, first to offer a summary of our critique of VR from a Christian ethical standpoint, and then to develop ideas about the ways in which VR as a concept may stimulate a development of *the Ethics of Christian Realism* in postmodernity. We have seen that VR is neither the giant leap forward in evolutionary progress which was heralded by the late Timothy Leary, nor is it to be demonized. It is both an opportunity and a threat, and the way it is developed will not depend merely on the technical possibilities which

[34] See above, pp. 66–74.

[35] *Cf.* 'It is much harder to purify the Mediterranean than to make an airplane fly' (Ellul 1990: 51).

are being discovered. We have rejected the technicistic imperative which states that what *can* be done (in technical terms) *should* be done. We have also indicated that technological determinism is to be rejected as an avoidance of the real issues. We are not being carried along by unseen forces which are inexorably leading us to produce certain kinds of technology. We are making choices based on cultural and ideological assumptions about what it means to be *Homo Faber*.[36] With that in mind, we must now conclude our discussion.

[36] A. Benjamin, 'Virtual Heritage '95: Opening Address', in *VR News* 5.1, Jan–Feb 1996, 25.

Chapter Seven:
Virtual Morality and postmodernity

7.1 Summary of discussion

We began this book by noting the effects computers can have on our personal lives, that we find them fascinating and that interacting with them may draw us into virtual worlds. This made us ask questions about the effects of environment on ethics and morality. We set our objectives as seeking to establish the extent to which entering into virtual environments may enhance perception and extend human capabilities, and examining whether, in contrast, it may distort perceptions and invite abuse. We began with a working hypothesis that there may be such a thing as *Virtual Morality*, that we may be subject to behaviour manipulation, shifting the thresholds of tolerance of certain behaviours in ourselves and others, that we might find ourselves engaging in practices within virtual environments which we would find repugnant in real life, and that we might even become addicted to such experiences. This discussion was grounded in an understanding of human values as objective and not just personal preferences, so that technology such as Virtual Reality could be laden with values such as novelty, efficiency, user-friendliness, *etc.*

We accepted arguments against technology being value-neutral, decided to adopt a development of natural law theory as an appropriate expression of *Homo Faber* (Human the Maker), and accepted a revision of classical moral order theory as our working paradigm of Christian ethics. We styled this paradigm the '*Ethics of Christian Realism*'. We noted the differences and similarities between ancient and modern technology but recognized both as human activities. We linked them with a covenantal understanding of biblical anthropology (*Homo Faber* as a reflection of *God the Worker*) and recognized that the combination of creation and fall as complementary themes means that it is inevitable that in biblical perspective technology must be viewed as both opportunity and threat.

We then explored the relationship between natural and moral order, and entered the debate over whether metaphysics or epistemology holds the key to an effective philosophical critique of modern technology, in view of the likely long-term effects of much technical advance. The gap between predictive and technical knowledge led us to recognize the need for stewardship of the environment and of technological systems, an eschatological concept readily found in the Judeo-Christian tradition. There followed an exploration of how biblical eschatology might be used to assess the long-term impacts of technology, and of the need to challenge futurology based on *technicism* (technology for technology's sake).

Technicism was the focus of the application of normative principles arising out of a Christian ethical analysis of technology, in which we acknowledged the need for limits to be placed on potentially harmful developments. We recognized many of the fears expressed by informed commentators and pinpointed some of the particular dilemmas raised by VR. This led to a discussion of concepts of moral responsibility in computer use, and of the need to include in such concepts some form of collective responsibility among system designers, operators and end users, and to link outcomes, agents and potential victims of abuse in VE. The key to this part of the discussion was the question of how technological intermediaries may influence what we do when we use them and how they may impose patterns of action on users. We concluded that computers can often do better than humans where closed systems of factors, data or tasks are in view. However, where there are open-ended, fluid systems which require judgment, humans are far superior to computers. Virtual Reality is such a system, and should be treated accordingly. This means that those who develop VR must take prospective moral responsibility for preventing disastrous consequences. Now is the time to engage in an ethical critique of VR, while the technology is in its relative infancy.

We must now gather the discussion together by drawing on the themes developed above, to attempt to answer four questions:

1. Is Virtual Reality essentially a *postmodern* phenomenon, as has been alleged?
2. What is the significance of the concept of Virtual Reality for our understanding of Christian ethics; is a new ethical category of '*Virtual Morality*' required?
3. What is the significance of the *Ethics of Christian Realism* for providing conceptual tools for an effective critical analysis of the ethical implications of Virtual Reality?
4. What may be some of the implications of *postmodernity* for the inter-relationship between philosophy of technology and Christian ethics?

7.2 *Virtual Reality, technicism and postmodernity*

In our discussion of postmodernity we have noted the claim that we are passing into a post-industrial era, into the mode of *information* rather than that of *production*. Egbert Schuurman has suggested that the relationship between modernity and postmodernity is much more complex than this (1995b: 6–7). Our industrial culture, from which we are supposed to be emerging into an information culture, is levelled and fragmented, suggests Schuurman, because of a rupture between nature and society which has led to the deepening ecological crisis and a fragmentation of society. In an assessment of modernity this appears to be a disaster, and yet one of the great products of late modernity has been information technology, which postmodernists are happy to use, despite its cultural and social implications and the creation of a new class of have-nots who lack access to computer systems and the Internet. This last point has been taken further by the Nigerian art historian Olu Oguibe[1] who raises ethical questions of

---

[1] See O. Oguibe in *5CYBERCONF* (1996: 28–29) for discussion of information poverty in the two-thirds world. Oguibe argues that discussion of VR and the Internet is largely irrelevant to the real world of poverty and illiteracy: 'Cyberspace, much as it may provide us with multiple and unguarded routes of interzonality across

fairness in the distribution of information.[2]

We have noted that some postmodernists are technologically pessimistic, yet seem to find comfort in new technological possibilities.[3] In industrially based societies, power has been concentrated and centralized and is resistant to attempts to undermine its domination. Schuurman notes:

> Modernists have been promoting high technology. Postmodernists are making use of it. It therefore follows that they will not accept responsibility for any technological developments and they are even 'technologically pessimistic' but this does not prevent them from using it in an equally irresponsible manner and thereby in a certain sense worshipping this technology in operation . . . In an industrially-based society, power was concentrated and centralised and it was possible to fight battles against it. The postmodern philosophers Lyotard and Foucault have remarked that, within a post-industrial society with digital highways and VR, power no longer plays a central, singular, decisive and controllable part. It would appear that, for the first time in history, concentrations of power and social hierarchies are disappearing (1995b: 6).

This is a challenge for philosophy of technology in postmodernity: to analyse information technology within a holistic understanding of human experience and not allow this to be absorbed and reduced into abstract-technological reality. Therefore the claim that the concept of VR is essentially postmodern is misplaced, in that it must be viewed as an outcome of the complex interaction between modern technicism and postmodern pluralism.

An illustration of such a complex interaction is seen in the underlying values of the cult TV series *Star Trek* and its various sequels, as noted in Chapter Three.[4] The original series displayed the mindset of modernity, which is presented, albeit in an extreme form, in the

---

the globe, nevertheless remains the preserve of a statistically negligible fraction of the world, unable as yet, and indeed unwilling, to undermine fundamental boundaries within and without our principal terrains' (p. 29).

[2] *Cf.* above, p. 25 n. 19, with reference to Rawls's theory of social justice.

[3] See Marx, above, p. 100.

[4] See above, pp. 102–103.

character Spock. He applies a detached rationalistic approach to all problems and his reasoning is unaffected by his emotions. All problems, for Spock, have a scientific explanation. This kind of scientism and technicism is perceived as a threat in the sequel series, but fascination with technology is still one of the hallmarks of *The Next Generation*.

Schuurman is surely right when he perceives that postmodernity has a love–hate relationship with technology. Perhaps we should think of the postmodern climate as one of *super-modernity* and should be critical of an over-readiness to declare that a new post-industrial age has dawned. We cannot ignore the continuing power of multi-national industrial corporations. It may be that the Western countries are increasingly devoid of manufacturing industries and are being dominated by information technology and the financial and service sectors. But such corporations rely on sweatshops in poorer countries to produce the consumer goods which our culture demands. The two-thirds world may not agree with a Western assertion that the new information age has dawned!

7.3   *Virtual Morality: significance of Virtual Reality for Christian ethics*

The author was a participant at *5CYBERCONF*, the Fifth Interna-tional Conference on Cyberspace, in Madrid during June 1996, which explored some of the socio-cultural, ethical and aesthetic implications of VR and the Internet, as well as providing an update on the latest developments in VR technology. Of the eighteen papers presented by scholars, technologists and artists, a number tackled human factors questions, but the most significant insights for an ethical perspective on VR came from a demonstration of the multi-media performance *EPIZOO*, created by the Spanish artist and software designer Sergi Jorda, in which he explores the distinctions between virtual and real morality.[5]

Jorda notes that, with the development of combat computer games, 'the bad guys are always the others and the violence and cruelty are free' (*5CYBERCONF* 1996: 22). This is different from real violent

[5] S. Jorda, 'EPIZOO: Cruelty and Gratuitousness in Real Virtuality', in *5CYBERCONF* (1996: 22–23).

sports or pastimes, and from real combat in warfare, where real antag-
onists are only relatively good or bad. However, the 1991 Gulf War
marked a shift in our understanding of this distinction. During that
conflict, combat scenarios were presented in the Western media as if
they were simulation games in which the 'bad guys' were the Iraqis,
and the laser-guided weapons delivery systems of allied aircraft were
seen providing 'clinical strikes' from the vantage-point of pilots
thousands of feet above the targets. The TV pictures seemed not to be
of a real, bloody war, but merely a celebration of technology. It was
only later that we discovered some of the awful effects of these
weapons, accurately delivered into the air-vents of a bomb-shelter in
Baghdad, for example, with resultant carnage.

Just as weapon systems delivered from such a distance can
seemingly lead to cruelty without a sense of remorse, Jorda argues that
the simulation interface can lead people to explore the subjective
experience of inflicting pain on others. He has developed *EPIZOO*,
in which a performance artist is fitted with pneumatically driven
devices connected to his nose, ears, mouth, chest and thighs, and
which are operated via the graphic interface of a computer. Participants can inflict minimum discomfort to the artist and produce
contortions and distortions on his body and facial surface, as well as
modifying graphic animation, music and lighting. The purpose of the
piece is to show how people can easily engage in activities which
might lead to sadism or gratuitous violence where there is a computer
interface which seems to detach the operator from effects. Jorda
suggests that there is a connection between real and virtual morality
– that behaviour which might not be sanctioned in normal real-life
interactions might come to be accepted where computers are
involved, especially by children who often assess situations involving
computers as somehow unreal. *EPIZOO* has been presented all over
Europe and in Latin America, and it is in the latter area, where
suffering and violence are more evident, that participation by
audiences has been most enthusiastic.

But is Jorda correct in making a distinction between virtual and
real morality, or is this a category error? The main point of Jorda's
work is to show that in 'real virtuality the moral price to pay for a
possible act of cruelty is absolutely subjective' (1996: 22). In other
words, the moral dilemma is not based on the potential effects of
causing real harm to the performer, but within the subjective

experience of the potential torturer. It is in the desires of the participant that moral principles are expressed, in, the choice to inflict or withhold the distortions which the system enables, limited as it is by mechanical checks and balances. The system demonstrates that a feedback loop system, even if it cannot produce really harmful effects in others, can radically engage the operator and encourage a salient experience of agency which is very similar in attitude and desire to real sadism and gratuitous expressions of violence. It demonstrates very powerfully what Gordon Graham has said about harm and consent.[6] Clearly, the performance artist has consented in advance to certain manipulations of his body being performed. The ethical issues are therefore to be seen in the subjective experience of the participants who accept the invitation to engage in such activity.

Virtual Morality, therefore, focuses on the subjective experience of the agent in a virtual environment, and is ethically significant because of the intentionality and desire involved and not because of any real or imagined harmful effects on others. Whether or not it can be established that such agency may lead to real interactive behaviour changes in individuals or tolerance of such changes in others, with harmful effects, is not the primary issue. As consenting adults enter virtual worlds, they take with them their sense of moral order and impose an interpretative framework on their understanding of agency in that environment, as they do in the real world. For children, consent in this sense is not possible, and Turkle's research on the potential of computers to influence the psyche of children must be taken very seriously by those who develop and market VR systems.[7]

In this way, we can see that *Virtual Morality* is a valid ethical category. If 'real' morality is customary behaviour arising from beliefs (conscious and subconscious) about goods and harms, rights and duties, virtues and vices, *etc.*, which are based on perceptions of objective reality, and which may or may not be expressed in terms of ethical principles, 'virtual' morality is behaviour which is based on perceptions of virtuality (*i.e.* artificiality, simulation and subjectivity). Such morality develops with interaction and becomes subject to moral evaluation and to discussion about rights and duties in cyberspace.[8]

---

[6] See above, pp. 134–136.

[7] See above, pp. 33–35.

[8] See J. P. Barlow, 'A declaration of the independence of cyberspace', in

The immediate interest in exploring the ethical implications of VR as a concept lies in its implicit claims about the nature of reality. The label 'Virtual *Reality*', for that reason, has been rejected by some who feel that it is another example of the kind of hype which led to great claims being made for AI (artificial intelligence).[9] The choice of a word to describe a technological phenomenon can bring with it metaphysical baggage which is not sustainable in a thoroughgoing analysis. We have noted some of the hype associated with the early days of VR development which mirrors claims made for AI in the 1970s.[10] However we may label the concept of VR, it clearly does raise questions about the existence of what Leibniz called 'possible worlds'.[11] As Michael Heim asserts:

> The philosophical echoes in the term 'virtual reality' serve perfectly well to suggest today's ambiguous merger of life with computers . . . 'Virtual' implies the computer storage model of life, software tricks, and the switch from industrial physics to information symbolics (1995: 65).

5CYBERCONF (1996), *addendum*, 17: a reaction to the Telecom Reform Act of 1996 (USA) in which restrictions on Internet access are planned. Internet use worldwide has doubled every nine months since 1968. Barlow speaks of cyberspace morality in this way: 'You [US government] do not know our culture, our ethics, our unwritten codes that already provide our society more order than could be obtained by any of your impositions . . . We are forming our own Social Contract . . . Cyberspace consists of transactions, relationships, and thought itself . . . We are creating a world that all may enter without privilege or prejudice accorded by race, economic power, military force, or station of birth . . . The only rule that all our constituent cultures would generally recognize is the Golden Rule . . . We must declare our virtual selves immune to your sovereignty, even as we continue to consent to your rule over our bodies.' This is based on the reductionist view that 'Life is information . . . Information is life', and on a mind–body dualism. Barlow's position is therefore untenable, and was subject to severe criticism at the conference.

[9] See above, p. 36, for reference to virtual or synthetic *environments*.

[10] See Weizenbaum (1984); *cf.* Mackay (1988). Weizenbaum argues that some of the claims made for AI in the mid-1970s were ridiculous, in that computers can only be programmed to mimic human instrumental reasoning and that they are unsuitable for reflective or evaluative thought. This is confirmed by J. Ladd (1989). On the other hand, Danielson (1992) describes a research project in which attempts were made to equip robots with powers of ethical decision-making.

[11] See Heim 1995: 65.

VR is a powerful medium which will continue to challenge the ontological basis of classical moral order theory and to encourage a dialogue between the *Ethics of Christian Realism* and moral thought in postmodernity. As David Lyon asks, 'Is the Babel of communicative society a situation to be welcomed for its liberating potential or resisted as disintegrative and destructive of human relationships?' (1994a: 52). The answer, as we have seen, is probably *both*, but as postmodernity evolves, further dialogue is necessary.

7.4   Order, freedom, judgment: significance of Christian ethics for Virtual Reality

The illustration of *EPIZOO* provides a link to discussion of the relevance of the *Ethics of Christian Realism* to the ethical questioning of Virtual Reality, both as a concept and in its applications. Following Ellul,[12] we have affirmed that Christian ethics is essentially an ethics of means rather than ends, which explores such notions as motivation, desire and intention as the basis of moral agency, and that an ethics of subjectivity is a major part of classical Christian moral thought. This is expanded by Oliver O'Donovan in his treatment of the moral subject (1994: 204–225). The salient experience of agency in a virtual environment brings the ethics of subjectivity into focus. 'Human morality is a series of disclosures in which reality (the heart) forces itself into the realm of appearances (deeds and words) and declares itself, tearing apart the veil of pretence which has hidden it' (1994: 206).

This insight shifts the focus from outward acts to inward character, and clearly is of fundamental relevance to our discussion. The fact that O'Donovan speaks of *reality* as the subjective realm is significant. Yet the inner character is only known through outward acts. We describe people as long-suffering because their actions (or withholding of action) display that quality. VR is not a passive medium, but inter-active, and it is therefore appropriate to consider its ethical signifi-cance in relation to deliberative questions about moral judgment as the basis for action. The *Ethics of Christian Realism* provides resources for a balanced and integrative approach to such an analysis. Subjec-tivity is taken to be the wellspring of action, but action within the

---

[12] See above, pp. 90–91.

virtual world is not excluded from the framework of moral order and moral freedom. Our moral judgment as to what constitutes appropriate applications must therefore take all these dimensions into account. Critical realism helps us to assess both opportunity and threat, means and ends, anthropology and eschatology, and to seek a dynamic of thought which can hold such diverse factors in creative tension. On this basis, the significance of the *Ethics of Christian Realism* for VR as an expression of information technology is in providing both *explanatory power* and tools for an *ethical critique*. The relevance of this approach in the context of postmodernity is in its implicit recognition of the value of a pluralistic approach, in which valid aspects of related ethical theories may be synthesized.[13]

The connection between concepts of order and freedom was found in the fact that human freedom is rooted in a response to reality, subjective and objective. Notions of judgment came into play when we considered how belief in responsibility for thoughts, imagination and desires is central to Christian ethics, and how that intention is of prime significance in the moral life. Commitment to Christian realism implies a framework for ethical judgment; this we found in the method of presumption, which takes account of positive affirmations about the goodness of creation, the value of individual life, *etc.*, but which also accepts notions of human finitude and sinfulness.[14]

7.5 Philosophy of technology and Christian ethics in postmodernity: compassionate holism

The cultural shift which is taking place from modernity to postmodernity has implications for the interface between philosophy of technology and Christian ethics. With the widespread acceptance of the critique of technicism which we have expounded, there is the possibility of what Frederick Ferré calls 'a deeper sustained meditation on the relationship between Christianity and technology' (1993: 54). As we become more aware of the way technological formation is influenced by styles of knowing and fundamental values, he wonders if, in future, we may be able to speak of *Christian technologies*. This idea sounds strange to modern Western ears, but if it is true that

---

[13] See above, pp. 81–91.
[14] See above, pp. 85–88.

technology is value-laden, why should technologies not be laden with *Christian* values as an alternative to *technicistic* values? Clearly, while values are important in technological development, they are not sufficient, in themselves, to account for the achievements of modern technology. Artefacts are laden not only with some value or values, but also with some level of knowledge, even if this is only the knowledge of craft skills passed down from craftsman to apprentice. Scientific knowledge, which emphasizes precision, quantification and analysis, is clearly embodied in today's hi-tech systems. Ferré suggests that if Christianity is really a distinctive approach to thinking and living, there is surely nothing wrong with Christian intellectuals' trying to develop a vision for technologies which might express 'characteristic Christian cognitive styles or epistemic norms and distinctive Christian values' (1993: 55).

This idea is linked with our analysis of postmodernity, which opens the way for a pluralistic approach to knowledge, taking account of various sources in order to achieve a holistic understanding.[15] In contrast to scientism and technicism, Ferré suggests that science and technology can be informed by a Christian cognitive style which is, at the very least, 'respectful of the object known' (1993: 55). The normative Christian cognitive style would be warm and compassionate, unlike both that of the officers of the Inquisition and that of the detached and cool approach which has followed from Cartesian logic, and seeks to know the parts of an object in terms of their relationship to each other. It would be a 'compassionate holism' (1993: 55). Ferré does not imagine that there is any likelihood of a utopia based on such principles being brought about, but he believes that compassionate holism can be used as a standard to test technologies within our culture, and that it is possible to modify technologies and to restrain negative tendencies.

As we have suggested,[16] such a holistic approach would be informed and directed by Christian love (*agape*), the self-forgetful concern for others as the supreme norm by which all norms must be tested. Such an approach would imply a shift in the dominant motivating values in Western society. First, community well-being would become more significant than private profit (although the two

[15] See above, pp. 95–105; *cf.* Oden (1990).
[16] See above, pp. 128–134.

are closely related in free market economies) as a priority. Secondly, linear, analytic solutions would be replaced by a concern to bring together insights from various disciplines, for application to an analysis of the complex effects of technological interventions on society and the environment. Thirdly, quantitative considerations would become secondary to qualitative issues in determining decisions. Fourthly, other more holistic concerns would counterbalance the drive for profit and efficiency, such as quality of life and long-term stability of communities. Yet such ideals would not become idealism if they were qualified by the critical realism of our paradigm of Christian ethics, in line with the thought of philosophers of technology such as John Ladd,[17] who affirms that information technology is often the bearer of negative outcomes and may impose patterns on our actions with unintended disastrous results.

7.6   Summary of main conclusions

7.6.1   VR is a product of a complex interaction between modern technicism and postmodern pluralism

The claim that VR as a concept is essentially postmodern has been refuted. VR is a phenomenon developed as the result of the technological drive for control which is expressive of technicism, and is often seen as a solution in search of problems to solve, yet it offers possibilities of decentralized and diffuse communications, interactive learning and entertainment and problem-solving in virtual environments. In this way, it displays the qualities of interactivity which characterize subject constitution in the second media age, and thus the cultural shift we have provisionally labelled '*postmodernity*'.

7.6.2   Virtual Morality is a valid ethical category

Morality within virtual worlds must be assessed by focusing on an ethics of subjectivity which emphasizes intention, imagination and desire, rather than on an ethics of consequentialism which focuses on objective effects. 'Virtual' and 'real' are interconnected concepts and not mutually exclusive, so morality in one sphere is presumed to influence morality in the other, following Wogaman's strategy of presumption.

---

[17] See above, pp. 136–144.

7.6.3 The Ethics of Christian Realism – *as a synthesis of the focus of Oliver O'Donovan on* moral order, *Jacques Ellul on* moral freedom, *and Philip Wogaman on* moral judgment – *provides explanatory power and tools for a normative critique of technology.*

This synthesis demonstrates the distinctive contribution which classical Christian ethics can make in the debate about the ethical implications of information technology in postmodernity, because of three affirmations that it makes. 1. Moral order is based on created order, which is confirmed by the resurrection of Christ and rooted in the gospel; 2. technological determinism is not necessary, because of the freedom won by Christ in whom all things hold together; and 3. it is possible to apply normative principles based on divine love, adopting a strategy of presumption, which enable a radical yet realistic approach to ethical decision-making. Such a critique is not only possible, as seen in the exposition of the *Ethics of Christian Realism*, but relevant, in its commitment to the view that ethics responds to reality, and therefore enables a dialogue with what may purport to be new levels of reality in virtual worlds.

7.6.4 *Kallman and Grillo's 'four-step analysis process' can be effectively adapted and applied to an ethical analysis of applications developments in VR*

The analysis of our example, the cave of Lascaux archaeological heritage project, indicated that a systematic process can elucidate ethical issues which may exist in even apparently non-controversial applications. It may be argued, therefore, that such a process has much wider potential, and enables the application of normative principles arising from paragraph 7.6.3 above in a systematic way, as in existing ethical codes for computer professionals which require further development in the light of specific ethical issues associated with VR.

7.6.5 *Christian ethics remain relevant and helpful in the computer era*

A synthetic approach to Christian ethics, in creative tension with the motifs of postmodernity, can provide powerful insights for the computer era. In this book we have drawn from a wide range of ethical approaches within the discipline of Christian ethics and we have also brought on board insights from the best of current secular treatments of ethical issues in information technology.

This is not so much a 'pick 'n' mix' approach as a recognition of the provisionality of all ethical systems and the need to be open to learn from all who have blazed the trail in the virgin territory of computer ethics.

Having said that, we need to affirm that the distinctive contribution we seek to make in the debate is on two levels. First, with regard to *anthropology*, we affirm the insight of Anthony Thiselton: 'A Christian account of human nature accepts the capacity of the self for self-deception and its readiness to use strategies of manipulation' (1995: 13). In an age of simulation, therefore, ethics must be based on truth rather than rhetoric, substance rather than style. Classical Christian ethics uniquely connects with, and offers a critique of, the postmodern climate, by affirming the objective reality of moral order and the primacy of the moral subject within that order. It provides a transcendent reference to challenge the self-referential nature of postmodern ideology. It interplays with fantasy, imagination, individualism, consumerism, isolation, distrust, community and identity in the multi-faceted age of simulation. It deals with people where they are in the contemporary world, realistically, as human beings in continuity with those who have gone before us (even in *pre*modern times!) and not as inhabitants of some imaginary postmodern island. In an interactive age we recognize patterns of action and interaction in virtual worlds, and that they have the hallmarks of authentic human experience – full of interest, attention and expectation. We see that an ethics which focuses merely on possible objective outcomes of action, such as utilitarianism, is useless in the analysis of morality within synthetic environments where subjective outcomes are paramount.

Secondly, with regard to *eschatology*, we have noted that Christian hopes for the future are not disconnected from technology. In some sense, our investment of time, talents and money to generate wealth and improve the conditions of the whole human race has eternal ramifications. We may not be sure where Western culture is going in postmodernity. We may accept that there is no longer a place for simplistic ideas of progress. We may recognize the all-pervasive influence of consumerism and face the fact that, despite all the problems generated by capitalism and prosperity, the two-thirds world wants to follow the West in almost every area except in its ideologies of democracy and individualism. But Christians are meant to be witnesses to *the presence of the future*, in some sense experiencing (and encouraging others to experience) a foretaste of the new heavens and earth in real *or* virtual worlds now.

7.7 Living in the real and virtual worlds

'. . . *reality is being broken down into images* . . .' *(Lyon 1994a: 48)*

At the outset of this book, we indicated that our discussion would explore the interface between philosophy of technology and Christian ethics. We have seen that there is indeed a 'locus of communication'[18] between those two systems of thought, and that many fruitful connections may be made which further the analysis of information technology in postmodernity. It is in the hope that the thesis proposed in this book will develop such connections, as well as elucidating the particular issues raised by the phenomenon of Virtual Reality, that we conclude this discussion. As with the concept of postmodernity, conclusions about the ethical implications of VR must be to a certain extent provisional. We are limited by virtue of the fact that VR is a nascent technology and by the awareness that modernity may not be the spent force which some philosophers have declared it to be. Yet we may affirm with some confidence as we move toward the close of this discussion that, in an age of simulation, reality is indeed being broken down into images and that there is a choice to be made, either to affirm an ethical stance based on notions of humankind made in the *imago Dei*, or to allow ourselves to be immersed, and our sense of centred selfhood lost, in a postmodern pastiche of apparently meaningless montage.

Christian ethics has ultimate value when, as a discipline, it provides an analytical basis for Christian lifestyle as a distinctive set of attitudes and approaches to action which may be commended to all people everywhere as embodying universal normative principles grounded on the objective basis of the resurrection of Christ from the dead. In this book we have seen how important it is to recognize the influence of the inner life, and especially of the imagination, in determining conduct. We have seen that the biblical writers think of inner experience and outward expression as forming a seamless robe. Recently there has been much debate in UK society about the private

---

[18] See above, p. 16 n. 2.

lives of politicians and members of the royal family, and about whether alleged immorality in one sphere may lead to corruption in the other. Much of the discussion has focused on whether private morality can be or should be connected with public morality. This question is similar to the one we have asked about the potential effects of entering virtual worlds and whether experiences there may or may not influence behaviour in real life. We have sought to affirm that, under God, morality is one and that, therefore, ethics must take a holistic approach. But this is an affirmation with a price attached, for we live in a Western world of fragmentation and isolation, where communication ideals are so often denied by rampant individualism. Part of the way of the cross for Christians living through postmodernity is to bear witness to the reality of the presence of God among people who so often are seeking presence within other realities. Perhaps our calling is not so very different from that of the apostle Paul on his mission to Athens (Acts 17:16–34).

Paul had left behind the world with which he was most familiar, that of Hellenistic Judaism and the Christian churches which grew out of the synagogues of the Diaspora in response to the message of Jesus as Messiah. He was now confronted, for the first time, with the *pluralism* of a city 'full of idols' (17:16) and the *modernism* whereby many of the inhabitants 'spent their time doing nothing but talking about and listening to the latest ideas' (17:21). It is significant that Paul held discussions with passers-by in the *agora* or market-place where ideas were exchanged as well as goods. This was the Internet of first-century times! The people's pluralism made them open to consider other gods than those of which they already knew; their modernism gave them a desire for novelty and the hope of always finding something better. Luke's ethical critique of the Athenians is limited to an aside about their doing nothing but talking and listening to the latest ideas. Today, a large number of people worldwide are spending inordinate amounts of time in the pursuit of information and the dissemination of ideas through the Internet. But, as Richard Epstein notes:

> Information is not knowledge. Knowledge is the result of the processing of information. Knowledge is actually diminished if there is too much information to process. Knowledge comes about when you have processed and digested the information you have

received. Information is a lot like food, and knowledge is like the tissues and structures that the body builds using the nutrition contained in food. There is nutrious information and there is 'junk' information. Too much information, even if it is of high quality, leads to excess fat. This excess fat manifests as incoherent ideas and confusion. This excess fat prevents the function of genuine knowledge (1997: 119–120).

Paul pinpointed the weakness of the Athenians' knowledge. All their exchange of ideas and information had not led them to know the living God in whom we live and move and have our being (16:28). God is not made in humankind's image, but vice versa (16:29). In other words, ultimate Reality is God-given, and is not to be simulated by idolatry. Idolatry is a sign of ignorance, of not knowing the living God. The call to repentance is directed at such ignorance and is undergirded by reference to the resurrection of Jesus in space and time (16:31). It is this mighty act of God which affirms the order of things, natural and moral, and provides a basis for his call to the Athenians to redirect their lives towards the God whom they should seek and find. Here are the seed thoughts of the *Ethics of Christian Realism*.

In postmodernity, many of our neighbours may feel that such talk of resurrection from the dead is another virtual reality, a construction of hopes and dreams, but nothing more. Others may suggest that this is merely the ultimate power-play to gain control of hapless individuals. But Paul simply invites his hearers freely to enter into the world of Ultimate Reality. As we see from his letters, this is the basis of his ethical teaching, found for example in his first epistle to the Thessalonians, written about the time his visited Athens and Corinth. They 'turned to God from idols to serve the living and true God' (1 Thes. 1:9). He 'instructed [them] *how to live* in order to please God' (4:1ff.) with self-control, brotherly love and hard work. Their daily lives were to win the respect of unbelievers. Throughout his writings Paul bases his ethical imperatives on the indicatives of what God has done in Christ. 'Oh, the depths of the riches of the *wisdom and knowledge* of God! . . . For from him and through him and to him are all things. To him be the glory for ever. Amen! *Therefore*, I urge you, brothers, in view of God's mercy, to offer your bodies as living sacrifices, holy and pleasing to God' (Rom. 11:33, 36; 12:1).

Christian ethics offers principles of conduct by which we may live lives pleasing to God in every environment, real or virtual. Such normative principles remain valid in the computer era. Virtual Reality would be well guided in its development by the Ethics of Christian Realism.

Appendix One:
A four-step process for ethical analysis and decision-making[1]

Step 1: Understanding the situation
A. List and number the relevant facts.
B. Which of these raises an ethical issue? Why? What is the potential or resulting harm?
C. List the stakeholders involved.

Step 2: Isolating the major ethical dilemma
What is the ethical dilemma to be resolved NOW? State it using the form: Should *someone* do or not do *something*? (Note: Just state the dilemma here; leave any reasoning for Step 3.)

Step 3: Analysing the ethicality of both alternatives in Step 2
Consequentialism
A. If action in Step 2 is done, who, if anyone, will be harmed?
B. If action in Step 2 is not done, who, if anyone will be harmed?
C. Which alternative results in the least harm, A or B?
D. If action in Step 2 is done, who, if anyone, will benefit?

[1] From Kallman & Grillo (1996: 34), *Ethical Decision-making and Information Technology*, 2nd ed. (reproduced with permission of the McGraw-Hill Companies).

E. If action in Step 2 is not done, who, if anyone, will benefit?
F. Which alternative results in the maximum benefit, D or E?

Rights and duties

G. What *rights* have been or may be abridged? What *duties* have been or may be neglected? Identify the stakeholder and the right or duty. When listing a right, show its corresponding duty and vice versa.

Kant's categorical imperative

H. If action in Step 2 is done, who, if anyone, will be treated with *dis*respect?
I. If action in Step 2 is not done, who, if anyone, will be treated with *dis*respect?
J. Which alternative is preferable, H or I?
K. If action in Step 2 is done, who, if anyone, will be treated *un*like others?
L. If action in Step 2 is not done, who, if anyone, will be treated *un*like others?
M. Which alternative is preferable, K or L?
N. Are there benefits if everyone did action in Step 2?
O. Are there benefits if nobody did action in Step 2?
P. Which alternative is preferable, N or O?

Step 4: Making a decision and planning the implementation

A. Make a defensible ethical decision.
    Based on the analysis in Step 2, respond to the question in Step 2.

    Indicate the letters of the categories that best support your response.
    Add any arguments justifying your choice of these ethical principles to support your decision. Where there are conflicting rights and duties, choose and defend those that take precedence. (Note: Just make and justify your choice here; leave any action steps for parts B and D below.)
B. List the specific steps needed to implement your defensible ethical decision.

C. Show how the major stakeholders are affected by these actions.
D. What other longer-term changes (political, legal, technical, societal, organizational) would help prevent such problems in the future?
E. What should have been done or not done in the first place (at the pivot point) to avoid this dilemma?

Appendix Two:
Current Virtual Reality applications[1]

Text 1: VR in education[2]

History of VR in education

The first educational VR developments were necessarily housed in research laboratories with expansive budgets for expensive equipment. The Human Interface Technology Laboratory at the University of Washington in Seattle and the Institute for Simulation and Training at the University of Central Florida in Orlando were early educational seedbeds for VR and still continue groundbreaking educational research and development today.

The first large school–based VR research and development project was in Europe at West Denton High School, Newcastle-upon-Tyne in the UK. The project developed three prototype VR environments using Virtus WalkThrough on the Macintosh and Superscape on a 486 PC. Major funding was from the Learning Technologies Unit, Training, Enterprise and Education Directorate, in the UK government's Department of Employment. Commercial support was from

[1] These texts are taken from the journal *VR News* (reproduced by permission of the publisher, Cydata Ltd., London N4 4JW).

[2] From *VR News* 5.6, July 1996, 31–32.

Superscape (at that time called Dimension International), NEI Parsons, Tyneside Training and Enterprise Council, Cadonmac Ltd, and Virus Corporation.

The developers were charged with answering whether they could create educationally useful VR environments, whether teachers and students could learn the use of VR environments effectively, and whether the new education/business partnership was mutually beneficial.

The West Denton project was in operation from October 1991 to September 1992. It is now five years later,[3] and VR technologies are not yet in common use in educational settings. VR's widespread integration into schools and universities is affected by cost, safety and the variable reducing nature of the educational institution itself. A broad-based educational VR market has not yet emerged.

Totally immersive educational experiences have been limited to situations with special funding, such as Virtuality's Nagoya project described later in this article. The Virtual Reality Roving Vehicle project from Division and the HIT Lab (also detailed below) is another example of a special funding consortium that created a high-level immersive science education experience.

Contemporary educational VR developments
In the late nineties, with costs of computer technology dropping as CPU power rises, VR is becoming economically practical for university and school classrooms. Immersion, navigation, manipulation and high resolution are becoming available on desktop computers. The integration of the Internet and VRML into the desktop configuration are also spurs to classroom usage. The 'cultural change pioneers' within education are responding to these technical opportunities. Innovators and early adopters[3] are beginning to set up labs (on their own initiative) and even conduct teacher-training in the use of VR. Cost is of major concern to these early adopters, and for that reason their conversations tend to turn toward lower-cost VR products such as the Virtual I-0 headmount or the Virtus VR packages. Sense8's WorldUp and Superscape VRT are also being used, particularly in US community college technology laboratories. Related to this discussion, it must be noted that the 1996 American

---

[3] See date of article, n. 2.

National Technology Teacher of the Year Award was given to Caroline McCullen for her use of Virtus WalkThrough Pro and the Virtus 3D Website Builder at the middle school where she teaches, in Cary, North Carolina.

The Virtual Reality and Education Laboratory (VREL) at East Carolina University has become the international focus for classroom educators interested in finding ways to use virtual reality in education. The goals of VREL are to identify suitable applications of virtual reality in education, evaluate hardware and software, examine the impact of VR on education, and disseminate information to the educational community worldwide. VREL publishes a journal entitled 'VR in the Schools' that is available in print or electronic form. Subscriptions are free. Co-Directors of VREL are Dr Veronica S. Pantelidis and Dr Lawrence Auld (VREL, School of Education, East Carolina University, Greenville, NC27858, USA; Ispantel@ecuvm.cis.ecu.edu or Isauld@ecuvm.cis.ecu.edu).

One of the first efforts to train classroom teachers in the use of VR technology in the classroom has been carried out by Dr Alan Evans at Kent State University in Kent, Ohio. The Instructional Technology Program in the College and Graduate School of Education at Kent State provides a class on the use of desktop VR in which teachers have a chance to construct, experience and critique virtual worlds constructed with Virtus VR. Evans reports that only ten to fifteen of the forty teachers in the pilot project have gone on to use VR back in their classrooms.

Examples of educational applications
Most possible configurations of virtual reality technologies have been used for educational purposes in VR's brief history. This article will now move to provide examples of VR's use in education. The potential educational applications for VR were categorized by Rory Stuart and John Thomas of NYNEX in a seminal article written for Multimedia Review in the early nineties. According to Stuart and Thomas, VR applications can enable learners to:

- *Explore existing places and things to which students would not otherwise have access.*
- *Explore real things that, without alterations of scale in size and time, could not otherwise be effectively examined.*

- *Create places and things with natural or altered qualities.*
- *Interact with people who are in remote locations.*
- *Interact with real people in non-realistic ways.*
- *Interact with virtual beings, such as representations of historical figures.*
- *Create and manipulate abstract conceptual representatives, like data structures and mathematical functions.*

Text 2: Medical training applications[4]

Healthcare systems are expected to account for as much as $15 billion expenditure on information technologies within the next five years.[5] Virtual reality is a very specific component of the total healthcare technology budget.

This report looks at the Virtual Reality technology developments within the medical marketplace at the opening of 1996. Colonel Richard Satava of the US Advanced Research Projects Agency (ARPA) estimated that less than $20 million is currently being spent annually on Virtual Reality Technologies for use in healthcare worldwide. US government funding is primarily coming from ARPA at about $6 million per year.

To date, developers for VR in Medicine have been faced by a 'tough, tough market' in the words of Cine-Med's Kevin McGovern. Venture money has been shy. Corporate investment has been limited to a few significant backers such as Johnson & Johnson, and Abbot Laboratories.

There are two sources of economic blocks for commercial market development. The first drawback has been the cost of the technology. In order to produce a sense of realism for medical purposes, developers are faced with providing organ fidelity, interactivity, physical and physiological properties of organs, and sensory input. Together, that integrated package requires extreme amounts of computing power. Heretofore, only expensive systems such as SGI's Reality Engine have had the capabilities to even begin to integrate all those requirements. The costs of such computing power for full-scale medical simulations have thwarted many interested healthcare professionals.

The second set of monetary drawbacks for VR's use in Medicine stems from medical economics and the cutbacks in medical funding.

---

[4] From *VR News* 5.3, April 1996, 34.
[5] See date of article, n. 4.

There are no easy ways for healthcare professionals to fund their use of Virtual Reality. As it currently stands, VR offers no revenue enhancement to medical practitioners. A medical procedure must directly affect the patient before it can become a direct billable to the patient. Neither a hospital nor a solo practitioner has a way to pass along the expense of VR to the patient as can be done with medication.

Medical researchers interested in Virtual Reality development also face stiff tests. While the payoff in VR is currently seen by medicine as being offered in basic research, purchases by medical colleges must be justified to a board typically headed by financial and CEO-type business professionals. Too many times, a request for a VR system is seen as expensive and/or frivolous. Especially with funding cutbacks for graduate medical education, state-subsidized medical schools may well feel that the money must be spent on basic needs today.

But over the next five years – certainly by the time the $15 billion information technology total has been expended by healthcare – the economic barriers to VR's use in medicine will be much lessened. Basic computing power is dropping in price and VR developers are already working on products based on lower-cost desktop systems. Further, an alternative solution is emerging that is based on part-task training or 'pieces' of a total learning experience.

Products that 'break apart' a total learning experience and provide training for subsets of a medical procedure typically require less computing power and less cost than a full-blown VR simulation. One of the first development firms to utilize this approach is London-based Virtual Presence, which has created MIST, a training package that teaches the standard psycho-motor skills necessary for laparoscopic surgery. Surgeons can practice movements such as tissue cut and lift, or arterial/duct clipping on MIST with the attached 'surgical scissors' (Immersion Corporation's Virtual Laparoscopic Interface). The individual user's movements are analysed against a large database that assesses specific physical skills.

Text 3: Architectural heritage applications[6]

Europe's architectural heritage is immensely rich and diverse; it contributes to the quality of life in our cities and attracts hundreds of

---

[6] From *VR News* 5.1, Jan-Feb 1996, 27.

thousands of visitors from all corners of the world. Yet it is under increasing threat from insensitive planning, atmospheric pollution and commercial exploitation.

There is urgent need to understand the complex evolutionary development of our urban habitats, to reconstruct what once existed, to archive what currently exists and to test, in context, proposed future architectural and planning interventions.

The emerging multimedia technologies offer an unprecedented opportunity to make all this accessible to a wide range of interested agents – from citizens to tourists, from students to scholars, from conservationists to developers.

The ABACUS Group, which is part of the Department of Architecture and Building Science at the University of Strathclyde, has been melding the technologies of Computer Aided Design (CAD) and Multimedia (MM) to provide tools and systems appropriate to the modelling and management of our urban heritage.

The group's first experiment in combining CAD and MM was carried out in collaboration with the University of Rome and the University of Cataluña and was funded by the European Community. The challenge was to offer an explanation of the extraordinary evolution of the modern city of Split on the Dalmatian coast, from its origins as the Diocletian Palace built at the height of the Venetian Empire.

The next challenge, offered by the Edinburgh Old Town Renewal Trust, was to provide a highly detailed and comprehensive model of the beautiful and ancient capital of Scotland which could be used on a day-to-day basis by the Trust, to explain the quality and value of the Old Town environment, and to test proposals for renovation, renewal and revitalization of Edinburgh's historical heart.

The challenge now facing the ABACUS group is in the run-up to 1999, when the magnificent and dynamic Victorian city of Glasgow celebrates its award as City of Architecture and Design. Students of the Strathclyde School of Architecture have, over the past five years,[7] created a massive geometric database of the city which includes its hilly topology, its road, rail and river networks, and the footprint and form of over 10,000 of its buildings. Over the next four years the ambition is to build the most comprehensive Virtual City this side of the Millennium.

[7] See date of article, n. 6.

Text 4: Virtual engineering applications[8]

(a) The Advanced Interactive Systems Division at CCL's Rutherford Appleton Laboratory in Oxfordshire, in the UK, is exploring how virtual reality can be used as a pre-installation planning tool for the assembly of the Atlas experiment for the Large Hadron Collider project at CERN, the European Centre for Nuclear Research, in Switzerland. The large 20-metre diameter particle detector, part of which is being constructed by the Laboratory's Applied Science Department, is very densely packed with equipment, making it essential that final assembly and subsequent maintenance of the system in the underground experimental hall in the CERN accelerator must be meticulously planned.

The aim is to use virtual reality techniques to help engineers test assembly procedures using digital CAD models of the detector apparatus. Dr David Boyd, head of the Advanced Interactive Systems Division at Rutherford Appleton Laboratory, says: 'We believe virtual reality will be an important tool for the engineers and physicists working on the project to use in planning and carrying out the system integration. It could also enable collaborators developing other parts of the detector system in different European countries to bring these parts together in a virtual environment before doing it for real at CERN. This is only one of a number of potential applications of these techniques in the science and engineering programme of the Laboratory. Much of our work involves building complex, one-off pieces of equipment where the ability to develop and test design concepts using virtual prototypes could be of great benefit.' The VR equipment being used by the Laboratory includes Division's dVS and dVISE, running on a Silicon Graphics Onyx Reality Engine.

(b) As a manufacturer of complex aerospace products, McDonnell Douglas must perform design analysis early in the product development cycle. The company began using VR in tandem with its CAD/CAM tools after a trial demonstration showed how VR could potentially reduce the need for costly prototypes. For the original demonstration, provided by Division, design geometry for an F/A-18 tactical strike fighter engine, the engine bay and various maintenance equipment was imported from a Unigraphics II CAD system into dVISE. McDonnell Douglas engineers were then able to interact with

---

[8] From *VR News*, 5.3, April 1996, 29.

the design to determine how easy or difficult it would be to install and remove the engine from its bay for maintenance.

The company says that it 'is moving ahead with its use of VR because it has helped us to evaluate designs earlier in the development cycle . . . this means fewer physical prototypes and reduced development costs'. In one application, two independently designed aircraft sub-systems were imported into a virtual environment and assembled. While evaluating the virtual prototypes, the engineers discovered that the support structures for one of the components protruded into a subsystem bay of the aircraft. This ability to identify problems at a very early stage in the design process has recently led the company to invest heavily in Division-based workstations for a major new aircraft program.

Text 5: Cave of Lascaux archaeological heritage project[9]
Professor Britton's brilliant reconstruction of the Lascaux cave defies textual encapsulation, as does the highly personal account of its background and significance he gave at Virtual Heritage 95 – as much a performance as the visual material it accompanied. The cave was closed to the public many years ago, for conservation reasons, and for most people virtual reality offers the only prospect of exploring and enjoying its huge gallery of paintings, many of which take advantage of the rock outlines and textures of the walls and ceilings to add depth or shape, or to puzzle or surprise the passing observer. The reconstruction, which continues to be developed, will tour the world for a number of years, before eventually becoming a permanent museum exhibit, probably in France. Prof. Britton offers the following description of how his work is presented as a museum installation.

In the gallery is a pool of light. In the light is a chair, a joystick, and wraparound video glasses. The viewer dons the glasses in which are displayed images of the reconstructed Cave of Lascaux. By turning one's head or by manipulating the joystick, the viewer may look in any direction and move around the cave guided by illuminated areas containing paintings of animal figures. As one searches through the cave one may find other images hidden in the niches. These images are interactive. If the viewer studies a figure for a period of time, an interactive sequence is triggered, and then the painting dissolves back

---

[9] From *VR News* 5.1, Jan–Feb 1996, 31.

into the cave. On video monitors the audience sees the view which the viewer with the glasses is selecting. The interaction is planned so each viewer will explore the cave for about ten minutes, though longer viewing is possible.

Hidden deep within the virtual cave is a painting on the wall of a human being which, like the other paintings, comes to life when the viewer finds it and concentrates on it. This image, in coming to life, can only be seen by the viewer wearing the wraparound video glasses. Viewers watching this interaction do not share in this totally private viewing experience unless and until they take their turn in the virtual environment. The figure which comes to life asks the viewer if they are willing to share in a secret. Those viewers who will not promise to keep this secret find that the piece ends, their time in the cave is over, and it is a ready for the next viewer. If they indicate they are willing, they receive a secret message regarding the hidden history of humanity.

Glossary of technical terms

Analytic/synthetic thinking   Analysis takes things apart; synthesis brings things together.

Avatar   Graphic representation of human body in computer-generated environment.

Bandwidth   Capacity of copper wire, cable or fibre-optic network in bits per second. The higher the bandwidth, the greater the speed of capacity of the network.

BBS   Bulletin board system, whereby messages can be posted electronically via a modem. There are more than 15,000 bulletin boards at the time of writing.

Casuistry   Approach to ethics based on case studies which may qualify the letter of the moral law.

CD-ROM   Compact disc read-only memory. One such disc can hold as much data as 700 floppy diskettes.

Cybernetics   The science of control and communication popularized by Norbert Wiener, describing not only the processing of information but also the use of information in a feedback system for the purposes of homeostatic control.

Cyberspace   The totality of information resources available through computer networks and other multimedia. The term can also refer to a shared virtual environment.

DataGlove   Glove fitted with connections to VR computer via position sensors which enables simulation of grasping virtual objects and directing movement through virtual spaces.

DataSuit   Full body suit fitted with electronic sensors to extend impression of presence in virtual spaces, based on same principle as DataGlove. The wearer's movements are tracked, providing constant input to the host computer so that the computer-generated environment and avatar can be updated according to the user's gestures and orientation.

Deconstruction   Theory in the science of interpretation (hermeneutics) that any interpretation must be undermined or 'deconstructed' by another. The strategy is to raise persistent questions to deny that any text is settled or stable.

Deontology   An explanation focusing inherent qualities or duties rather than goals or purposes.

Epistemology   Theory of knowledge, which explores such notions as knowing, perceiving, feeling sure, guessing, remembering, *etc.*, and involves studying the sources, limits and validation of human knowledge.

Eschatological   Pertaining to the end-times or ultimate destiny of humanity.

EyePhones   Trade name coined by Jaron Lanier, VR pioneer, for head-mounted display (HMD) gear which usually involves stereo sound and stereoscopic vision of graphics generated by the host computer.

Flame   Insulting, derogatory or crude messages sent by e-mail or online postings. Discussions in newsgroups can degenerate into 'flame wars'.

Haptic   Perception which involves not only the sense of touch but also awareness of the position of limbs in relation to each other and the surrounding space.

Holism   The general thesis that wholes are more than the sum of their parts.

Homo Faber   Anthropological term describing humankind as maker and user of tools for work and craft.

Iconocentrism   Focus on images and their significance, typical of postmodernity.

Individualism   The view that in social philosophy, political theory and practice, and in moral thought and deed, individual human beings must be regarded as prior to society.

Interface   Where two or more information sources come together. The term can also refer to the result of a human user's connecting with the system and the computer's becoming interactive.

Katharsis   An experience of inner release or cleansing.

Logical   positivism   Philosophical   movement   emphasizing so-called scientific empiricism or the belief that all knowledge is ultimately derived from experience. Ethical judgments are thought of as mere expressions of the speaker's emotions.

Logocentrism   Focus on language and its meaning, typical of modernity.

Metanarrative   A 'big story' (such as God's plan, progress or Marxism-Leninism) which provides an interpretive framework for the component small stories of individuals.

Metaphysics   The study of the first principles of reality, exploring ideas about possible worlds, intrinsic goals, meaning and ultimate purpose.

Modem   Device which enables a computer to transmit data over a phone line.

MUD   'Multi-user domain, or dungeon': programmed concept of spaces, time zones or worlds.

Newsgroups   A generic term for discussion areas. To read the news a news server must be accessed via service provider. Groups are divided according to interest.

Panopticon   Anti-vision, popularized by Foucault, of a society dominated by surveillance as a tool of political repression, originating in Bentham's idea for a prison where all inmates could be observed by the warders at all times.

Paradigm   A standard of scientific achievement in terms of which scientific work is conducted and evaluated.

Positivism   The view that the description of phenomena and the order in which they occur is all that human beings can know. Value judgments and statements of belief or aesthetical appreciation fall outside these limits.

PC   Any personal computer, but specifically those cloned from IBM equipment.

Robotic telepresence   Science of controlling robots remotely and attaching video cameras to enable hazardous tasks, such as underwater and space construction, to be carried out with the operator at a safe distance.

Simulacra Baudrillard's world of hyperreality where the only 'reality' is TV ads and other signifiers.

Spaceball Device which enables desktop VR-users to navigate simulated spaces by turning a ball.

Technoptimist Term coined by the author for those who believe that technology will always be able to solve the problems which it creates.

Teleology An explanation focusing on goals or purposes rather than inherent qualities or duties.

Trackers Position-tracking devices which monitor the user's physical (hand, head or eye) movements and feed the user's action into the host computer; these are interpreted as changes in the synthetic environment.

Utilitarianism Ethical theory based on the premise that the rightness of an action is to be judged by the contribution it makes to human happiness or to the diminution of human misery. Pleasure is seen as the only good in itself, and pain as the only evil in itself.

VDU Visual display unit. The monitor which is attached to a PC.

Website Files (pertaining to a particular organization or individual) containing text, audio or pictorial material stored on a computer file-server which may be accessed by users of the Internet (or World Wide Web).

Bibliography

Aquinas, Thomas (1964), *Summa Theologica*, ET T. McDermott, London: Chapman.

Arthur, C. (1992), 'Did Reality Move for You?', *New Scientist* 134.1822: 22–27.

Barbour, I. G. (1992), *Ethics in an Age of Technology*, London: SCM Press.

Barth, K. (1936–69), *Church Dogmatics*, ET, Edinburgh: T. & T. Clark.

Beardon, C. (1992), 'The Ethics of Virtual Reality', *Intelligent Tutoring Media* 3.1: 23ff.

Bereano, P. L. (1976), *Technology as a Social and Political Phenomenon*, New York: Wiley.

Billington, R. (1993), *Living Philosophy*, 2nd ed., London: Routledge.

Blocher, H. (1984), *In the Beginning*, ET, Leicester: IVP.

Bolter, J. D. (1986), *Turing's Man*, Harmondsworth: Penguin.

Bonhoeffer, D. (1955), *Ethics*, ET, New York: Macmillan.

Boulton, W. G., T. D. Kennedy & A. Verhey (eds.) (1994), *From Christ to the World: Introductory Readings in Christian Ethics*, Grand Rapids: Eerdmans.

Brod, C. (1984), *Technostress: The Human Cost of the Computer Revolution*, Reading MA: Addison-Wesley.

Brown, C. (ed.) (1976), *New International Dictionary of New Testament Theology*, 3 vols., Grand Rapids: Zondervan.

Buber, M. (1970), *I and Thou*, Edinburgh: T. & T. Clark.

Calvin, John (1960), *Institutes of the Christian Religion*, ET F. Battles, Philadelphia: Fortress Press.

Carr, D. (1991), *Educating the Virtues*, London: Routledge.

Carr, D., & J. Haldane (1993), *Values and Values Education*, St Andrews: Centre for Philosophy and Public Affairs.

Clarke, N. (1982), 'Technology and Man: A Christian Vision', in Mitcham and Mackey (1982: 250ff.).

Clowney, P. (1993), 'The Triumph of Illusion', *Third Way* 16.4: 12–15.

Cook, D. (1983), *The Moral Maze*, London: SPCK.

Cook, S. D. (1991), 'Technological Revolution and the Gutenberg Myth', in Pitt & Lugo (1991: 175–189).

———(1993), 'Eden Revisited: Technology and our Relationship to Nature', in Hickman & Porter (1993: 27–47).

Cromby, J. (1995), 'Using Virtual Environments in Special Education', *VR in the Schools*, 1.3: 1–4.

Cullmann, O. (1962), *Christ and Time*, ET, London: SCM Press.

Cupitt, D. (1989), *Radicals and the Future of the Church*, London: SCM Press.

5CYBERCONF(1996), *Proceedings of Fifth Annual Conference on Cyberspace*, Madrid: Fundacíon Arte y Tecnología.

Danielson, D. (1992), *Artificial Morality*, London: Routledge.

Davies, P. (1984), *God and the New Physics*, Harmondsworth: Pelican.

———(1993), *The Mind of God*, Harmondsworth: Penguin.

Davis, H., & D. Gosling (1985), *Will the Future Work?* Geneva: WCC.

Dennett, D. C. (1991), *Consciousness Explained*, London: Penguin.

Don, A. (1992), 'Anthropomorphism: From Eliza to Terminator 2', in *Computer–Human Interaction Symposium*: 67–70.

Donaldson, J. (1989), *Key Issues in Business Ethics*, London: Academic Press.

Dreyfus, H. (1979), *What Computers Can't Do*, 2nd ed., New York: Harper Colophon.

Durlach, N. I., & A. Mavor (eds.) (1995), *Virtual Reality: Scientific and Technological Challenges*, Washington DC: National Academic Press.

Ellul, J. (1965), *The Technological Society*, ET, London: Jonathan Cape.

———(1976), *The Ethics of Freedom*, ET, London: Mowbrays.

———(1990), *The Technological Bluff*, ET, Grand Rapids: Eerdmans.

Emerson, A., & C. Forbes (1990), *The Invasion of the Computer Culture*, Leicester: IVP.

Epstein, R. (1997), *The Case of the Killer Robot*, New York: Wiley.

Evans, C. S. (1982), *Philosophy of Religion*, Downers Grove IL and Leicester: IVP.

Fang, J. J., *et al.* (1995), 'Collision Detection Methodologies for Rigid Body Assembly in a Virtual Environment', *VR-Research, Development, and Applications*, 1.1: 41–48.

Featherstone, M., & R. Burrows (eds.) (1995), *Cyberspace/Cyberbodies/Cyberpunk*, London: Sage Publications.

Ferguson, R. (1994), *Technology at the Crossroads*, Edinburgh: St Andrew Press.

Ferkiss, V. (1969), *Technological Man*, London: Heinemann.

Ferré, F. (1988), *Philosophy of Technology*, Englewood Cliffs NJ: Prentice-Hall.

———(1993), *Hellfire and Lightning Rods*, New York: Orbis.

Ferrell, O., & J. Fraedrich (1994), *Business Ethics*, Boston: Houghton Mifflin.

Fletcher, J. (1966), *Situation Ethics: The New Morality*, Philadelphia: Westminster Press.

Forester, T., & P. Morrison (1993), *Computer Ethics*, 2nd ed., Cambridge MA: MIT Press.

Francis, J., & P. Abrecht (eds.) (1976), *Facing up to Nuclear Power*, Edinburgh: St Andrew Press.

Frankena, W. (1971), *Ethics*, 2nd ed., Englewood Cliffs NJ: Prentice Hall.

———(1973), 'Is Morality Logically Dependent on Religion?' in Outka & Reeder (1973: 313–314).

Freeman, A. (1993), *God in Us: A Case for Christian Humanism*, London: SCM Press.

Gaarder, J. (1995), *Sophie's World*, ET, London: Phoenix.

Gill, R. (1985), *A Textbook of Christian Ethics*, Edinburgh: T. & T. Clark.

———(1991), *Christian Ethics in Secular Worlds*, Edinburgh: T. & T. Clark.

Goodman, N. (1978), *Ways of Worldmaking*, Indianapolis: Hackett Publishing.

Goodman, P. (1976), 'Can Technology be Humane?', in Bereano (1976: 6ff.).

Goudzwaard, B. (1984), *Idols of our Time*, Downers Grove IL: IVP.

Gould, C. (ed.) (1989), *The Information Web: Ethical and Social Implications of Computer Networking*, Boulder CO: Westview Press.

Graham, G. (1988), *Contemporary Social Philosophy*, Oxford: Blackwell.

Green, M. (1987), *2 Peter and Jude*, 2nd ed., Leicester: IVP.

Haldane, J. (1990), *Environmental Philosophy: An Introductory Survey*, St Andrews: Centre for Philosophy and Public Affairs.

Harries, R. (1994), *The Real God*, London: Mowbray.

Harris, R., G. Archer & B. Waltke (eds.) (1980), *Theological Wordbook of the Old Testament*, 2 vols., Chicago: Moody Press.

Hart, D. (1993), *Faith in Doubt*, London: Mowbray.

Hasker, W. (1983), *Metaphysics*, Downers Grove IL and Leicester: IVP.

Hauerwas, S., & W. Willimon (1989), *Resident Aliens*, Nashville TN: Abingdon Press.

Heidegger, M. (1977), *The Question Concerning Technology and Other Essays*, ET, New York: Harper and Row.

Heim, M. (1990), 'The Metaphysics of Virtual Reality', in Helsel & Roth (1990: 27–34).

———(1993), *The Metaphysics of Virtual Reality*, New York: OUP.

———(1995), 'The Design of Virtual Reality', in Featherstone & Burrows (1995: 65–77).

Helsel, S. K., & J. A. Roth (eds.) (1990), *Virtual Reality – Theory, Practice and Promise*, London: Meckler.

Hickman, L., & E. Porter (eds.) (1993), *Technology and Ecology*, Carbondale IL: Society for Philosophy and Technology.

Holmes, A. F. (1984), *Ethics*, Downers Grove IL and Leicester: IVP.

Hooykaas, R. (1972), *Religion and the Rise of Modern Science*, Edinburgh: Scottish Academic Press.

Horizon (TV) (1991), 'Colonizing Cyberspace', London: BBC.

Houston, G. (1989), *Prophecy Now*, Leicester: IVP.

———(1994), review of J. Polkinghorne (1991) in *Scottish Bulletin of Evangelical Theology*, 12.1: 72–75.

Houston, J. (ed.) (1984), *Is it Reasonable to Believe in God?* Edinburgh: Handsel Press.

Hughes, P. E. (1989), *The True Image*, Grand Rapids: Eerdmans; Leicester: IVP.

Hunter, G. (1992), *How to Reach Secular People*, Nashville TN: Abingdon Press.

Illich, I. (1973), *Tools for Conviviality*, New York: Harper & Row.

Jeremias, J. (1954), *The Parables of Jesus*, ET, London: SCM Press.

Jiggins, A. (1988), *Human Future?* London: Scripture Union.

Johnson, D. (1993), *Computer Ethics*, Englewood Cliffs NJ: Prentice-Hall.

Jonas, H. (1984), *The Imperative of Responsibility*, Chicago: University of Chicago Press.

Jones, S. (ed.) (1995), *Cybersociety*, London: Sage Publications.

———(1997), *Virtual Culture*, London: Sage Publications.

Kallman, E. (1993), 'Ethical Evaluation: A Necessary Element in VE Research', *Presence* 2.2: 143–146.

Kallman, E., & J. Grillo (1996), *Ethical Decision-making and Information Technology*, 2nd ed., New York: McGraw-Hill.

Krueger, M. (1991), *Artificial Reality II*, Reading MA: Addison-Wesley.

———(1993), 'The Experience Society', *Presence* 2.2: 162–168.

Kuhn, T. S. (1970), *The Structure of Scientific Revolutions*, 2nd ed., Chicago: University of Chicago Press.

Kung, H. (1991), *Global Responsibility*, London: SCM Press.

Ladd, G. E. (1964), *Jesus and the Kingdom*, London: SPCK.

———(1976), *The Presence of the Future*, Grand Rapids: Eerdmans.

Ladd, J. (1970), 'Morality and the Ideal of Rationality in Formal Organisations', *Monist* 54.4: 142–143.

———(1989), 'Computers and Moral Responsibility: A Framework for Ethical Analysis', in Gould (1989: 207–227).

Larijani, L. C. (1994), *The Virtual Reality Primer*, New York: McGraw-Hill.

Laurel, B. (1991), *Computers as Theatre*, Reading MA: Addison-Wesley.

Lockhart, T. (1993), 'Technological Fixes for Moral Dilemmas', in Hickman & Porter (1993: 332–346).

Lowe, D. (1995), *Memory Management for Dummies*, Foster City CA: IDG Books.

Lynch, J. (1996), *Cyberethics*, Leighton Buzzard: Rushmere Wynne.

Lyon, D. (1984), *Future Society*, Tring: Lion.

———(1986), *The Silicon Society*, Tring: Lion.

———(1994a), *Postmodernity*, Buckingham: Open University Press.

———(1994b), 'Hazard Warning', *Third Way* 17.8: 22–25.

Lyotard, J. F. (1984), *The Postmodern Condition: A Report on Knowledge*, ET, Minneapolis: University of Minnesota Press.

McComiskey, T. (1987), *The Covenants of Promise*, Grand Rapids: Baker Book House; Leicester: IVP.

McDonald, J. I. (1993), *Biblical Interpretation and Christian Ethics*, Cambridge: Cambridge University Press.

McDonnell, J., & F. Trampiets (eds.) (1989), *Communicating Faith in a Technological Age*, Slough: St Paul Press.

McGrath, A. (1994), *Christian Theology: An Introduction*, Oxford: Blackwell.

Mackie, J. L. (1974), *Ethics: Inventing Right and Wrong*, London: Penguin.

MacIntyre, A. (1985), *After Virtue*, 2nd ed., London: Duckworth.

Mackay, D. (1988), *The Open Mind*, Leicester: IVP.

McLuhan, M. (1987) *Understanding Media*, London: Ark Paperbacks.

Marx, L. (1994), 'The Idea of Technology in Postmodern Pessimism', in Y. Ezrahi *et al.* (eds.), *Technology, Pessimism and Postmodernism*, Dordrecht: Kluwer: 12ff.

Mill, John Stuart (1859), *On Liberty*, London: Nisbet.

Milton, R. (1992), *The Facts of Life*, London: Fourth Estate.

Mitcham, C. (1991), 'Rediscovering the Ethical Dimension of Science and Technology', in Pitt & Lugo (1989: 137–143).

————(1994), *Thinking through Technology*, Chicago: University of Chicago Press.

Mitcham, C., & J. Grote (eds.) (1984), *Theology and Technology*, Lanham MD: University Press of America.

Mitcham, C., & R. Mackey (eds.) (1982), *Philosophy and Technology*, New York: Free Press.

Moberg, D. (1973), *The Great Reversal: Evangelism versus Social Action*, London: Scripture Union.

Molinari, M., *et al.* (eds.) (1987), *The Letters of Marshall McLuhan*, New York: Oxford.

Moltmann, J. (1985), *God in Creation*, ET, London: SCM Press.

————(1992), *The Spirit of Life*, ET, London: SCM Press.

Monsma, S. (ed.) (1986), *Responsible Technology*, Grand Rapids: Eerdmans.

Montefiore, H. (ed.) (1992), *The Gospel in Contemporary Culture*, London: Mowbray.

Moore, G. E. (1903), *Principia Ethica*, London: Nisbet.

Morgan, T. C. (1995), 'Cybershock', *Christianity Today* 39.4: 78–86.

Moulthrop, S. (1993), 'Writing Cyberspace: Literacy in the Age of Simulacra', in Waxelblat (1993: 78ff.).

Murphy, N. (1990), *Theology in the Age of Scientific Reasoning*, New York: Cornell University Press.

Negropont, N. (1995), *Being Digital*, London: Hodder & Stoughton.

Nelson, T. (1987), *Computer Lib/Dream Machine*, Redmond WA: Tempus.

Newbigin, L. (1989), *The Gospel in a Pluralist Society*, London: SPCK.

————(1991), *Truth to Tell: The Gospel as Public Truth*, London: SPCK.

Newlands, G. (1985), *Making Christian Decisions*, London: Mowbray.

Niebuhr, H. R. (1963), 'The Meaning of Responsibility', in Boulton *et al.* (1994: 195–204).

————(1975), *Christ and Culture*, New York: Harper & Row.

Norris, C. (1985), *The Contest of Faculties*, New York: Methuen.

O'Donovan, O. (1994), *Resurrection and Moral Order*, 2nd ed., Leicester: Apollos.

Oden, T. (1990), *After Modernity – What?* Grand Rapids: Zondervan.

Outka, G., & J. Reeder (eds.) (1973), *Religion and Morality*, New York: Doubleday.

Pantelidis, V. (1994), 'VR and Ethics: Questions to be asked'; and

————(1995), 'VR and Education: Information Sources' (Unpublished papers; Greenville NC: VR and Education Laboratory).

Pepperell, R. (1994), 'What is Human?', *Intelligent Tutoring Media*, 5.1: 35–43.

Pfeiffer, J. (1982), *The Creative Explosion*, New York: Cornell University Press.

Pimental, K., & K. Teixeira (1993), *Virtual Reality – Through the New Looking Glass*, New York: Windcrest.

Pirsig, R. (1974), *Zen and the Art of Motorcycle Maintenance: An Enquiry into Values*, New York: Morrow.

Pitt, J., & E. Lugo (eds.) (1991), *The Technology of Discovery and the Discovery of Technology*, Blacksburg VA: Society for Philosophy and Technology.

Polanyi, M. (1962), *Personal Knowledge*, London: Routledge & Kegan Paul.

————(1964), *Science, Faith and Society*, Chicago: University of Chicago Press.

————(1969), *Knowing and Being*, Chicago: University of Chicago Press.

Polkinghorne, J. (1986), *One World*, London: SPCK.

————(1991), *Reason and Reality*, London: SPCK.

du Pont, P. (1992), 'Overview of Virtual Reality Applications with *Division*', *Symposium on Virtual Representations for Design and Manufacture*, Coventry University.

Poster, M. (1990), *The Mode of Information*, Cambridge: Polity Press.

——(1995), 'Postmodern Virtualities', in Featherstone & Burrows (1995: 79–95).

Poythress, V. (1988), *Science and Hermeneutics*, Grand Rapids: Zondervan; Leicester: Apollos.

Prickett, S. (1986), *Words and the Word*, Cambridge: Cambridge University Press.

Ramsey, P. (1961), 'The Problem of Protestant Ethics Today', in Boulton *et al.* (1994: 212–214).

Ratzsch, D. (1986), *Philosophy of Science*, Downers Grove IL and Leicester: IVP.

Rawls, J. (1972), *A Theory of Justice*, Cambridge MA: Harvard University Press.

Regan, C. (1995), 'An Investigation into Nausea and Other Side-effects of Head-coupled Immersive VR', *VR-Research, Development and Applications*: 1.1: 17–31.

Rheingold, H. (1991), *Virtual Reality*, London: Secker & Warburg.

——(1994), *The Virtual Community*, London: Secker & Warburg.

Rivers, T. J. (1993), *Contra Technologiam – The Crisis of Value in a Technological Age*, New York: University Press of America.

Rookmaaker, H. (1973), *Modern Art and the Death of a Culture*, Leicester: IVP.

Rorty, R. (1980), *Philosophy and the Mirror of Nature*, Princeton NJ: Princeton University Press.

Rossman, P., & R. Kirby (1990), *Christians and the World of Computers*, London: SCM Press.

Roszak, T. (1988), *The Cult of Information*, London: Paladin.

Russell, C. A. (1985), *Cross-currents*, Leicester: IVP.

——(1989), 'The Conflict Metaphor and its Social Origins', *Science and Christian Belief*, 1.1: 3–26.

Schaeffer, F. (1968), *The God Who is There*, London: Hodder & Stoughton.

Schroeder, R. (1995), 'Learning from Virtual Reality Applications in Education', *VR: Research, Developments and Applications*, 1.1: 33–39.

Schumacher, E. F. (1974), *Small is Beautiful*, London: Abacus.

Schuurman, E. (1980), *Technology and the Future*, Toronto: Wedge Publishing.

———(1995a), 'A Confrontation with Technicism as the Spiritual Climate of the West' (4th Annual Lecture on Technology and Belief, unpublished; Heriot-Watt University).

———(1995b), 'The Myth of the Information Highway and VR' (unpublished paper).

Sheridan, T. (1993), 'My Anxieties about VE', *Presence*, 2.2: 141–142.

Sherman, B., & P. Judkins (1992), *Glimpses of Heaven, Visions of Hell*, London: Hodder and Stoughton.

Skinner, B. F. (1972), *Beyond Freedom and Dignity*, London: Jonathan Cape.

Slouka, M. (1995), *War of the Worlds: The Assault on Reality*, London: Abacus.

Spinello, R. (1997), *Case Studies in Information and Computer Ethics*, New Jersey: Prentice Hall.

Stanney, K. (1995), 'Reaching the Full Potential of VR: Human Factors Issues that could Stand in the Way', *VR Annual International Symposium*: 28–34.

Stone, R. (1992), 'VR Interactive Visualisation for British Industry', *Virtual Representations for Design and Manufacture*, Coventry University Symposium, KN2.

Stone, V. (1993), 'Social Interaction and Social Development in VE', *Presence* 2.2: 153–161.

Sviedrys, R. (1991), 'Discovering the Long-range Impacts of Technology', in Pitt & Lugo (1991: 25–40).

Tart, C. T. (1990), 'Multiple Personality, Altered States and Virtual Reality', *Dissociation* 3.4: 222–223.

Taylor, M. (1984), *Erring: A Postmodern Atheology*, Chicago: University of Chicago Press.

Thiselton, A. C. (1995), *Interpreting God and the Postmodern Self*, Edinburgh: T. & T. Clark.

Tillich, P. (1987), 'Ethical Principles of Moral Action', in Boulton *et al.* (1994: 248–251).

Torrance, T. F. (1969), *Theological Science*, London: Oxford University Press.

Turkle, S. (1984), *The Second Self: Computers and the Human Spirit*, London: Granada.

———(1995), *Life on the Screen*, London: Weidenfeld & Nicholson.

Ucko, P., & A. Rosenfeld (1967), *Palaeolithic Cave Art*, London: Weidenfeld.

Unger, S. (1982), *Controlling Technology*, New York: SRW.

Urmson, J. O., & J. Ree (eds.) (1991), *Concise Encyclopedia of Western Philosophy and Philosophers*, London: Routledge.

Vallee, J. (1982), *The Network Revolution*, Berkeley CA: And/Or Books.

Van Til, H. R. (1972), *The Calvinistic Concept of Culture*, Philadelphia: Presbyterian & Reformed Publishing Co.

Wann, J. P. *et al.* (1992), 'Assessing Human Response to Virtual Environments', in *Virtual Representations for Design and Manufacture*, Coventry University Symposium, B6.

Weizenbaum, J. (1984), *Computer Power and Human Reason*, Harmondsworth: Pelican.

Welby, J. (1992), *Can Companies Sin?* Bramcote, Nottingham: Grove Books.

Wexelblat, A. (ed.) (1993), *Virtual Reality: Applications and Explanations*, Redmond MA: Academic Press.

Whitbeck, C. (1993), 'VE: Ethical Issues and Significant Confusions', *Presence* 2.2: 147–152.

Whitby, B. (1993), 'The Virtual Sky is Not the Limit', *AIS* 1.2: 1–10.

White, L. (1968), 'The Historical Roots of our Ecological Crisis', in *Dynamo and Virgin Revisited*, Cambridge MA: MIT Press.

Wilson, J. R., *et al.* (1995), 'VR Health and Safety: Facts, Speculations and Myths', *VR News* 4.9: 20–24.

Winner, L. (1977), *Autonomous Technology*, Cambridge MA: MIT Press.

Wogaman, J. P. (1989), *Christian Moral Judgment*, Louisville KY: Westminster & John Knox Press.

Wolfe, D. L. (1982), *Epistemology*, Downers Grove IL: IVP.

Wolterstorff, N. (1983), *Until Justice and Peace Embrace*, Grand Rapids: Eerdmans.

Woolley, B. (1992), *Virtual Worlds*, Oxford: Blackwell.

World Council of Churches (1979), *Faith, Science and in the Future*, Geneva: WCC.

———(1980), *Faith and Science in an Unjust World*, Geneva: WCC.

———(1985), *Science Education and Educational Values*, Geneva: WCC.

Zachary, G. P. (1990), 'Artificial Reality: Computer Simulations One Day may Provide Surreal Experiences', *Wall Street Journal*, 23 Jan, A1(E).

Index